A THEORY OF POSSIBILITY

A THEORY OF POSSIBILITY

A Constructivistic and Conceptualistic Account
of Possible Individuals and Possible Worlds

NICHOLAS RESCHER

UNIVERSITY OF PITTSBURGH PRESS

Published in Great Britain in 1975
by Basil Blackwell & Mott Limited.

Published in the U.S.A. in 1975
by the University of Pittsburgh Press.

© Basil Blackwell, 1975

ISBN: 0-8229-1122-1
Library of Congress Catalog Card No: 75-10540

Printed in Great Britain by
William Clowes & Sons, Limited
London, Beccles and Colchester

Howard J. B. Ziegler
IN MEMORIAM

CONTENTS

PREFACE

This is an essay in the formal systematization of certain fundamental notions in metaphysics, specifically in the ontology and epistemology of possibility. The framework of its approach to the *modus operandi* of possibility may be indicated by rehearsing the key names of the chain of the tradition upon which it draws (often without explicit acknowledgment)—Aristotle, the Scholastics, Leibniz, Meinong, McTaggart, and the later Carnap. These writers are linked by a common tendency of metaphysical concern and perspective that no amount of substantive disagreement can altogether remove, a tendency which the present work obtains from theirs.

Giambattista Vico said somewhere that we men only understand what we have made ourselves, and in my view this dictum applies with full force to possibilia; possible worlds and possible individuals being most properly viewed as actual or potential conceptual artifacts. The elucidation and support of this thesis constitutes the task of the book

Possible worlds and possible individuals are decidedly in philosophical vogue nowadays. Logicians, analytic metaphysicians, semanticists of modal logic, and even linguistic theorists are all active contributors to the presently flourishing discussions of possibilia. But while the ranks of those who invoke the conception of possible individuals and worlds are legion, few attempts have been made to elucidate their *nature* and to clarify their metaphysical and ontological foundations. It is precisely to these issues that the present book is addressed. Its primary aims are four: (1) To present a specific theory of possible individuals and possible worlds, a theory of a fundamentally conceptualistic cast. (2) To exhibit how this theory is adequate to the demands put upon possibilia—in particular in the development of the standard possibilistic semantics for modal logic. (3) To apply the theory to the elucidation of relevant philosophical issues—in the analysis of dispositions, laws, counterfactual conditionals, and cognate concepts. And finally,

(4) to examine various issues in the metaphysics of possibility in the light of the theory presented. In this last regard a wide range of metaphysical problems will be dealt with, including such issues as essentialism, the individuation of possibilia, the cross-world identification of individuals, and the doctrine of internal relations.

My own concern with this problem-area goes back some 25 years, to 1949 when I began work at Princeton on my doctoral dissertation on the philosophy of G. W. Leibniz, that principal architect of the theory of possible worlds. In 1959 I published in *The Philosophical Review* a paper "On the Logic of Existence and Denotation" (vol. 68, pp. 157–80),[1] which constituted a main step in the development of my thinking about "merely possible individuals." Since then I have dealt with various facets of the problem through a variegated series of publications.[2] The present book represents the latest stage in the development and synthesis of this facet of my work.

The book is related in a particularly intimate way to my previous volume on *Conceptual Idealism* (Blackwell, 1973), for it attempts to spell out formally at the logico-semantical level the approach to possibility articulated in this previous publication. *Conceptual Idealism* presupposed a conceptualistic and idealistic theory of possibility. The present book seeks to substantiate in detail that such a theory can be made to work—i.e., that it can be elaborated in rigorously systematic fashion so as to meet the demands put upon possible individuals and possible worlds in those contexts, such as the semantics of modal logic, where these ideas are actually put into service.

Hopefully, the discussion manages to achieve in reasonable measure the difficult compromise between formal development and informal motivation. No doubt, a more extensive treatment of examples and illustrative material would be in principle

[1] Reprinted in W. Sellars (ed.), *New Readings in Philosophical Analysis* (New York, 1972).

[2] *Hypothetical Reasoning* (Amsterdam, 1964): "The Concept of Nonexistent Possibles" in *Essays in Philosophical Analysis* (Pittsburgh, 1969); "Counterfactual Hypotheses, Laws, and Dispositions," *Nous*, vol. 5 (1971), pp. 157–78; "Possible Individuals, Trans-World Identity and Quantified Modal Logic," *Nous*, vol. 7 (1973), pp. 330–350, co-authored with Zane Parks; *Conceptual Idealism* (Oxford, 1973).

desirable, but the book is already long, and additions in some places would require cuts in others. Certainly any further curtailment of the exploration of philosophical ramifications would have been a most undesirable impoverishment. It cannot be gainsaid that each chapter could itself readily be expanded into a book. But the price of this gain in adequacy at the local level would have been a sacrifice of the main global aim of the book—the presentation of a synoptic theory of the nature of the possible.

The book presents in revised and expanded form a series of lectures delivered during the Trinity Term of 1973 in the school of Literae Humaniores of the University of Oxford at the kind invitation of the Sub-Faculty of Philosophy. I also very much appreciate the kindness and hospitality of Corpus Christi College for affording me an academic foothold during my stay in Oxford on this as on several previous occasions.

I am indebted to my student Thomas C. Vinci for reading a draft of this material and suggesting some improvements, and to Professors Gerald J. Massey and Nino Cocciarella for helpful discussions of some of the issues. I also want to thank the participants in a seminar at the University of Pittsburgh to which I presented this material in the Winter of 1974, and in particular Mark Ylvisaker, for their helpfulness. And I wish to thank Mrs. Kathleen Reznik for preparing the typescript through many revisions with great patience and competence. Finally, I owe a debt of gratitude to Paolo Dau, William C. House, and my wife for their help in checking the proofs.

Work on this book was supported by a National Science Foundation research grant (GS-37883) during 1973–4, and I wish to avail myself of this occasion to thank the Foundation for this help.

Pittsburgh
Spring, 1974

GLOSSARY OF NOTATION

¬, &, ∨, ⊃, ≡	the standard connectives of propositional logic
$p, q, r, \ldots$	propositional variables
$x, y, z, \ldots$	individual variables (ranging over possible and actual individuals)
$x_1, x_2, x_3, \ldots$	individual constants
$w, w', w'', \ldots$	possible world variables
$w_1, w_2, w_3, \ldots$	possible world constants
w^*	the actual or real world (constant); the set of all real individuals
v	the set of all *actual-variant* individuals
s	the set of all *supernumerary* individuals
$\phi, \psi, \chi, \ldots$	predicate variables (including multi-place predicates in their range)
$F, G, H, \ldots$	predicate constants ("atomic")
$R, R', R'', \ldots$	relational constants
∀, ∃	quantifiers over actual individuals
Π, Σ	quantifiers over individuals (actual and possible alike)
A, E	quantifiers over possible worlds (occasionally also used for properties and relations)
≐	identity of individuals within a given world (usually the actual one)
≅	identity of individuals in general
∼	the correlation of an individual with its fully individuating characterization (*fic*)
ϕx	ϕ characterizes x (ϕ is an *actual* property of x)
$\phi! x$	ϕ characterizes x essentially (ϕ is an *essential* property of x)

$\phi?x$	ϕ characterizes x possibly (ϕ is a *possible* property of x—this embraces the actual)
$\phi\P x$	ϕ characterizes x D-essentially (ϕ is a dispositionally essential property of x)
$\phi\dagger x$	ϕ characterizes x N-essentially (ϕ is a *nomically* essential property of x)
$(\psi/\phi)x$	the disposition from ϕ to ψ characterizes x (x must have ψ if [or *since*] it has ϕ)
$\phi \Rightarrow \psi$	ψ is lawfully resultant from ϕ
E	existence (Ex iff $x \in w^*$)
$\mathscr{P}(x)$	the set of all *actual* properties of x, i.e., $\{\phi: \phi x\}$
$\mathscr{E}(x)$	the set of all *essential* properties of x, i.e., $\{\phi: \phi!x\}$
$\mathscr{Q}(x)$	the set of all *possible* properties of x, i.e., $\{\phi: \phi?x\}$
$\mathscr{D}_\psi(x)$	the set of all dispositionally resultant properties of x relative to ψ, i.e., $\{\phi: (\phi/\psi)x\}$
i	represents an ostensive indicator with respect to *actual* individuals
p	represents a positional placement-operator with respect to (actual or possible) individuals

$\in, \subseteq, =, \Lambda, V$ the usual set-theoretic conceptions

$\{X:\ldots X\ldots\}$ the class of all X such that $\ldots X\ldots$ obtains

$x \in w$	the individual x is a member of (the population of) the possible world w
$Rw(p)$	the proposition p is realized (obtains) in the world w
S_{xy}^w	in the world w, the individual y is the *surrogate* for the (actual) individual x

D_x	$\{y: (Ew)S_{yx}^w$ & $(Aw)(A\phi)(A\psi)(\Pi z)[[(\psi/\phi)\,x$ & $S_{zx}^w]$ $\supset Rw\,(\phi z \supset \psi\,z)]\}$
$\varDelta_x$	$\{w: (\Sigma y)\,[S_{yx}^w$ & $y \in D_x]\}$
$\mathscr{N}$	$\{x: (A\phi)(A\psi)[(\phi \Rightarrow \psi) \supset (\psi/\phi) \in \mathscr{P}(x)]\}$
$\varXi$	$\{w: (\Pi x)[x \in w \supset x \in \mathscr{N}]\}$

d, d', d''	individual descriptions
$(\lambda x)dx$	the property characterizing an individual x iff x meets the descriptive condition d
$(\imath x/w)dx$	the (one and only) individual in the world w that answers to the (possibly incomplete) description d
$(\imath x)dx$	$(\imath x/w^*)dx$
$=,$	descriptive identification (as in $z =,(\imath x/w)dx$
$[\phi]_A$	$\{x: \phi x\}$
$[\phi]_N$	$\{x: \phi!x\}$
$[\phi]_P$	$\{x: \phi?x\}$
$\Box, \Diamond$	the modalities of necessity and possibility, respectively

Chapter I

PROPERTY ATTRIBUTION AND ITS MODES

1. MOTIVATION AND BACKGROUND

The domain of the possible plays a prominent part in our thought about the affairs of nature and of man. Deliberation about alternatives, contingency planning, reasoning from hypotheses and assumptions, and thought-experiments are but a few instances of our far-flung concern with possibility. The rational guidance of human affairs involves a constant recourse to possibilities: we try to guard against them, to prevent them, to bring them to realization, etc. The theory of possibility thus represents a significant part of our understanding of man's ways of thought and action.

The historical ancestry of the theory of possibility is most substantial and respectable. The range of "mere possibilities" has been given a prominent place by philosophers from the days of Plato and Aristotle in antiquity—and even by their Presocratic predecessors—continuing through the medieval schoolmen, via rationalists like Leibniz and Malebranche in the 17th century, until we reach Peirce and our numerous contemporaries who recognize genuinely chance eventuations in nature ("stochastic processes").[1]

To be sure, in the world of experientiable fact one inevitably encounters the actual and never the (merely) possible. The range of possible things and states of affairs is not the discovery of acute observers of nature; it is at bottom of the theoreticians' devising. It is thus not surprising that this conception has usually been displeasing to those who find metaphysical speculation distasteful, from Hume to the logical positivists of the 1930's and their later congeners, such as W.V.O. Quine and Nelson Goodman. In fact, by the end of the 1940's this product

[1] On the historical issues see Chapter IV, "The Concept of Nonexistent Possibles," of N. Rescher, *Essays in Philosophical Analysis* (Pittsburgh, 1969).

of philosophical theorizing was in very bad repute. In recent years, however, the stock of the possible has risen sharply in the wake of the development initially by Rudolf Carnap, and then by Saul Kripke and others, of the "possible world" semantics for modal logic. The resulting conceptual solidification of modal logic—not only in its standard, alethic guise, but also in the direction of such applications as epistemic, temporal, and deontic logic—has made talk about possibilities and possible worlds once again philosophically respectable, not to say fashionable.

And yet, the subject of possible things, states of affairs, and "possible worlds" remains underdeveloped and has not received the extensive and detailed attention that is its philosophical due. As a result, most discussions of the theoretical and semantical foundations of modal logic have been forced to start more or less *in medias res*. They assume that possible worlds are forthcoming *somehow*, neither knowing nor caring whence, and go on from there.[2] The machinery of possibilities—possible things and states of affairs and entire possible worlds—is involved in the pursuit of other purposes rather than studied in their own right. The aim of the present inquiry is to propose and to elaborate considerations that can serve to remedy this deficiency.

The motivating idea of this book is the view that *actual* individuals and the sundry properties they *actually* have are epistemically and ontologically basic, in that "merely possible" individuals (and states of affairs and worlds) are *intellectual constructions (entia rationis)* developed from a strictly actually-pertaining starting-point. Accordingly, we shall strive here to develop an approach that does not ask for its possible worlds (and their furnishings) to be given *gratis*, but is willing to put its shoulder to the wheel of the honest work of constructing them from actualistic ingredients. We shall endeavor to contend *that* —and to show *how*—the "sphere of the possible" is to be under-

[2] The modal logician need not, after all, concern himself with just what sorts of "possible worlds" are at issue because his theses are deliberately designed to be invariant under alternative answers to this question. But he may surely wonder ("in his nonprofessional moments," as Russell put it) what sorts of things go on behind the scenes, as it were, of the stage on which his own drama is enacted.

stood as a construction from materials afforded by that of the real. The present task is thus the elaboration of a theory of possibility according to which the domain of unrealized possibility comes to be seen in the light of *a rational construction proceeding from the domain of the actual*.

There is, of course, little hope of somehow *demonstrating* that there is no Platonic realm where possible worlds are graven on crystalline tablets or neatly stored away row on row on museum shelves. Demonstrations of nonexistence are seldom promising. No attempt will be made here to offer one. The aim is simply to show that one need not espouse a Platonic realism to obtain the instrumentalities of possibilia—that a conceptualistically constructive theory affords a resource of possible individuals and worlds amply adequate to all demands generally made upon machinery of this sort. Thus we shall not show that Platonic realism is blocked as an option, but simply that it is not a *forced* option, because genuine alternatives are open.

At the very outset we shall have to decide which comes first: the "chicken" of our logic or the "egg" of our theory of possible worlds. On the one hand, one can take the manifold of possible worlds as basic and given, defining the central concepts of formal logic with retrospective reference to it. (For example: an argument is defined to be *valid* if all possible worlds in which its premises obtain are such that its conclusion also obtains.) Or else we can take our logic as a given basis, and then develop the manifold of possible worlds by its means (so that, for example, it is a *derivative* consequence of the process of constructing possible worlds that those arguments which logical considerations determine to be valid turn out to have true conclusions in all possible worlds in which their premises are true). It is clear that the present line of approach takes this second route, treating possible worlds as *constructs* in whose manufacture the machinery of an already *available* logic plays a decisive role. The crucial advantage of this procedure is an epistemological one: we know reasonably well how to get a logic so as to be able to go on from there by constructive means, but we have no intellectual intuition to provide us with *direct*, nonconstructive access to a realm of possible worlds (nor is there any *deus ex machina* to waft us thither). Moreover, we can in principle obtain our logic from an analysis of actuality-orientated reasoning, and do not require in its development any inescapable recourse to the sphere of possibility.

To be sure, semantical analysis has accustomed one to look to possible worlds as a starting-point. Rather than constructing the possibilities on the basis of the "meanings" of propositions and their constituent components as given inputs, the orthodox semantical program seeks to explicate these "meanings" through *truth-conditions*, that is, by means of determination of their truth status in the various (*ex hypothesi* available) possible worlds.

The sort of semantical meaning-explication to be obtained in this way may be illustrated by the following examples:

1. p is (logically) *possible* iff p obtains (is true) in some possible world
2. p is (logically) *necessary* iff p obtains (is true) in every possible world
3. p is *nomically possible* iff p obtains in some nomically possible world
4. p is nomically *necessary* iff p obtains in every nomically possible world
5. p *entails* (logically implies) q iff q obtains in every possible world in which p obtains
6. p *nomically implies* q iff q obtains in every nomically possible world in which p obtains

Now it is clear on the very surface of the matter that all such specifications of truth-conditions are inherently *formal* in nature: they take the purely hypothetical form of claims to the effect that one thesis is true *if* another is, and so *correlate* the truth-status of related theses without ever requiring (or enabling) us materially to *determine* the truth-status of any specific thesis. As long as we remain at the strictly hypothetical level ("If a thesis obtains in all possible worlds, then . . ."), such principles remain ineffective abstractions. Until we are able to apply them concretely—to identify some specific possible world and to determine whether some particular thesis holds true in it—this mechanism of abstract truth-conditions is simply so much disconnected machinery with its wheels spinning about unavailingly. As *hypothetical* claims, they have no motive power of their own; they become serviceable only if certain external conditions are realized. And these "external conditions" require us to know about "*logically* possible" worlds (and perhaps even to know which among them are to count as "*nomically* possible"). To be in a position to *apply* this purely formal machinery we must already know about possible worlds. And, of course, at just *this* point of determining what sorts of worlds are to count as logically (or nomically) "possible" all the old problems come upon us once again.

To resolve this issue of deciding in the first instance what a "possible world" is, one must be in a position to determine of a putative world whether or not it is possible, so that we must *already* know the principles of logic to make any operative use of the right hand side of equivalence (1). We cannot hope to *rely* on this equivalence to tell us what a logical principle is, since we must already have this information as an input to its use.

Necessary truths, from this standpoint, are not necessary *because* they are "true in all possible worlds"; *au contraire*, possible worlds are so—i.e., are *possible—because* they do not conflict with truths that qualify as necessary on independent grounds. The sphere of our logic and the range of possibility do indeed stand in a relationship of inseparable coordination, but in this relationship logic is (on our approach) the independent, determining variable and the manifold of possibility the dependent, and superveniently determined one.

Again, to determine of a given (logically) possible world if it is a *nomically* possible one, we must *already* know the relevant laws, and so must, in effect, already know what the nomic possibilities are. Here too we cannot hope to decide about nomic possibility by using equivalence (3), since we must already know about the laws to make any use of its right hand side. We cannot expect to rely on this equivalence to tell us what a nomic principle is, since we must already have this information as an input to its use. Equivalences of the sort at issue in these various truth-conditions are correct enough in their own way in the *semantical* order of things, where our concern is with abstract relationships alone. But they are unhelpful in the *explanatory* order, because their application to specific cases requires as an input precisely the sort of information they are being used to determine when they are regarded as explanatory principles. To be in a position to *apply* the machinery of such truth conditions one must *already* be able to make determinations regarding "possible worlds." That is, one must be in a position to carry out the very task that is the aim of the constructive theory of possibility whose development is being undertaken here.

2. THINGS AND PROPERTIES: BACKGROUNDS FOR ESSENTIALISM

On the line of approach now to be explored, metaphysics roots in science: the possibilistic ontology we propose to develop begins in the observational and cognitive exploration of the real. The starting-point is provided by a survey of *actual individuals and their properties*, a survey that embraces two items:

(1) a *population census* or *item-inventory* of real individuals, comprising their systematic *identification*, and including the specification (be it exhaustive or partial) of the extant particulars that make up "the furniture of the world."

(2) a *feature-inventory* for these individuals, indicating those properties (features, characteristics) that pertain to the actual individuals, going beyond this actualistic basis only insofar as is needed to round off this descriptive machinery into a systematic taxonomy.

The first of these items (the census of individuals) is a relatively straightforward matter, or at any rate poses no greater difficulties in the present context than elsewhere. The second item (the properties of individuals) bears the stress of most of the theoretical difficulties.

Care must be exercised in interpreting the thesis that the spectrum of the properties of things emerges from a scrutiny of the real. There can, of course, be properties, perfectly genuine and "real" properties, that are not actually exemplified in nature. The range of the properties of things is not to be determined solely by *inspection* but is a matter of the *theoretical systematization* and rounding off of our inspectional data. (On a modest scale, think of Hume's famous example of the missing shade of blue. A more complex case is that of continuous predicate families of quantitative measure—length, temperature, etc.—in a world, as we may suppose it, of finitely many objects.) Properties must admit of exemplification, but they need not be exemplified.[3] Our theory that the range of descriptive properties is to be developed on the basis of a study of the real is thus not committed to the view that this range is in principle restricted to those properties that are actually exemplified.

On the line of theoretical approach to be pursued here, possibility is taken to root in actuality, it being maintained that the descriptive machinery which has come to be developed for characterizing actualities affords the sole effective means for a characterization of the possible. But to say this is not to say that the descriptive horizons of the possible are limited by those properties that are in fact instantiated. Unactualized descriptions can be compounded from actualized ones (winged horses). Moreover, no demand for any actual instantiation of descriptive elements need even be made. Not only can those actualized properties that come in suitably structured families be rounded off into unactualized sectors of the range (Hume's missing shade of blue), but also theoretical devices of a character far more intricate than such mere extrapolations can be used (as in theory-construction in the sciences) to lead to the conceptualization of properties that may well fail to be actualized.

Again, to say that descriptive possibilities must root in actuality is not to say that the only descriptive possibilities are those that one can *now* describe with the descriptive machinery of present-day conceptions. We do not want to say that television is somehow impossible because the Romans could not

---

[3] Many philosophical doctrines embody such a view—that of Leibniz preeminently. Compare also Santayana's oft-criticized conception of unenacted essences, regarding which see the articles on Santayana in *The Journal of Philosophy*, vol. 51 (1954), pp. 29–64. ("Santayana at Harvard," by C. I. Lewis, pp. 29–31; Donald C. Williams, "Of Essence and Existence and Santayana," pp. 31–42; F. A. Olafson, "Skepticism and Animal Faith," pp. 42–6; Ernest Nagel, "Some Gleanings from The Life of Reason, pp. 46–9; J. H. Randall, Jr., "George Santayana—Naturalizing the Imagination," pp. 50–2; Justus Buchler, "One Santayana or Two?", pp. 52–7; Daniel Cory, "God or the External World," pp. 57–61; Irwin Erdman, "Philosopher as Poet," pp. 62–4.) For modern discussions of cognate views see Nicholas Rescher, "Definitions of 'Existence'," *Philosophical Studies*, vol. 8 (1957), pp. 65–80, and Jack Kaminsky, *Language and Ontology* (Carbondale and Edwardsville, 1969).

describe it fully. Of course, the Romans could conceptualize it in terms of incomplete and "merely indicative" descriptions given wholly to their own terms of reference (say as a contrivance for transmitting pictures over large distances by sending lightning-like waves through space somewhat as pressure-impulses may be transmitted through water).

Again we do not want to deny that certain possibilities come to be opened up to view by incorrect rather than actually correct ways of characterizing real phenomena (the evil eye, the philosopher's stone, the elixir of eternal youth). Wrong theories about the actual may well provide the descriptive mechanisms for conceptualizing certain possibilities.

The key point is that actuality, and the descriptive apparatus we frame—rightly or wrongly—to describe it, is *for us* the measure of all things: of that which is, what it is, and of that which is possible, what manner of thing is at issue. The only specific possibilities that can exist *for* us are those that are conceived *by* us—those that lie within the range of the cognitive grasp of our reality-descriptive mechanisms. When this perspective is objectivized, we are led to the stance that the only possibilities that can exist *per se* are those articulated in terms of reality-descriptive mechanisms that are available in principle (even though they have not as yet been devised, and perhaps never shall be in practice).

The line of thought to be explored here thus envisages a process which embeds the articulation of possibilities in the theoretical study of the real in roughly the following manner:

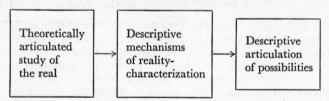

It is in the sense of this progression that we propose to adopt the Artistotelian dictum that actuality is prior to possibility.

Among contemporary philosophers, Nelson Goodman has insisted more emphatically than all others that the descriptive machinery of the real is the indispensable basis for all discourse about the possible. Thus Goodman writes:

However, the question naturally arises whether, if we restrict ourselves to predicates of actual things, we shall have enough equipment to say about the actual everything we need to say that ordinarily passes for talk about the possible. It is comforting to observe that if there are only three atomic elements, then there are seven individuals in all, and these supply differing extensions (none of them null) for some 127 one-place predicates. For any normal system that admits at least hundreds of atomic elements, either phenomenal or physical, the number of available extensions runs into billions. The threat of enforced silence is remote.

My main purpose here, then, has been to suggest that discourse, even about possibles, need not transgress the boundaries of the actual world. . . . We have come to think of the actual as one among many possible worlds. We need to repaint that picture. All possible worlds lie within the actual one.[4]

Our present position agrees with that of Goodman in this basic respect: it too takes the stance that, as regards the mechanisms for the descriptive specification of things, the manifold of possible worlds must, in the final analysis, be seen to originate from within the actual one.[5]

With the building blocks of the preceding discussion—the census of individuals and the inventory of properties—the first and crucial issue is simply this: does a certain property characterize a given individual or does it not? But one can also go beyond this (strictly factualistic) starting-point to raise the question of whether this possession or lack of a property is (categorically or hypothetically) *essential* to the individual or not.[6] Let us for the present moment put aside the question of the *grounds* for this distinction—a question to which the whole

---

[4] *Fact, Fiction and Forecast* (London, 1955), p. 56.

[5] As will appear below, Goodman takes this stance of actuality-boundedness not only as regards properties but also as regards individuals. However in this latter respect our own theory will depart sharply from his. See section 7 of Chapter III.

[6] We construe essentiality in its generic sense, so that distinct individuals can (in principle) share an essential property in common. A property that is "essential" to an individual thus forms a *part* of the "essence" of this individual and need not exhaustively constitute it.

of the next chapter will be devoted—and review the systematic position of our ontological perspective.

The machinery whose availability we presuppose is as follows:

1. A family x_1, x_2, x_3, ... of *actual* individuals, comprising the set of all reals.
2. A family F, G, H, ... of elemental (atomic) properties that either characterize reals or are systematic extensions of those that do (in the sense of Hume's missing shade of blue and its more complex theoretical congeners).
3. Given an individual x and *any* property ϕ, we can raise (and expect an answer to) the questions (i) of whether this property does or does not characterize the individual in question, and (ii) of whether this property is or is not *essential* to the individual in question.

Thus various sorts of situations can arise with respect to a property ϕ and an individual x:

(i) ϕx, that is, ϕ is an *actual* property of x: ϕ actually characterizes x.
(ii) $\phi! x$, that is, ϕ is an *essential* or *necessary* property of x: ϕ essentially characterizes x.
(iii) $\phi? x$, that is, ϕ is a *possible* property of x. (This is so related to the preceding that $\phi? x$ iff not: $\bar\phi! x$.)

(Here $\bar\phi$ represents the property-complement of ϕ, i.e., the property that belongs to a thing iff it lacks ϕ: $\bar\phi = (\lambda x)(\neg \phi x)$.)

One further complication must be introduced. The properties of a given individual may stand in a relationship of *nomic requirement* to one another. That is, the individual may not just have ϕ and ψ, but may have ϕ *because* it has ψ, if it does have ψ— or, if it lacks ψ, then be such that it would have to have ϕ as a result of its possession of ψ, if this possession of ψ were hypothetically the case. When we carry the scientific study of the real beyond the stage of purely phenomenal description and enter into the *explanatory* order of understanding, such relationships of nomic requirement must enter into our ken. We thus arrive at the following further item of machinery:

4. Given an individual x and any pair of properties ϕ and ψ, we can raise (and expect an answer to) the question of

whether the individual has the dispositional property
ϕ/ψ, that is, of whether, in the context of this individual, ψ
constrains or requires ϕ in the manner considered above
(i.e., whether, should the individual have ϕ and ψ, it has ϕ
because of its possessing of ψ). (We shall not for the present
make much of these dispositional properties, but shall deal
with them in detail in Chapter VII.)

For concreteness, consider a microworld of three individuals
x_1, x_2, x_3 and three basic (atomic) properties F, G, H. And let it
be supposed that the relevant description of this world is as
given by the following property-census tabulation:

	F	G	H
x_1	$+$	$[+]$	$-$
x_2	$+$	$[+]$	$[+]$
x_3	$[-]$	$[+]$	$+$

The following points should be noted with respect to this
tabulation:

(1) The mark $+$ indicates that an individual has the pro-
    perty at issue (at the top of the column), and the mark $-$
    indicates that it lacks it. (Thus x_1 has F and G but lacks
    H.)
(2) The property-indicating sign is placed within brackets to
    convey that this property is *essential* to the individual at
    issue; and accordingly the omission of brackets would
    convey that possession (or lack) of the property is in-
    essential. (Thus lack of F and possession of G are both
    essential to x_3, but its possession of H is inessential to it.)

One special complication deserves note here: Properties
can be *elemental* (i.e., be treated as such in a given context of
discussion), or else they can be *logically composite* in involving a
logical combination of other properties. For example, when
ϕ and ψ are given properties, then consider

$$\phi \vee \psi = (\lambda x)(\phi x \vee \psi x) = \text{possessing at least one of } \{\phi, \psi\}$$
$$\phi \supset \psi = (\lambda x)(\phi x \supset \psi x) = \text{possessing at least one of } \{\bar\phi, \psi\}$$

Such composite properties do not introduce anything fundamentally new. Since they are mere *logical* constructs from

atomic ones, the empirical inquiry into the elemental (atomic) properties of things also provides the information needed for determinations about their applicability.

Special complications enter with respect to these logically derivative (composite or nonelemental) properties once the factor of essentiality is introduced. Of course, the *de facto* status of all such properties can be settled from the tabulated information about the states of atomic properties. Thus that x_1 has $G \vee H$ and lacks $F \supset H$ is at once determinable in this way. But $F \vee H$ may also be an *essential* property of x_1 (without either F or H being separately essential), and *this* fact is not available from the tabulated information regarding the status of atomic properties. (Of course that $G \vee H$ is essential to x_1 does follow at once as a logical consequence of its essential possession of G.) Thus, in giving complete information about the properties of an individual, we must also indicate specifically those of its nonelemental (nonatomic) properties whose *possession* is, of course, logically derivable, but whose *essentiality* status remains an additional, nonderivable datum.

Further issues regarding essentiality arise with respect to dispositional properties. Assume an individual x has the dispositional property ϕ/ψ indicative of the circumstance that x does (or else *would*) have ϕ because it does have (or, alternatively, *if it were to have*) ψ. We may now confront the additional question of whether or not this dispositional property characterizes the individual *essentially*. Three policies confront us:

(i)   to treat *all* dispositional properties as essential.
(ii) to treat *no* dispositional properties as essential, i.e., to treat all dispositional properties as accidental.
(iii) to treat *only some* dispositional properties as essential, and some not.

In the framework of our discussion we shall adopt the third policy, and treat dispositional properties as in principle uncommitted in point of essentiality—a dispositional property is not, in short, automatically essential. Accordingly, we take the view that an individual may have dispositions in the *actual* scheme of things that need not of necessity characterize it in every alternative dispensation—even as people can have merely *acquired* habits. (Our reason for adopting this view will be developed in section 3 of Chapter VII below.)

We propose to adopt the following taxonomic nomenclature with respect to the properties of things:

(i) The distinction between *absolute* and *modalized* properties (or rather, between the absolute and modalized possession of properties). Thus if ϕx and ψx then ϕ and $\bar{\psi}$ are absolute properties of x, but if $\phi!x$ or if $\phi?x$ (without ϕx) —that is to say, if ϕ is a necessary or a (merely) possible property of x—then x will be said to possess ϕ in a *modalized* way (and not just absolutely).

(ii) The distinction between the *categorical* and the *conditionalized* properties of a thing. Thus if ϕx and ψx (or $\phi!x$ and $\psi!x$), then ϕ and $\bar{\psi}$ and ϕ & $\bar{\psi}$ are categorical properties of x while if $(\phi \vee \psi)x$ or $(\phi/\psi)x$, then $\phi \vee \psi$ and ϕ/ψ are conditionalized properties of x. Categorical properties are such that we are in a position to say definitely with respect to the elemental properties at issue whether or not they characterize the item in view.

(iii) The distinction between the *manifest* (or *phenomenal*) properties of an object, namely those of its actual properties that are absolute and categorical; and all the rest, which are said to be *covert* (or *nonmanifest*).

3. A DIGRESSION INTO RELATIONS

One important sector of the characteristics of individuals has been left out of account in the preceding discussion. Individuals can also have *relational* properties, properties reflecting their connections with other individuals. Consider again the micro-world conforming to the following feature-census tabulation:

	F	G	H
x_1	+	[+]	−
x_2	+	[+]	[+]
x_3	[−]	[+]	+

Given some relationship R between individuals (with Rxy obtaining when, for example, x is placed in the spatial proximity of y), we may have it that x_1 possesses the *relational* property of bearing R towards x_3. Clearly, in this specific case, the relational property of x_1 that is in view (viz., $(\lambda x)Rxx_3$) is *individual-involving* because of its invocation of x_3. But, of course, relational properties can also be *generic* in being devoid of any reference to other specific individuals, for example "being proximate to something" (viz, $(\lambda x)(\exists y)Rxy$) or "having something proximate to it" (viz., $(\lambda x)(\exists y)Ryx$).

A relational property is *reducible* if its obtaining between the individuals that it relates can be determined solely on the basis of information about the nonrelational properties of these relata. Thus for example "being like y in point of F-ness" (viz., (λx) $[(Fx\ \&\ Fy) \lor (\bar{F}x\ \&\ \bar{F}y)]$) or generically "being like *some* other individual in also having G" (viz., $(\lambda x)\ (\exists y)\ [y \neq x\ \&\ Gx\ \&\ Gy]$) are instances of reducible relations, the former relation being individual-involving, the latter generic.

The descriptively complete specification of the individuals of a world need make no mention of their (inessential) reducible relational properties, since these can always be obtained from the nonrelational rest of the descriptive picture. But the *irreducible* relational properties must be mentioned explicitly; they cannot be derived by inference from nonrelational information.

It is important to acknowledge the need for a policy prepared in principle to recognize that its relational properties may figure among the essential properties of an individual. For it may well prove to be the case that distinct individuals are distinguishable only in terms of their relational properties, as in the example:

	F	G	H	R
x_1	[+]	[+]	+	to x_3 only
x_2	[+]	[+]	+	to nothing
x_3	+	[−]	+	[to x_2 only]

Note that here the distinctness of x_1 and x_2 is discernible only in terms of the former's having and the latter's lacking the relational property $(\lambda x)(\exists y)Rxy$, which could, accordingly, be viewed as an essential aspect of these two individuals.

There is, clearly, no reason of principle why its relational properties cannot also count among the essential properties of an individual. And hence it is important to observe that even when a relational property is itself reducible, its essentiality need not be. Consider once more the property of "being like y in point of F-ness" (see two paragraphs above). If this property is essential to x, this fact itself will need not be derivable from information about x and y taken one at a time—even essentialistic information—for neither F nor F need *separately* be essential to the two of them, but merely the fact of *likeness of condition* in this regard. When essentiality enters in, relational properties may need to be specified explicitly and as such if a complete description is to be forthcoming. For the fact (for example) that it is essential to x that some other individual be like it in point of also having F, is something we cannot derive from a descriptive picture of the world from which this fact itself has been omitted. This issue of the essentiality of relations will be dealt with in greater detail in Chapter X. In the intervening discussion we shall for the most part simplify matters by putting aside the special complications regarding relational properties.

4. THE MODALITIES OF ATTRIBUTION

The key fact of *any* essentialistic approach is that it enables one to divide the properties which characterize an individual into those that do so essentially and those that do so merely *de facto*, accidentally. A complex and useful structure can be erected on this foundation. Specifically, it becomes possible to deploy the following mechanisms for dealing with the properties of individuals.

We shall suppose: (i) a domain **D** of individuals, and (ii) a family Γ of properties. The following four sets of properties can now be defined:

(1) The *actual-property set* of an individual. For every $x \in \mathbf{D}$ there is a set $\mathscr{P}(x) \subseteq \Gamma$ of all of the properties that x *actually* has:

$$\mathscr{P}(x) = \{\phi : \phi x\}$$

(2) The *essential-property set* of an individual. For every $x \in \mathbf{D}$ there is a set $\mathscr{E}(x) \subseteq \Gamma$ of all of the properties that x *necessarily* has, i.e., that are *essential* to x (in some appropriate mode of this protean conception):

$$\mathscr{E}(x) = \{\phi : \phi ! x\}$$

(3) The *possible-property set* of an individual. For every $x \in \mathbf{D}$ there is a set $\mathscr{Q}(x) \subseteq \varGamma$ of all of the properties that *x possibly* has, i.e., properties the complements (or contradictories) of which are not essential to x:

$$\mathscr{Q}(x) = \{\phi: \bar{\phi} \notin \mathscr{E}(x)\} = \{\phi: \phi?x\}$$

(4) The *dispositional-property set* of an individual with respect to each one of its possible properties:

$$\mathscr{D}_{\psi}(x) = \{\phi: (\phi/\psi)x\}, \text{ where } \psi \in \mathscr{Q}(x)$$

Thus $\mathscr{D}_{\psi}(x)$ is the set of those properties that x *must* have when ψx is the case.

It has to be said someplace, and we might as well say it here, that not everything that can truly be said of an individual corresponds to a property of it, so that not *every* context of the form $(\ldots y \ldots)$ need give rise to a feature $(\lambda y)(\ldots y \ldots)$ that qualifies specifically as a *property*. Thus for example, "being identical with x_1" or $(\lambda y)(y \equiv x_1)$, certainly represents what might, broadly speaking, be called a *feature* of x_1, but this need not be counted among its *properties*. We need not count this "feature" of x_1-hood, $(\lambda y)(y \equiv x_1)$, as an element of $\mathscr{P}(x_1)$, nor include it in the range of our property-variables ϕ, ψ, χ, etc.

The ensuing theory of essentiality revolves around the four property-sets indicated above. This very fact shows that our essentialism lends itself to an effectively *extensional* (i.e., set-theoretic) treatment, it being understood that sets of *properties*—duly correlated with individuals—are at issue, not sets of *individuals*. The semantics of the situation dictates that these property-sets must conform to certain "logical" laws, among which the following are prominent:

(i) $\mathscr{P}(x) \subseteq \mathscr{Q}(x)$

(ii) $\mathscr{D}_{\psi}(x) \subseteq \mathscr{Q}(x)$

(iii) Whenever $\psi \in \mathscr{P}(x)$, then $\mathscr{D}_{\psi}(x) \subseteq \mathscr{P}(x)$

(iv) Whenever $\psi \in \mathscr{Q}(x)$, then $\psi \in \mathscr{D}_{\psi}(x)$

(v) $\psi \notin \mathscr{Q}(x)$ iff $\mathscr{D}_{\psi}(x) = \varLambda$

(vi) $\mathscr{P}(x)$ satisfies the condition of *determination*:

Either $\phi \in \mathscr{P}(x)$ or $\bar{\phi} \in \mathscr{P}(x)$, for any x

(vii) $\mathscr{P}(x)$ satisfies the condition of *consistency*:

$$\phi \notin \mathscr{P}(x) \lor \bar{\phi} \notin \mathscr{P}(x), \text{ for all } \phi$$

(viii) $\mathscr{P}(x)$ satisfies the condition of *compatibility*:

$$(\exists x)[\phi \in \mathscr{P}(x) \ \& \ \psi \in \mathscr{P}(x)] \supset \phi \text{ compat } \psi.$$

(ix) $\mathscr{Q}(x)$ in general satisfies the condition of *overdetermination*; since $\mathscr{P}(x)$ is in general a *proper* subset of $\mathscr{Q}(x)$, $\mathscr{Q}(x)$ must meet the condition of determination but not in general that of consistency.

(x) $\mathscr{Q}(x)$ in general fails to satisfy the condition of *compatibility*, since it will in general contain properties not compatible with one another.

(xi) $\mathscr{D}_\psi(x)$ in general satisfies the condition of *underdetermination*, since in general there will be properties ψ such that neither $\phi \in \mathscr{D}_\psi(x)$ nor $\phi \in \mathscr{D}_\psi(x)$. That is, *x may or may not have ϕ even if x does ex hypothesi have ψ.*

(xii) $\mathscr{D}_\psi(x)$ satisfies the conditions of *compatibility* and of *consistency*.

(xiii) The dispositional property sets need to satisfy the condition of transitivity:

$$[\phi \in \mathscr{D}_\psi(x) \ \& \ \psi \in \mathscr{D}_\chi(x)] \supset \phi \in \mathscr{D}_\chi(x).$$

Given such property-sets, the whole of an essentialistic theory can be articulated in *extensionalistic* terms—to be sure, with an extension with respect to properties rather than individuals.

5. ESSENTIALISTIC EXTENSIONALISM

The direction of our analysis has to this point moved from actual individuals to their properties. It is helpful to reverse this direction and to look at properties from the orthodoxly extensional angle of the individuals that exemplify them. On this extensional approach we begin with a doman **D** of individuals and a set $\varGamma$ of properties. (Note that we could obtain a highly actualistic version of essentialism by taking as our domain **D** the domain w^* of real (i.e., actual) individuals pure and simple.)

For each $\phi \in \varGamma$, two subsets of **D** are to be given, namely

(1) the set of all those individuals in **D** that have ϕ *in actual fact*:

$$[\phi]_A = \{x \in \mathbf{D} : \phi x\}$$

(2) the set of all those individuals in **D** that have ϕ *essentially* (E-necessarily):

$$[\phi]_N = \{x \in \mathbf{D} : \phi!x\}$$

Given this mechanism, we can also introduce the related set of possible or potential exemplifiers of a certain property:

(3) the set of all those individuals in **D** that have ϕ *possibly* (i.e., E-possibly):

$$[\phi]_P = [\bar{\phi}]'_N$$

where in general **S'** represents the set-complement of the set **S** (in the domain **D**). Accordingly,

$$[\phi]_P = \{x \in \mathbf{D} : \phi ? x\}.$$

Note that if **D** = w^*, this yields a theory of possible property-exemplifiers that is wholly devoid of any involvement with a theory of possible *objects* as such.

The sets at issue will obviously have the feature that:

$$[\phi]_N \subseteq [\phi]_A \subseteq [\phi]_P$$

On the basis of this machinery of sets of individuals, various of the key conceptions of our essentialism can be developed in a strictly "extensionalistic" way.

Of course, the introduction of this machinery is pointful only if its inherent distinctions obtain, that is only if we do *not* in general have it that

$$[\phi]_A = [\phi]_N$$

and so only if it happens that:

$$\text{For some } x : x \in [\phi]_A \ \& \ x \notin [\phi]_N$$

Unless some actual properties of individuals are not essential (E-necessary) to them, there is no warrant for these distinctions.

Again, the machinery would be pointful only if we did not in general have it that *everything is E-possible for every individual*. We want a sphere of *restricted possibility* where one does not have the thesis that "anything is possible":

$$[\phi]_P = \mathbf{D} \quad \text{(for arbitrary } \phi\text{)}$$

For this is equivalent to

$$[\bar{\phi}]'_N = \mathbf{D}$$

which amounts to

$[\bar{\phi}]_N = \varLambda$, where $\varLambda$ = the null class (correlative with **D**) whose generality entails that of

$$[\phi]_N = \varLambda.$$

If universal with respect to ϕ, this principle would, in effect, abolish the whole mechanism of essential properties.

Again, we would not want to have it that, in general

$$[\phi]_P = [\psi]_P \quad \text{(for every } \phi, \psi)$$

or equivalently

$$[\bar{\phi}]'_N = [\bar{\psi}]'_N$$

whose generality entails that of

$$[\phi]_N = [\psi]_N.$$

To accept this as obtaining generally would be unfortunate, since it maintains that all those things that have essential properties have all of their essential properties in common, so that there can be no *differentially* E-necessary (and E-possible) properties, that is, properties belonging necessarily (or possibly) to some things but not others.[7]

It is worth noting that the sets $[\phi]_P$ and $[\bar{\phi}]_P$ are *not* in general disjoint, i.e., that there can be individuals among whose possible properties there figure not only some property ϕ, but also its complement $\bar{\phi}$. For consider the thesis

$$x \in [\phi]_P \ \& \ x \in [\bar{\phi}]_P$$

which is equivalent with

$$x \in [\bar{\phi}]'_N \ \& \ x \in [\phi]'_N$$

or equivalently

$$x \notin [\bar{\phi}]_N \ \& \ x \notin [\phi]_N$$

To see graphically the points at issue here, consider the micro-world (with individuals x_1, x_2, x_3 and properties F, G, H) whose description is as given in the following feature-census tabulation:

	F	G	H
x_1	$+$	$[-]$	$+$
x_2	$-$	$[+]$	$[-]$
x_3	$-$	$+$	$[+]$

---

[7] Some writers are prepared to accept this consequence. See Terence Parsons, "Essentialism and Quantified Modal Logic," *The Philosophical Review*, vol. 78 (1969), pp. 35–52; see especially pp. 37ff.

Note that:

$$[F]_A = \{x_1\} \qquad [G]_A = \{x_2, x_3\} \qquad [H]_A = \{x_1, x_3\}$$
$$[F]_N = \Lambda \qquad\qquad [G]_N = \{x_2\} \qquad\quad [H]_N = \{x_3\}$$
$$[F]_P = \{x_1, x_2, x_3\} \quad [G]_P = \{x_2, x_3\} \qquad [H]_P = \{x_1, x_3\}$$
$$[\bar{F}]_A = \{x_2, x_3\} \qquad [\bar{G}]_A = \{x_1\} \qquad\quad [\bar{H}]_A = \{x_2\}$$
$$[\bar{F}]_N = \Lambda \qquad\qquad [\bar{G}]_N = \{x_1\} \qquad\quad [\bar{H}]_N = \{x_2\}$$
$$[\bar{F}]_P = \{x_1, x_2, x_3\} \quad [\bar{G}]_P = \{x_1, x_3\} \qquad [\bar{H}]_P = \{x_1, x_2\}$$

This illustrates how ϕ can be *contingent* for x, with neither ϕ nor $\bar{\phi}$ essential to x (for neither H nor $\bar{H}$ is essential to x_1).

It is important to observe that *none* of the following entailments obtain:

(i) If all actual ϕ's are ψ's, then all E-necessary ϕ's are E-necessary ψ's:

$$\text{if } [\phi]_A \subseteq [\psi]_A, \text{ then } [\phi]_N \subseteq [\psi]_N$$

(i') The converse of (i)

$$\text{if } [\phi]_N \subseteq [\psi]_N, \text{ then } [\phi]_A \subseteq [\psi]_A$$

(ii) If all actual ϕ's are ψ's then all E-possible ϕ's are E-possible ψ's.

$$\text{if } [\phi]_A \subseteq [\psi]_A, \text{ then } [\phi]_P \subseteq [\psi]_P$$

(ii') The converse of (ii):

$$\text{if } [\phi]_P \subseteq [\psi]_P, \text{ then } [\phi]_A \subseteq [\psi]_A$$

(iii) If all E-possible ϕ's are E-possible ψ's then all E-necessary ϕ's are E-necessary ψ's.

$$\text{if } [\phi]_P \subseteq [\psi]_P, \text{ then } [\phi]_N \subseteq [\psi]_N$$

(iii') The converse of (iii):

$$\text{if } [\phi]_N \subseteq [\psi]_N, \text{ then } [\phi]_P \subseteq [\psi]_P$$

We have suggested that the set **D** of the preceding discussion should be construed as that of all *actually existing* individuals. The considerations of this entire section would lead to very different results if one were to fix upon a strictly possibilistic approach and construe the basic domain **D** as that of all *possible* individuals. For while on the actualistic construction $[\phi]_A$ is

> the set of all *actual* individuals
> that have ϕ,

on the revised construction of actuality-transcending purport, $[\phi]_A$ becomes

> the set of all *possible* individuals
> (actual or *merely* possible) that have ϕ

and analogous differences arise with respect to $[\phi]_N$ and $[\phi]_P$. To be sure—and this fact deserves emphasis—such a difference in the construction of **D** will make no difference in the purely *formal* relations that obtain among these items of machinery. But, of course, it will make a *decisive* difference for the *interpretative meaning* of the theses at issue. We shall now turn to this issue of nonexistent and "merely possible" individuals. But first, it certainly warrants stress that one can maintain an essentialism of reality-divergent possibilities without thereby necessarily transgressing the boundaries of the realm of actually-existing individuals.

Throughout this preliminary discussion we have presupposed *that* an essentialism of properties can be established without considering *how* this is to be done. The next chapter will address itself to this crucial issue.

Chapter II

ESSENTIALISTIC FOUNDATIONS

I. ESSENTIALISM

The issue of differentiating the properties of an object into those that are essential to it and those that are not so (i.e., are accidental) is basic to the whole of the ensuing discussion. While we shall indeed maintain that this distinction *can* be implemented, only a rather relaxed view of such an essentialistic stance will be taken here. For we are not going to hold that there is some single uniquely right and proper construction of essential properties—a construction somehow inherent in the very meaning of the conception of *being essential*. Rather, our essentialism adopts the posture of a pragmatic *pluralism*. For we shall maintain that there are various different and *alternative* bases upon which the essential/accidental distinction can be placed, and that one cannot establish any one of these as uniquely and universally *correct*, but rather can only maintain one or another of them as functionally *suitable* within the concrete setting of a particular problem-context. Viewing the distinction between the essential and the accidental as one to be developed along *various distinct lines*, no one of which is specially privileged, we regard the implementation of one or another of these as a matter not to be settled at the theoretical level of general principles, but at the concrete level of specific contexts of application. Moreover, there is nothing occult or mysterious about the mode of approach to essentialism we propose to adopt: it is—as will be seen—wholly factualistic, and seeks to proceed along effectively contingent and empirical lines. There is no sound reason for adopting the view that essentialism can bear only one monolithically unique interpretation—and moreover, one that renders the entire doctrine inherently objectionable.

One further point must be settled at the outset. The concept of essentiality that concerns us is not inevitably and in principle correlative with that of a *natural kind* (i.e., genus or species).

To be sure, there will inescapably (by the very definition of a *natural kind*) be some essential property that an individual shares with all others of its natural kind, and with these alone. But while kinds must be able to serve to determine essential properties, the converse does not hold, essential properties need not determine kinds. Indeed, it is important that this not be so, for if we are ever to be in a position to operate with the idea of a *complete* (i.e., individuating) essence, then the *differentiae* of an individual—those features which distinguish it from others of its kind—will also have to qualify for inclusion among its essential properties, and these are inherently unable to serve of themselves to define a natural kind. There is, accordingly, no reason of general principle why the individuals sharing a given essential property must constitute a natural kind. And there is no adequate ground for rejecting in principle the idea of *kind-internal differentially essential properties*, properties essential to some individuals of a certain kind but not to others of this selfsame kind.

2. APPROACHES TO ESSENTIALISM

(i) *Essential Properties from Canonical Description Families*

The starting-point of one approach to essentiality is posed by the issue of the *introduction* of individuals into the sphere of consideration and discussion. One of the key procedures for this is to proceed by way of descriptive identification. In particular, let it be supposed that an individual x answers to any of a number of different "basic" or "canonical" *identifying descriptions* of it (which need *not* be complete descriptions):[1]

$$x: d_1, d_2, \ldots, d_n$$

Now those properties of x which follow from at least one of these canonical descriptions can be held to be the (basic) essential properties of x:

> ϕ is a *basic essential* property of x iff $d_i x \vdash \phi x$ for at least one of the individuating descriptions d_i in x's family of canonical descriptions.

---

[1] An *identifying description* of a real individual is simply a (partial) description of it to which no other real individual in fact answers.

Accordingly, those properties are *basically essential* to an individual which must (i.e., *demonstrably must*) characterize it on *some one* of its (incomplete) individuating descriptions that qualifies as "canonical."[2]

Thus, suppose that x answers to the following two canonical definite descriptions:

$$x =, (\imath y)(Fy \ \& \ Gy)$$
$$x =, (\imath y)(Fy \ \& \ \neg Hy).$$

(Here '$=$,' is to be read as "is descriptively identified by the definite description . . .".) Clearly the two properties

$$F = (\lambda x)Fx$$
$$\bar{H} = (\lambda x)(\neg Hx)$$

are now both essential properties of x according to the proposed construction of this idea. And, of course, any property that is entailed by essential properties must also be an essential property, so that the basic essentiality of (for example) F and $\bar{H}$ entails the essentiality of $F \ \& \ \bar{H}$.

One important facet of this approach must be recognized. Suppose we were to *drop* the second of the just-given definite descriptions of x from the list of its "canonical" descriptions. Then immediately $\bar{H} = (\lambda x)(\neg Hx)$ would be subtracted from the list of the essential properties of x. Thus, on this present approach, the issue of which of the properties of an individual is essential to it is not an *absolute* matter, but is clearly *relative* to the way in which certain of its descriptions are given precedence over others in being designated as "canonical." And this is an issue not resolved by matters of abstract inevitability, but determined rather by considerations that are context-relative and depend upon the standpoint of the particular range of applications in view. (This is presumably a matter of the

---

[2] It is possible to contemplate the variant version of this criterion obtained by altering "*some* one" to "*every* one" of the canonical descriptions. Though we shall not pursue it here, this prospect is by no means devoid of interest. For the ramifications of this approach to essentialism by way of canonical descriptions see Saul Kripke, "Naming and Necessity" in D. Davidson and G. Harman (eds.), *Semantics of Natural Language* (Dordrecht, 1972), pp. 253–355, and also John R. Searle, "Proper Names," *Mind*, vol. 67 (1958), pp. 166–73.

particular scientific issues operative within the framework of discussion.)

Now W. V. Quine has objected against the recognition of essential properties that

> Essentialism is abruptly at variance with the idea, favored by Carnap, Lewis, and others, of explaining necessity by analyticity. For the appeal to analyticity can pretend to distinguish the essential and the accidental traits of an object relative to how the object is specified, not absolutely.[3]

Here Quine patently construes essentialism as committed to the view that the distinction between the essential and inessential properties of an individual must be an absolute one that is independent of how we may choose to describe this individual, and functions in an altogether description-invariant and context-independent way. But this view is not adopted here. On the approach presently in view, for example, an individual (regardless of how specified) has certain canonical descriptions, and these determine its essential properties, and in *this* sense, the absolutistic thesis is satisfied. However, if some *other* group of its descriptions had been canonized—that is, if we had taken a different stance towards the descriptions of the individual at issue—then the family of its essential properties might well have been altered. In this sense, the present essentialism is quite prepared to take a relativistic rather than absolutistic stance standing, ready to allow the issue of essentiality to hinge upon the "pragmatic" features of the problems and interests of a particular range of scientific discussion.

It is, of course, quite clear that this approach to essentiality via canonical descriptions leaves much in suspension until the crucial matter of the "canonicity" of a description is settled. We propose to implement this idea as follows: One would characterize just *some* of the atomic properties as determinative in this regard, and then count any individuating description that specifies the individual with respect to all (or most) of *these* properties

---

[3] "Reference and Modality" in *From a Logical Point of View* (Cambridge, Mass.; 2nd ed., 1961), pp. 139–59, see p. 155. Quine's objections to quantified modal logic are largely based upon his view that its acceptance would commit one to an unpalatable "Aristotelian essentialism" of absolutist character.

as representing a canonical description.[4] Thus suppose some item is introduced into the framework of discussion as, e.g., "this wooden kitchen chair." Then from the carpenter's perspective it would be essential that it be a wooden piece of furniture (whether a chair or table might be incidental); from the home decorator's perspective it would be essential that it is a *kitchen* chair (that it is wooden might be incidental); from the fire marshal's perspective that it be something wooden; and so on.[5]

This approach to essentialism can be implemented in terms of the background of a plurality of "functional perspectives." These are to operate in such a way that when an object is specified by such a description as

$$(\imath x)(\phi x\ \&\ \psi x\ \&\ \chi x\ \&\ \ldots)$$

then those predicates (ϕ, ψ, χ, etc.) that are definitive of the given perspective at issue become the determinants of the canonical identifying descriptions. In what would perhaps be the standard application of this machinery, these canonicity-determinative properties would presumably be those at issue in the descriptive parameters (or "boundary values") needed for the purposes of scientific explanation within the sphere of interest of some particular context of consideration. In any event, however, this sort of approach to the determination of canonical descriptions is a *pragmatic* matter of the orientation of one's interests which hinges on the specific purposive context that is at issue in the determination of what we have called a "functional perspective." For example, another way of implementing the idea of a canonical description is to take a causally ontogenetic approach. On such a view all of those descriptions that deal with the causal origination of a thing are to be taken as canonical. Accordingly, all those descriptive features of an individual that

---

[4] This formulation of the essentialistic doctrine at issue will serve for our present immediate purposes, though its fully adequate development requires the introduction of some refinements. For further details see Daniel Bennett, "Essential Properties," *The Journal of Philosophy*, vol. 66 (1969).

[5] For an eloquent statement of the case for supplementing the more orthodox logico-conceptual essentialism based on a definitional approach by this context-perspectival mode of essentialism, see Amelie Oksenberg Rorty, "Essential Possibilities in the Actual World," *The Review of Metaphysics*, vol. 25 (1972), pp. 607-24.

deal with its origins are essential, but the historical vicissitudes of its later development becomes an accidental matter. Thus being the offspring of his parents, being born on such-and-such a date, developing as a male, and in general all facets of some suitably "initial" period of his biography—and, *a fortiori*, of his causal antecedents would all be essential to Napoleon, but his subsequent contingent history—e.g., becoming emperor of France (rather than dying on a distant battlefield as an obscure major of artillery)—would be accidental to him.

(ii) *Essential Properties From Difference-Maintaining Properties*

On the approach now to be considered, a (basic) essential property is one needed *to maintain the descriptive differentiation of an individual from all others*. For the sake of illustration, consider a set of individuals described—so we shall assume—*completely* with respect to a certain given family of properties:

	F	G	H
x_1	$+$	$+$	$-$
x_2	$+$	$+$	$+$
x_3	$-$	$-$	$+$

On the present criterion we shall obtain results such as the following:

(1) $\bar{H}$ is essential to x_1; for if $\bar{H}$ were changed to its complement H, then x_1 would coincide descriptively with x_2

(2) H is essential to x_2; for if H were changed to its complement $\bar{H}$, then x_2 would coincide descriptively with x_1

(3) $\bar{F} \vee \bar{G}$ is essential to x_3; for if $\bar{F} \vee \bar{G}$ were changed to its complement F & G, then x_3 would coincide descriptively with x_2.

On this approach, a property will qualify as essential if it is such that replacement by its complement results in a "descriptive collision" with the over-all description of another individual. In effect, we use the principle of the "identity of indiscernibles" as a guide to allocating the status of basic essentiality to properties. Note that, on this approach, the existence of an individual answering to the complete description

$$(\imath x)(F_1\,x\ \&\ F_2 x\ \&\ F_3 x\ \&\ \ldots)$$

presumptively entails that all other individuals will have the essential property $F_1 \lor F_2 \lor F_3 \ldots$, since each will differ from the one initially at issue in *some* respect the world satisfies the principle of the "identity of indiscernibles."

One complication must be taken into account. On the present criterion, the maintenance of descriptive differentiation must be taken as a *sufficient* condition of essentiality, not as a necessary one. For we should certainly wish once again to maintain the principle that the logical consequences of an essential property are themselves essential. Thus since H is essential to x_2, so by this principle is $F \lor G \lor H = (\lambda x)(Fx \lor Gx \lor Hx)$. But clearly this property is not "basically" essential to x_2 in the sense of the present criterion: when changed into its complement $\bar{F}$ & $\bar{G}$ & $\bar{H}$ there results no descriptive collision with any individual whatsoever.

(iii) *Essential Properties From Uniformity-Maintaining Properties: Typological or Taxonomic Essentialism*

The leading idea of a typological essentialism is (1) that the individuals in view are (somehow) distinguished into mutually disjoint types, and (2) that the basic essential properties of an individual are to be these that it shares with *all* others of its type. On this approach, a property is to count as basically essential if its presence is needed to preserve an existing uniformity across the whole of a type-family.

For the sake of illustration consider the microworld with the following description and typology (one may assume that the type-distinctions are drawn on the basis of considerations external to the tabulation itself):

	F	G	H	Type No.
x_1	+	−	+	1
x_2	+	−	−	1
x_3	+	+	+	2
x_4	+	+	−	2
x_5	−	+	+	3
x_6	−	+	−	3

Here F and $\bar{G}$ are both basically essential to the members of

Type No. 1 (viz., x_1 and x_2), and analogously both F and G are similarly essential to members of Type No. 2 (x_3 and x_4,) and $\bar{F}$ and G to members of Type No. 3.

On this approach, individuals of different types can share the same essential properties (as x_1 and x_3 both have F in common as a basic essential property, or as *all* the individuals share the nonbasic essential property $F \vee G = (\lambda x)[Fx \vee Gx]$). But it is clear that one should be prepared to reject a sorting out into types as improper—or at least to view it as highly problematic—when it leads to the one of the following results:

(1) the members of a certain type have no property in common (so that no "essential" properties at all—on the concept now at issue—are shared in common by the members of this type).

(2) There are two distinct types that share *all* of their essential properties, so that there are types that cannot be differentiated with respect to their corresponding essential properties. (Accordingly, the fact that two individuals share *all* of their essential properties ought to have the consequence that they belong to the same type.)

We are still, of course, left to face the unresolved issue of what is to constitute a "type." Undoubtedly, the simplest and most satisfactory way to proceed here would be to designate certain properties as type-determinative, and then to class as "of the same type" those individuals that share a common pattern with respect to these type-determinative properties. Consider for example the microworld with the following description:

	F	G	H	J	K
x_1	+	+	+	−	+
x_2	+	−	+	+	+
x_3	+	+	−	+	+
x_4	−	+	+	−	−
x_5	+	−	+	−	+
x_6	+	−	−	+	−
x_7	+	+	−	+	−

If here one were to class the properties G and K as type-determinants, we will clearly obtain four types:

Type No.	Descriptive Constitution	Members of the Type	Basic Essential Properties
1	$G \,\&\, K$	x_1, x_3	G, K, F
2	$G \,\&\, \bar{K}$	x_4, x_7	$G, \bar{K}$
3	$\bar{G} \,\&\, K$	x_2, x_5	$\bar{G}, K, F, H$
4	$\bar{G} \,\&\, \bar{K}$	x_6	$\bar{G}, \bar{K}, F, \bar{H}, J$

This taxonomic scheme produces the indicated distribution of basic essential properties. (It is, obviously, inevitable that an individual's status with respect to the type-determinative properties should be essential to it on the present criterion.)

Of course, the preceding indications for implementing the idea of a taxonomically based essentialism are highly schematic, and thus somewhat unsatisfying. Any realistic application of this machinery would have to proceed in terms of the concrete detail of a realistic taxonomy of "natural kinds," duly based on scientific theories as to how things work in the world.

(iv) *Essential Properties from Temporally Invariant Properties*

What is now at issue is perhaps the very first and oldest idea of essentiality, viz., temporal invariance. The conception is that just precisely those properties that an individual retains throughout its entire lifespan are to count as essential to it. (Of course, we must here construe *property* in the time-indefinite sense of —for example—"is red" rather the time-definite sense of "is-red-at-t.") Thus that he is a human being and that he is male are to count as essential to Napoleon, not that he is an emperor or the husband of Josephine. Essential properties are to be those that persist under historical (temporal) change throughout the period when the individual or type of individual at issue exists.[6] This conception of essentiality has been operative

---

[6] To implement this idea we must, of course, be in a position to determine when the things at issue begin and cease to exist. And this is clearly a description-relative matter: the child's pile of blocks exists as a plurality of blocks under one set of criteria and as a block-tower under another (and their existence in the former condition can survive their destruction in the latter). This correlative issue of existence criteria thus represents another cognate approach to the present issue of essentiality as inherent in temporal invariance.

in Aristotle, the Church Fathers, the Arabic logicians, the medieval schoolmen, and a host of others.[7]

This temporal approach to essentialism is intimately linked to the root conception of an essential property as one that a thing "must retain, come what may," and which it must continue to bear throughout all changes—with "changes" here construed very literally in terms of the root idea of the actual processes of historical change, instead of the subsequent, more sophisticated conception of purely conjectural or hypothetical changes. This last consideration points to the shortcoming of this conception: it is insufficiently systematic. Consider Napoleon again. He never set eyes on the Pacific, and thus had, throughout his life, the property of "not being a person who has seen the Pacific Ocean." But it is surely a matter of contingence and chance that this is so. It is surely, nowise a matter of deeper principle that Napoleon never saw this vast ocean. (The British could have imprisoned him in Tasmania as easily as on St. Helena.) The point is that just because a person maintains throughout his life some clearly contingent and in principle changeable property (being a resident of France, a property owner in Bordeaux, a man who never read Shakespeare, etc.), we might well not feel comfortable about regarding this as an *essential* property of his, as the present criterion of essentiality would oblige us to do. Continued possession of the property will, of course, be necessary to essentiality, but—so one might well feel—it should not be counted as sufficient.

For reasons such as these one might well feel reluctant to adopt a view of the essentiality of properties that sees these as forthcoming in terms of temporal invariance alone. But if one is willing to overlook these drawbacks and is prepared to follow this route to essentiality, the result provides a perfectly meaningful and clearly defined basis for articulating the distinction between the essential (now = permanent) and the accidental (now = changeable) properties of things.

One qualification or complication must, however, be introduced. It is clear that among the features that an individual

---

[7] Cf. N. Rescher, "The Theory of Modal Syllogistic in Medieval Arabic Philosophy" in *Studies in Modality* (Oxford, 1974; APQ Monograph Series, No. 8). See also St. Augustine, *De Trinitate* V, v, 6 (cited in Joseph Ratzinger, *Introduction to Christianity* [New York, 1970], p. 132n).

will have throughout its lifespan is that of existence itself. Thus if one adopts the present mode of essentiality and yet wishes to avoid the (surely unpalatable) Spinozistic result that whatever exists actually is such that it exists essentially, then one must refuse to recognize the existence as a candidate essentiality.[8] One must place existence outside the operative domain of the principle that those properties which it exhibits at all times throughout the timespan of its existence are to count as essential to a thing.[9]

(v) Essential Properties From Invariance Under Transformations

The essentialism of the preceding section was articulated in terms of the constancy of properties throughout *temporal* change. But strictly analogous considerations can be applied whenever a certain family of specified transformations other than simply temporal changes is at issue. For example, just those properties that a metal maintains throughout a specified range of natural processes—exposure to high and low temperatures, placement within electromagnetic fields, subjection to high-intensity vibration, etc.—might be regarded as essential to it. By deploying our scientific knowledge we can determine the properties of things that remain unaffected (actually or hypothetically) by various relevant natural processes, and this in turn can guide our imputations of essentiality. Thus it is an essential feature of every elephant-tusk that it be less than 30 feet long (to adapt an example of Meinong's): given the biological laws governing the development of *elephants*, it is not possible that this should happen. Accordingly, one would say, for example, that—the laws of nature being the same—Napoleon's blood type is essential to him relative to hypothetical transformations relating to the vicissitudes of his career (it would have remained the same if he had won at Waterloo, been imprisoned in Tasmania, etc.).

---

[8] Of course, if, with Kant, we refused in principle to count existence as a *property*, we would *a fortiori* rule it out as a feasibly *essential* property. But we need not go so far. On this whole issue, see Chapter VI.

[9] And we might well extend this exemption principle also to "being located in (real) space (or time)" and "being located in *this* (or such-and-such) a position in space (or time)."

It is helpful to assimilate this case of the assumptive transformation of things to that of their causal modification in the course of actual events. The actual physical transformation of things can be distinguished into two kinds: the *destructive* and the *preservative*. A *destructive* transformation destroys a thing (burning a letter, smashing a glass, stuffing an owl), a preservative transformation simply modifies it (folding the letter, emptying the glass, clipping the owl's wings), while preserving it as a thing of its kind (*sui generis*). Of course, a destructive transformation still leaves us with *something* (e.g., the ashes of the burnt letter, the fragments of the smashed glass); it is not *totally* destructive, but destroys an object the kind of thing it is (a letter, a glass). The melted wax in the example of the second of Descartes' *Meditations on First Philosophy* is still *the same chunk of matter* as the solid piece, but it is no longer *the same piece of wax*. The octogenarian is *the same person* as the 17-year old, but he is no longer *the same youth*. Throughout, examples of this sort deal with identity and difference not in the absolute sense (the same item), but in a kind-relativized sense of identity *sui generis* (the same X). In this sense, then, the transformationally essential properties are type-correlative. The criteria of re-identification *sui generis* determine those features which are essential to an item as an instance of the kind at issue. The essential properties are exactly those whose alteration is outside the scope of preservative transformations; the accidental properties those whose alteration lies within this range. When we replace the tire we still have unproblematically *the same car* on our hands—just this makes its possession of a certain tire an accidental rather than essential feature of a motor vehicle.

In ways such as these one arrives at a conception of a mode of essentiality to be articulated in terms of invariance under a specified family of *assumptive transformations* in the conditions and circumstances of things. This variant transformationist approach to essentiality via *physical* or *natural* transformations is calculated to obviate some of the limitations of the strictly temporal transformationism considered in the preceding section. (We shall return to this important issue of assumptive transformations in Chapter VII.)

One can, of course, only apply this essentiality criterion based on the preservation of identity *sui generis* when the relevant genus is determined. Thus this version of the transformationist criterion harks back to the conception of a typology of practical perspectives considered in subsection (i) above.

* * *

These five criteria for essentiality do not, of course, exhaust the reasonable prospects. But they should suffice to show that various more or less plausible constructions can be given to this idea, constructions which avoid obscurantism of any sort, and which, moreover, are by and large linked closely to some section or other of the historic tradition of essentialism in philosophy. This last point is clearly important. A workable separation of the predicates of objects into the "essential" and "accidental" cannot be simply arbitrary. It must qualify by way of historical affinities as an implementation of this distinction as it has evolved in the context of philosophical discussion. And the core idea at issue, one implemented by all the preceding constructions of the idea, is that an essential property is one that an individual is bound to exhibit "come what may."

3. NATURALISTIC ESSENTIALISM: THE ROLE OF FACTUAL FOUNDATIONS

It is plain that on most such approaches to essentialism the issue of which properties of an individual are essential to it becomes very much a question of the nature of its world environment and is contingent upon the make-up of the *other* individuals to be found there. (Think, for example, of the cases of difference-maintaining or of uniformity-maintaining properties as being essential.) The critical fact is that, beginning with a purely phenomenal description of the world (i.e., of its entire population), we *derive* the specifications of essentiality on the basis of this strictly *de facto* information. The key to the present lines of approach to essentialism is that essentiality-specification become something *calculable* given a sufficiently far-reaching basis of purely factual information.

The point is that ours is throughout an altogether *naturalistic* essentialism which proposes to settle the issue of the essential properties of individuals on the basis of what the world is like. There is nothing occult about an essentialism of this sort. No "mind's eye" faculty for *Wesensschau* need be assumed over and above the standard mechanisms of scientific observation and theorizing.

One immediate consequence of this stance is that we can rule out the prospect of finding the *actual* world to be as in the following example of an essentialistic description characterizing the three individuals (x_1, x_2, x_3) comprising a certain microworld:

	F	G	H
x_1	[+]	+	−
x_2	+	[+]	−
x_3	[−]	+	+

That is, it could not happen that in the *actual* world two otherwise indistinguishable individuals should differ solely with regard to the *mode* in which they bear these properties. For if we are to *begin* with the merely phenomenal descriptions of individuals, and proceed to determine the issue of essentiality through *systematic* considerations articulated on this basis—as we propose to do throughout—then we clearly could not (by the "Principle of Sufficient Reason") proceed to differentiate essentialistically between descriptively indistinguishable individuals. Essentiality considerations thus cannot of themselves play a decisive role when the individuation of actual individuals is at issue.

Accordingly, its fundamentally factual and contingent basis is a critical aspect of the sort of essentialism we have espoused here. It merits stress that on all of the various essentialistic approaches mooted above, the issue of essentiality is made to rest on a fundamentally factual and thus *contingent* foundation. Our essentialism is not absolute (categorical) and metaphysical, but relative (hypothetical) and empirical in nature. It sets out from considerations relating to the (by no means inevitable) circumstances of a factual starting-point. In all these cases, if the actual world that furnishes our *de facto* starting point were different, we would arrive at a different view of the "essential" properties of an individual. In this sense, our essentialism is not absolute but empirically relativized to the descriptive constitution of the actual world.

It is thus a critical feature of the essentialist perspective of the present discussion that it is actuality-derivative. It takes the stance that the essentiality of a property of a thing is not something occult and rationally inaccessible, but is altogether naturalistic in posing an issue that can be resolved, in the final analysis, on the basis of a scientific investigation into the workings of the world. Ours is thus an *empiricistic* essentialism, one that rests on a contingent and factual foundation determined in the scientific study of the real.

Accordingly, it is crucial for our purposes to distinguish between the *contingent* and the *accidental*. Presumably all of the factual arrangements of the actual world might be otherwise and thus obtain only contingently. And our approach has it that the distinction between the accidental and the essential is to be drawn *within* this contingent domain. The sort of absolute necessity that is opposite to contingency is not now operative. The sort of "necessity" at issue in essentiality is merely relative or hypothetical—*given* that "things are as they are," each thing must have those features that (correlatively) are "of its very nature."

It may sound strange to say that the essential properties of an individual could have been different. But one must heed the needed distinctions. To say that (because of the contingency of the world's arrangements) it could have turned out that some essential property of an individual might not have been essential (so that "it"—in a manner of speaking—would not have been the thing it is) is to say something quite different from saying that this selfsame individual could have differed in point of some property that, as matters stand, in fact qualifies as essential to it.

To be sure, though essentiality is, as just indicated, a "factual" matter, the issue of what features of a thing are essential to it is not an *observational* fact to be discovered by scrutinizing this thing in isolation. Essentiality is not to be arrived at by inspection but poses wider issues in the theoretical context of the description and explanation of the real. It is a matter of a theoretical *imputation*, but an imputation that is not a thing of haphazard, but is rationally founded on the empirical study of reality at the global level. The essentiality of some property of a thing is not to be detached by its inspection in isolation (neither with the eye of the body, nor with the eye of the mind in a speculative *Wesensschau*); it is *imputed* to the thing on the basis of *synoptically holistic or global* considerations regarding the make-up of the wider world to which it belongs. The essentiality of certain of its properties does not just hinge upon the individual make-up of the thing, but is a *relational* feature which depends on the relationship obtaining between this thing and those others that make up its environing world.

Neither its pluralism nor its cognate factualism should be misconstrued as somehow abrogating the fundamentally essentialistic nature of the enterprise. Any theory that makes effective use of the distinction between essential and accidental properties deserves to be qualified as "essentialistic", regardless of whether the basis on which this distinction is drawn itself derives from necessary or from contingent considerations.

As we see it, questions of the type listed at the outset of this section do not admit of a stable resolution arrived at in a uniform way on grounds of general theoretical principle. Their answer hinges upon the prior specification of some particular mode of essentiality/accidentality in whose specific terms the issues can be resolved meaningfully.

4. THE "PLASTICITY" OF INDIVIDUALS

Any essentialistic theory invites the posing of meta-theoretical questions of the type:

> Must every actual individual have (some) essential properties, or could it be that *all* of the properties of an (actual) individual might be inessential or *accidental* to it?

> Must every actual individual have (some) accidental properties, or could it be that *all* of the properties of an (actual) individual might be *essential* to it?

On the present line of approach, questions of this sort are not to be settled directly and immediately. Their standing becomes a secondary and supervenient one, in that they can be dealt with only after the issue of specifying a particular mode of essentiality/accidentality has first been resolved. And at *this* point their answer becomes derivative, and is forthcoming along relatively straightforward lines determined by the specific mode of essentiality at issue. The upshot is as follows:

Sense of Essential/Accidental	Q: Can an individual lack accidental properties?	Q: Can an individual lack essential properties?
(i) Canonical Descriptions	Yes	No*
(ii) Difference-Maintenance	Yes	Yes¶
(iii) Taxonomic Placement	No†	No†
(iv) Temporal Invariance	Yes#	Yes
(v) Transformational Invariance	No‡	No‡

* At any rate not as long as there are descriptions that have been designated as "canonical."
† The reason for a negative response lies in the fact that if these prospects *were* realized, this would simply establish the inadequacy or impropriety of the putatively "taxonomic" scheme at issue.
‡ At any rate not as long as the range of transformations is plausibly constituted.
¶ But only under the two conditions: (i) that there is only one individual, and (2) that while there are several individuals, they are all qualitatively indistinguishable.
# Given that relational properties are also at issue, this would, however, lock the individual into a wholly unchanging world.

It is thus useful to observe that, on each of the various conceptions of "essentiality/accidentality," the *extent* to which the properties of an individual are essential to it can vary from individual to individual; they can differ drastically in this regard—some can have all (or almost all) of their properties essentially, others only a few of them. Accordingly, we can introduce (relative to any fixed, *given* sense of essentiality) the conception of the *plasticity* of an individual—i.e., the extent to which it can be revamped by purely hypothetical remoulding. The fewer of its properties are essential to it, the more plastic it is in this sense, that is, the more hypothetical alterations we can effect in its descriptive specification without thereby ceasing to deal with *this* individual. Accordingly, a theory which, like that of Leibniz, views *all* of properties of an individual as essential to it stipulates zero plasticity for individuals, being committed to denying that one can alter them in *any* respect. On the other hand, a theory of "bare particulars" that views all of the properties of an individual as in effect accidental to it, would consider individuals as *totally* plastic in our sense.

One other point warrants stress. It might seem on first view that if one were to adopt the doctrine of universal and complete determinism, then the philosophically useful role of the idea of possibility would be confined to the epistemological domain of "what is possible for all one knows." But this is not necessarily so. The sort of possibilities that concern us here are those which lie within the sphere of essentialistically permissible variations. And—as the preceding approaches indicate—these need not be articulated with a view to *causal* possibilities at all, but may inhere in more fundamental issues as to the nature (i.e., the *factually descriptive* nature) of the actual world. The sort of possibility at issue will thus not be a causal possibility but a functional-descriptive one, exactly as in the example of that classic exclamation: "There, but for the Grace of God, go I."

This perspective is particularly important because it shows that our horizons of consideration need not be confined to the standard sort of "real possibilities" as distinct eventuations in an indeterministic world. For surely the most common sorts of "possible things" are those which evolve through a putatively indeterministic causality out of the actualia of the world (the cake I might have baked from the batter, instead of the cookies I actually did bake). In such cases, "possible things" are viewed as potentially projected upon the stage of world-history as the suitably resultant causal result of the (unrealized) actualization of an non-determined process (my "decision to bake cookies"). The critical upshot of such considerations is that this case of indeterministic causality is by no means the only avenue of access to "real possibilities."

The preceding discussion has focused upon the categorical or unconditionalized type of essentiality, in contradistinction to that which is hypothetical or conditionalized (i.e., that F is essential to x, as compared with its being essential to x that it have F *if and when* it has G). This latter type of (conditionalized) essentiality will be dealt with in the discussions devoted below to dispositions and laws. In general terms it does, however, warrant stress at this stage that our theoretical understanding of the lawful structure of the world provides what is unquestionably the securest guide we have in shaping our views as to the essential features of things—even the categorically essential ones.

This line of thought leads towards yet another important point. Precisely because of their different "natures," different sorts of things behave according to different laws—as copper comports itself differently from iron or the behavior of snails differs from that of snakes. It is thus only to be expected that the various approaches to essentialism lead to the common result that certain properties can be essential to one thing but not another—i.e., that there can be *differentially essential properties* that apply divergently to diverse things.

Some writers have found this particular essentialistic principle distasteful.[10] Assimilating *essential* properties to (suitably) *necessary* ones, their reasoning seems to go somewhat as follows:

If one is prepared to admit the *de dicto* necessity of certain universal propositions (as is pretty much inevitable) one is committed to the following chain of inferences:

(1) $\Box(\forall x)\phi x$ by a conceded assumption re, lawfulness

(2) $(\forall x)\Box\phi x$ from (1) by a standard inference of quantified modal logic

(3) $\Box\phi y$ from (2) by instantiation

(4) $(\exists x)\Box\phi x$ from (3) by existential generalization

So one may have to concede the prospect of *de re* necessities in *such* cases. But in the final analysis these are the *harmless* cases because they envisage *de re* necessity only in the in-

---

[10] See, for example, the discussion in Terence Parsons, "Essentialism and Quantified Modal Logic," *The Philosophical Review*, vol. 78 (1969), pp. 35–52 (see in particular, pp. 37–9).

herently universalized "lawful" cases (i.e., only when it is traceable back to a universal *de dicto* necessity of the type of (1)). What is *not* harmless is the sort of *differential* necessity *de re* of the sort at issue with a thesis of the type:

$$(\exists x)\Box\psi x \ \& \ (\exists x)\neg\Box\psi x$$

However, the shortcoming of this line of objection is that no one has succeeded in clarifying just why this result should be regarded as obnoxious. Agreed!—differentially necessary properties are *ex hypothesi* not of universalized bearing, but what is wrong with that? Indeed there would, in the final analysis, be little point in an essentialism that did not embrace this prospect —i.e., that was prepared to regard as essential to an individual only those rather jejune properties that belong to everything whatsoever (like the "entity" and "unity" of the medievals).

Chapter III

INDIVIDUATION AND THE CONSTRUCTIVE THEORY OF POSSIBLE INDIVIDUALS

I. ACTUALS AND THEIR POTENTIALITIES

It is advantageous (and well-advised) to approach the consideration of *nonexistent* things and states of affairs—those which are not actual but "merely possible"—from the obviously less problematic angle of those that are actual. Accordingly, the starting point of our present inquiry into the "merely possible" is afforded by a consideration of the nature of the real.

With respect to an *actually* existing thing it is, presumably, always possible to determine the following items in a relatively straightforward way, along the lines of thought set forth in the preceding chapter.

(1) Its *actual* properties: those properties it actually *does* have.

(2) Its *necessary* properties: those among its actual properties which are (on some appropriate mode of approach) to be regarded as *essential* to it, and which, accordingly, it necessarily *must* have.

(3) Its (merely) *possible* properties: those properties which, though it lacks them, it yet possible *might* have. These can be derived from (2) by the principle that a thing's possible properties are those whose property-complements (negations) are not essential to it.

(4) Its *dispositional* properties: those inherent in the conditional realization-relationships among its absolute (nondispositional) possible properties, taking either the factualistic form "since it has such and such properties, it must also have these-and-those" or the contra-factualistic form "if it had such and such properties, it would also have to have these-and-those." Such dispositional properties represent its (as it were) *hypothetically necessary* features.

Such an elaboration of the modally differentiated properties of the actual will provide the starting-point for an elaboration of the domain of the possible.

2. THE INDIVIDUATION OF ACTUALIA (ACTUAL INDIVIDUALS)

The *descriptively complete property-specification* of an individual must indicate two items with regard to every suitable property: (1) whether this property is to be included or not, and (2) the mode of inclusion of this property in point of its being accidental or essential. We shall refer to these essentialistically complete descriptions as C.D.S., short for "[essentialistically] complete descriptive specifications." By contrast, a *weakly* complete descriptive specification (c.d.s.) of an individual is that component of its C.D.S. that is "purely" descriptive in content—its "full" description minus any essentiality-specifications. The C.D.S. of an individual x is given by $[\mathscr{P}(x), \mathscr{E}(x)]$; its c.d.s. by $\mathscr{P}(x)$ itself. In *both* cases, however, we take $\mathscr{P}$ to be so constituted as to *exclude* accidental relational properties involving other *individuals* (be they *specific* like "having R to x_1," or *generic* like "having R to something (else)." The reason for this exclusion will be set out in Appendix I to Chapter IV.

How can even a complete description assure individuational uniqueness? Very significant issues revolve about this fundamental question. To begin with, it must be recognized that since we must suppose dealing here with *genuine* description, description given in purely *qualitative* terms, honestly free of any and all ostensive elements, there simply cannot be any purely *conceptually warranted guarantee* of the uniqueness needed for individuation. To be sure, it is wholly possible—nay probable— that the contingent arrangements of the world are such that purely descriptive information is *de facto* sufficient for individuation. But no guarantee of this sufficiency can be issued as a matter of theoretical principle.

One must thus not suppose that actual individuals are to be *individuated* on a merely descriptive basis of the sort set out in the preceding chapter. As long as descriptions are given in *genuinely* qualitative terms, the possibility of multiple instantiations always remains open in principle. (This point may be taken to have emerged from the substantial literature of "The Problem of the Identity of Indiscernibles.") To be sure, *within* the actual world (or for that matter any particular possible world) the description of an individual—even an incomplete, partial description—may well suffice to individuate it as a matter of the contingencies of the composition of that world. But one must distinguish between *practical* and *theoretical* sufficiency. If we are to seek a logically secure *guarantee* of individuation (i.e., seek something on the order of the traditional "logically proper name" of a thing), then we must go beyond mere description. It becomes necessary to have resort to the *this* of ostensive reference—or in the case of communication to rely upon some interactional causal contact between the object, the speaker, and the hearer.[1]

By what sort of identifying procedure can one conceivably introduce a *thing* into the framework of consideration and discussion? *Actually existing* things can be identified in two ways:

(1) by *experiential encounter* in terms of their placement within the spatio-temporal matrix. That is, we may indicate the item either ostensively—as, e.g., "*this* chair (pointing)" or by means of locational instructions that—by indicating "how to get there from here"—can terminate in a comparable experiential confrontation (e.g., "the chair in the south-west corner of the adjacent room").

(2) by *description* in terms of their purely qualitative features. For example, by specifying the dimensions and make-up of the chair, specifying if need be its patterns of dents and scratches, etc. (One must here exclude from "purely qualitative description" spatio-temporal placement in terms of A-series indicators in the sense of McTaggart— viz., those which, like "three miles to the north of us" or "a fortnight hence," involve an ineliminable reference to *here* and *now*. This would carry us back to the preceding item. Accordingly, descriptive placement into *a* space

---

[1] For philosophical discussions of the relevant issues see P. F. Strawson, *Individuals: An Essay in Descriptive Metaphysics* (London, 1959); David Wiggins, "Individuation of Things and Places," *Proceedings of the Aristotelian Society*, Supplementary Volume XXXVII (London, 1963), pp. 177–208; and Saul Kripke, "Naming and Necessity" in D. Davidson and G. Harman (eds.), *Semantics of Natural Language* (Dordrect, 1972), pp. 253–355.

defined relative to other described objects is admissible, but placement in *our* space is not.)

Theoretically airtight guarantees of nonduplication are only available on an *ostensive* basis, where the element of experiential confrontation or confrontability ("how to get there from here") enters in through the presence of appropriate *indicators*.[2] The full individuating characterization of an actual individual is thus only to be had through a pair of data $\langle d, i \rangle$, the first member of which, *d*, is a *description* of the individual (which need not be a *complete* description, but may be a partial one), and whose second member, *i*, represents an ostension-involving *indicator* of the individual which reflects a *transaction* placing it within the context involving others. Thanks to the potential nonspecificity inherent in any genuine description, the individuation of a real individual demands the presence of a suitable ostensive indicator if a theoretical guarantee of particular-individuation is to be issued. This ostensive-indicator, being here-and-now connective, provides the basis for an *experiential confrontation* that is inherently item-selective. And it is not surprising that descriptive machinery should require such a supplementation: we are only in a position to *describe* a particular once IT has been identified—otherwise, while we may be describing an indefinite something, we are not describing IT as an individuated item.

The "descriptive sameness" of objects (in the relevant sense) thus cannot afford a theoretically failproof guarantee of identity in the case of *actual* objects. For example, distinct albeit qualitatively indistinguishable actualia—actuals, that is, which share all of their purely qualitative description features—can simply be located in different spatial positions. But this holds only for actual objects which do and must—by virtue of their status as such—have a spatial position that makes it possible, in principle, for an experiencing agent to confront them in this world. Thus in regard to *actualia* we cannot postulate the principle of the Identity of Indiscernibles. (Whether this principle can in fact be maintained in the case of nonexistents remains to be seen.)

Thus *in relation to the real* there will and must be concretizing mechanisms of identification (viz., ostensive ones) which go

---

[2] See P. F. Strawson, *op. cit.*

beyond the abstractive mechanisms of descriptive taxonomy. Being experience-correlative (in envisaging an actual or potential experiential confrontation with the thing at issue), these ostensive indicators are *egocentric* in orientation ("here and and now," or "there and then"—with directions as to "how to get there from here"). Positional locators given in objective, non-egocentric terms (e.g., "being in position No. 432," "being placed in the proximity of an X") are to be counted as *descriptive*. Hence, nonegocentric locators can be taken to represent *properties* and to form part of the content of the $\mathscr{P}$-sector of the c.d.s. of individuals. These particular spatial/positional properties would—in general—have to be counted among the *contingent* properties of individuals. It is appropriate to take the view that properties of this particular *positional* category should *in principle* be excluded from ever counting as essential to individuals of the ordinary sort.

But ostensive *indicators* are simply excluded from the sphere of *descriptive* taxonomy. Not being located in the descriptive, *property*-specifying realm, they are neither essential nor accidental, but lie outside the operative sphere of this distinction. Positionally *coordinate* (objective) placement is thus seen as altogether different in *modus operandi* from *ostensive* (subject-relative) placement: the former being regarded as descriptive in character, the latter not. (Cf. p. 68 below.)

3. THE PROLIFERATION OF ACTUAL-VARIANT DESCRIPTIONS

Given the sort of information about its properties that has been surveyed above, one can proceed to articulate the conception of a potentially *variant description* of an actual individual, by means of the following definition:

A (potentially) *variant description* of some actual individual is one that differs from it in only inessential respects, that is, one that includes all of the same essential properties, be they absolute or dispositional.

The crucial feature of this conception of "variant descriptions" for an actual individual is that it implements the idea that this selfsame individual can exist in descriptively different versions.

In saying that certain features of an individual are *accidental* to it, we are, in effect, committed to the thesis that *it*—this selfsame individual—might conceivably have taken on descriptively variant forms. Insofar as it is subject to "accidental" features one looks upon an individual as chameleon-like in that its descriptive coloration can, in principle, change in moving from one setting to another. (It is clear, however that, since an individual can have but one actual descriptive constitution in the real world, these "different settings" must be construed by way of hypothetical alteration rather than spatial relocation, and lead to "other possible worlds" rather than merely to other stage-settings within the actual world.)

For the sake of an illustration, consider an individual x_1 in a microworld based on the predicates F, G, H, such that x_1 answers to the following (*ex hypothesi* complete) descriptive specification:

$$\begin{array}{cccccc} & F & G & H & F/H & F/\bar{H} \\ x_1 = x_1^0 & + & [-] & + & + & [+] \end{array}$$

In accordance with the specified definition, this individual x_1 will have the following potentially variant forms:

	F	G	H	F/H	$F/\bar{H}$	*Comments*
1.	$+$	$[-]$	$+$	$-$	$[+]$	x_1^1
2.	$+$	$[-]$	$-$	$+$	$[+]$	impossible by $F/\bar{H}$
3.	$+$	$[-]$	$-$	$-$	$[+]$	impossible by $F/\bar{H}$
4.	$-$	$[-]$	$+$	$+$	$[+]$	impossible by F/H
5.	$-$	$[-]$	$+$	$-$	$[+]$	x_1^2
6.	$-$	$[-]$	$-$	$+$	$[+]$	x_1^3
7.	$-$	$[-]$	$-$	$-$	$[+]$	x_1^4

Thus x_1 will have a total of five admissible variant descriptive specifications, viz., that of x_1^0, its actual specification, and x_1^1, x_1^2, x_1^3, and x_1^4 answering to cases 1, 5, 6, and 7 respectively. Descriptions of form 2, 3, and 4 are *ineligible* or *inadmissible* as x_1-descriptions, given the commitments of the basic description x_1^0, for reasons indicated in the "comments" column. (After all, the very point of characterizing certain properties of an individual as essential to it is to rule out some descriptive specifications as *in principle* infeasible for it.)

Consider the microworld including a somewhat enlarged

population over and above the indicated x_1 (forgetting for the moment about *their* dispositional properties):

	F	G	H
x_1	+	[−]	+
x_2	−	[+]	[−]
x_3	−	+	[+]

Now the further variants of x_2 and x_3 would be individuals answering to the following specifications. (Note that here, and throughout, the *lack* of a property-disposition may be taken to be essential to the individual at issue unless otherwise indicated.)

x_2-variants				x_3-variants		
	F	G	H		F	G	H
x_2^1	+	[+]	[−]	x_3^1	+	+	[+]
				x_3^2	+	−	[+]
				x_3^3	−	−	[+]

Here x_3^2 is *qualitatively* indistinguishable from x_1 (absolute properties alone count for a purely qualitative or *phenomenal* description, and their essentiality status does not enter in).

The preceding survey of the individuals x_1, x_2, x_3 leads to the following results as regards occupancy of the various phenomenally descriptive compartments:

Inventory of Individual-Variant Descriptions

	F	G	H	x_1	x_2	x_3	Comments
1.	+	+	+			#	
2.	+	+	−		#		
3.	+	−	+	@		#	
4.	+	−	−				$\bar{F}/\bar{H}$ is essential to x_1
5.	−	+	+			@	
6.	−	+	−		@		
7.	−	−	+	#		#	
8.	−	−	−	#			

KEY: #: a possible descriptive specification of the individual
@: the actual descriptive specification of the individual

Note that descriptive compartment No. 4 $(F, \bar{G}, \bar{H})$ is necessarily unoccupied by any variants of the actual individuals x_1, x_2, x_3. This description is simply *inadmissible* for any real individual: it is *reality-disqualified*.

It warrants note in connection with this inventory that the suppression of explicit essentiality-indications costs us nothing; it can always be reconstructed from each tabulation. This is also true of *essential* property-dispositions. A complete variant-survey in the phenomenal (manifest) mode permits the covert (nonmanifest) situation to be reconstructed.

Let us consider the matter from a more generalized point of view. Abstractely formulated, we suppose that once a descriptive base is given in terms of some suitable set of properties Γ (i.e., {F, G, H} in our example), one can formulate the set S of all the theoretically available complete descriptive specifications (C.D.S.) for the actual individuals. Each of these C.D.S. that is not totally essentialistic will by its very nature have certain others as variant revisions—viz., those that differ from it in only inessential respects. And, accordingly, one can then proceed to indicate for every actual individual $x \in w^*$ (where w^* is the set of all individuals of "the real world," namely the set $\{x_1, x_2, x_3\}$ in the example) and every complete description $d \in S$, whether d does or does not qualify as a variant of x's actual description. This whole process proceeds simply by means of a purely formal proliferation of the combinatorial possibilities—subject to strictly logical constraints inherent in considerations of essentiality, based on the way in which the real individuals of w^* display the real properties of Γ.

4. THE REALM OF SUPERNUMERARIES ("MERELY POSSIBLE" INDIVIDUALS)

When one considers the full range of the various descriptive specifications for individuals that can be formulated, one recognizes that such individual-descriptions can be divided into three classes:

(1) those which describe actually existing individuals
(2) those which describe variant (i.e., possible but un-realized) alternative versions of actual individuals

(3) those which, given an essentialistic characterization of the real, cannot possibly (in the very logic of the situation) qualify as describing actual individuals.

Consider once more the tabulation of descriptive specifications developed in the example of Section 3 above:

	F	G	H	x_1	x_2	x_3
1.	+	+	+			#
2.	+	+	−		#	
3.	+	−	+	@		#
4.	+	−	−			
5.	−	+	+			@
6.	−	+	−		@	
7.	−	−	+	#		#
8.	−	−	−	#		

Here descriptions No. 3, 5, and 6 characterize actual individuals, descriptions No. 1, 2, 3, 7, and 8 represent possible variations of actual individuals, and description No. 4 is altogether reality-disqualified: it characterizes neither actual individuals nor any of their possible variants; this description could not be associated with alternative versions of the individuals that populate the microworld at issue in the example. If anything is to realize such a description, it must be some *"merely possible"* individual, one altogether outside the range of the actual and its feasible variations. That is, if one is to discuss the possibility of an individual that answers to this description, one must resort to an altogether new item, entirely *additional* to the domain of actual things. Such individuals that are wholly new rather than being old individuals in new descriptive guises will be characterized as *supernumeraries*.

An individual whose description is infeasible as a variant of an actual individual must, of course, be regarded as "new" individuals, altogether distinct from the actual ones. But there is no reason of principle why (at least under certain circumstances) a "new" individual should not take on a descriptive form that an actual individual could possibly bear. For example, in a world in which x_3 took on description 3, why should not a "new" individual, x_4, be permitted to take on description 1 (which among reals is admissible only for x_3)? There is, of course, no reason. Accordingly, we must also admit the prospect of *super-numerary* individuals that share descriptions with actual ones.

The following nomenclature will be adopted: The *possible* will be construed broadly as a genus embracing three species: the *actual*, the realm of *actual-variant possibility* (i.e., the actual in its possible albeit unactualized guises), and the *merely* possible (or supernumerary). The latter two categories, taken together, comprise the realm of *unactualized* possibility. The following taxonomy results

$$\text{the possible} \begin{cases} \text{the actual} \\ \text{unactualized possibility} \begin{cases} \text{actual-variant} \\ \text{possibility} \\ \text{mere (or super-} \\ \text{numerary) possibility} \end{cases} \end{cases}$$

The actual together with its actual-variant possibilities may be said to comprise the range of the *proximately* possible, in contrast with the greater remoteness of the *merely* possible.

Our adhesion to Aristotle's dictum that actuality is prior to possibility is not abrogated by the admission of supernumeraries upon the stage of consideration. It is important to stress that while the recognition of supernumerary individuals as genuinely possible may well lead outside the arena of the variations of the actual, they do not actually break the umbilical cord that links them to the domain of what actually exists—albeit at the level of universality rather than particularity. For the descriptive machinery in terms of which alone such possibilia are to be conceived and characterized is itself developed through an inquiry into the nature of the real, so that the real remains in this descriptive/conceptual sense altogether determinative for the realm of the possible.

5. RULES OF INDIVIDUATION: (A) INDIVIDUATING ACTUALS

Before examining theories regarding the individuation of actuals, it is desirable to pass some useful bits of machinery in review.

Any individual x (be it actual or possible) will determine, via its essentialistically complete descriptive specification (C.D.S.), the two associated sets of properties already adverted to above:

$$\mathscr{P}(x) = \text{the set of all (actual) properties of } x$$
$$\mathscr{E}(x) = \text{the set of all essential properties of } x.$$

Note that the property set $\mathscr{P}(x)$ is "complete" in the sense that for every property ϕ, either ϕ itself or its complement $\bar{\phi}$ must belong to x. As a concrete particular, every individual is property-decisive: whatever property may be specified, the individual either possesses or lacks it. Any concrete particular will, in this way, effect a "cut" across the entire range of available properties, dividing them into the yeas and nays. Moreover, it is clear that $\mathscr{P}(x)$ must always be a set of *mutually compatible* properties. (But cf. p. 65 below.)

Among the properties of $\mathscr{P}(x)$, some will be essential to x and others merely accidental. Accordingly, we specify $\mathscr{E}(x)$ as a certain subset of $\mathscr{P}(x)$ —possibly a subset that is null. This second property-set is, of course, "incomplete" (in the just-specified sense): there will in general be purely accidental properties of an individual x, properties that belong to x, but not essentially.

Let us consider some of the principal traditional theories of individuation. On a "Scotist view of essence," the essence of an individual is *particularistic*: every actual individual has its own specific, idiosyncratically definite, individualizing essence that makes it what it is, and no two distinct individuals can share the same essence. Thus essence-sharing individuals of the actual world must—on this view—be identical:

$$\mathscr{E}(x) = \mathscr{E}(y) \vdash x = y.$$

Should we adopt this position? Are the essential properties of an individual jointly sufficient to individuate it? Presumably not. For surely there is no reason of principle why—as in the metaphysics of Aristotle—distinct individuals should not share a common essence, so that accidental (contingent, non-essential) properties are needed to individuate. And the rationale for this position can also be seen from the standpoint of our technical explication of various modes of essentiality as presented in the preceding chapter. For it is clear that all these can work themselves out in such a way that not only can essentiality-confined descriptions fail to individuate, but an individual may even fail to have any essential properties whatever.

On a "Leibnizian view of identity," no two distinct individuals can share all of their properties in common, so that property-sharing individuals must be identical

$$\mathscr{P}(x) = \mathscr{P}(y) \vdash x = y.$$

In this, its "classical form" the Principle of the Identity of Indiscernibles may be formulated as follows:

No two distinct possible individuals can have *all* their properties in common (i.e., can be descriptively indistinguishable).

This is essentially a principle of exclusion, i.e., the possession of one (complete) description by one individual preempts the possession of the same description by another. A principle of collision-avoidance is at issue: No two distinct individuals can come together in the same descriptive compartment. In the formulation of this principle we begin with the seemingly obvious thesis, "Individuals having mutually distinct descriptions must be distinct individuals," and proceed also to assert its converse, the by no means equally obvious thesis, "Distinct individuals must have mutually distinct descriptions." The difficulties of this theory of individuation are well known and widely canvassed. If our descriptions are formulated in *strictly qualitative* terms, there is (as the longstanding controversy over the Leibnizian principle of the Identity of Indiscernibles serves to make clear) no decisive reason of theoretical principle why two distinct individuals could not share the same (complete) descriptive specification. As long as our descriptions remain at the genuinely qualitative level, we cannot justifiably deny the prospect that distinct and distinguishable (albeit not *qualitatively* distinguishable) individuals share one common description in having the same properties in common.

One can also contemplate the *combination* of the two aforementioned requirements, and thus to base a theory of particular-individuation on the rule

$$\mathscr{P}(x) = \mathscr{P}(y),\ \mathscr{E}(x) = \mathscr{E}(y) \vdash x = y.$$

In this present, essentialistic context one no longer accepts the Leibnizian version as a viable construal of the general idea of the identity of indiscernibles; rather, one goes over to its essentialistic counterpart:

No two distinct possible individuals can be such that they (1) have all their properties in common and (2) do so in each case with the same modal status (necessary or accidental).

The result is an "Artistotelian view of individuation." For Aristotle, many distinct individuals can share the same essential properties (Plato and Socrates share their common essence of humanity) and the individuation of such species-kindred (i.e., co-essential) individuals is effected through their accidents (for this, in effect, is what their individuation through "matter" comes to).

We ourselves are certainly not at liberty to adopt this Aristotelian theory of individuation. It has consequences incompatible with the naturalistic cast of our essentialism, with its insistence upon extracting the essential properties of things from their factualistic descriptions. For our approach must rule out the prospect that individuals which are indiscernible in point of their properties should be discriminable solely through differences as regards the essentiality-status with which these properties are possessed. When properties are shared in common, a theory that purports naturalistically to extract essentiality-considerations from these properties cannot (by symmetry or the principle of sufficient reason or whatever) admit of difference in essentiality status.

Thus none of these three theories of individuation which proceed solely in descriptive terms (though sometimes essentialistically descriptive ones) will be adopted here. Rather, we shall have to take seriously the idea inherent in the traditional criticisms of the principle of the Identity of Indiscernibles, that *ostensive* indications (let them be represented by i over and above the *descriptive* ones at issue in the $\mathscr{P}$-sets) are ineliminably requisite to the individuation of actualia, and that demonstrative indicators of placement must supplement any purely qualitative descriptions before a theoretical guarantee of individuation can be issued:

$$\mathscr{P}(x) = \mathscr{P}(y), \ i(x) = i(y) \vdash x = y$$

Here i represents an ostensive operator that indicates a certain item in a demonstrative (and ultimately at least in part "token-reflexive" way). Of course, the prospect of such "demonstration" will inherently be limited in its range to the actual world.[3] (It should be noted that it is *not* being said that the ostensive indication *i* suffices to individuate regardless of the descriptive data of $\mathscr{P}$, but only in the context thereof.)

These considerations then, suffice to define our position as to the problem of individuation within the range of *actual* individuals (i.e., within the actual world). We have arrived at a theory of identity in which *sameness of indication* plays a crucial role. But how is the issue of individuation to be resolved in the other, nonactual cases?

A crucial disanalogy between actualia and possibilia obtains with respect to *ostension*, in that an ostension towards "mere possibilities" is in principle not possible. Of course a certain parity remains: ostension remains as an intra-world principle, be the world actual or merely possible. And to say this is certainly to concede the prospect of ostension within a possible world. But the crucial point is that, while an individual in a possible world might (*ex hypothesi*) be in a position to identify something in that possible world ostensively, *we* are not. For us, the individuation of possibilia must proceed by very different means.

6. RULES OF INDIVIDUATION: (B) INDIVIDUATING POSSIBLES

The problem of individuating nonexistents was raised in a very forceful and lively manner by W. V. Quine, in his classic essay "On What There Is," first published a generation ago:

> Take for instance, the possible fat man in that doorway; and, again, the possible bald man in that doorway. Are they the same possible man, or two possible men? How do we decide? How many possible men are there in that doorway? Are there more possible thin ones than fat ones? How many of them are alike? Or would their being alike make them one? Are no *two* possible things alike? Is this the same as saying that it is impossible for two things to be alike? Or, finally, is

[3] No doubt the hypothetical beings of "other possible worlds" can also resort to ostension for the purposes of mutual indication of items assumed to be co-present with them in *their* world. But this presumed fact cuts no ice against the inherent actual-world-boundedness of any ostensive procedures by us who are fortunate enough to inhabit this actual world.

the concept of identity simply inapplicable to unactualized possibles? But what sense can be found in talking of entities which cannot meaningfully be said to be identical with themselves and distinct from one another?[4]

The key issues of the theory of possibilia crowd around these Quinean puzzlements.

Is one to take such difficulties as blocking the prospect of any talk of "merely possible individuals" at the very outset? Should one dismiss possibilia as *entia non grata* in Quine's elegant phrase?[5] In view of the price we would have to pay in restricting the realm of permissible assumption and supposition about the order of things, it is well to explore the prospects of a theory of possibility that does not require the adoption of so drastic a self-denying ordinance.

What Quine is after in the just-cited passage is a principle of individuation (*principium individuationis*) for nonexistent possibles. But this problem does not in fact pose any insuperable obstacles. Presumably an altogether nonexistent possible is to be identified by means of a *defining description*. And on this, the classical approach to the matter, the problems so amusingly posed by Quine pose no decisive theoretical difficulties. How many "merely possible" objects are there? As many as can be described—an *infinite* number. When are such objects to count as identical? When their defining descriptions are logically identical—that is, equivalent. The doctrine of merely possible objects entails no major logical anomalies. With nonexistents, everything save existence alone (and its implications) remains precisely as with objects which "really" exist, with the exception of this, that existents can be differentiated by purely ostensive processes, whereas nonexistents cannot be pointed to but must be differentiated by essentially descriptive means. It is clear that description must be the principal instrument of identification for nonexistent individuals, because ostension as well as other

---

[4] "On What There Is," *The Review of Metaphysics*, vol. 2 (1948), pp. 21–38; reprinted in L. Linsky (ed.), *Semantics and the Philosophy of Language* (Urbana, 1952), pp. 189–206. See pp. 23–4 (pp. 191–2 of the Linsky reprint). A cognate denial of nonexistent individuals and of the "reality" of unrealized possibilities is found in J. M. E. McTaggart, *The Nature of Existence*, Vol. I (Cambridge, Mass., 1921), Bk. I, chap. 2.

[5] W. V. Quine, *Word and Object* (Cambridge, Mass., 1960), p. 245.

modes of indication from within the orbit of the actual is in their case, in principle, infeasible.

It is important to note that *merely* possible individuals (i.e., supernumeraries) are at issue here, so that we are in fact confined to descriptive means of individuation. Actual-variants are another matter: since their individuation can be made to hinge on that of their actual originals, the issue becomes more straightforward. Of course, even here the question can be raised: How many variations does an actual individual admit of? But *this* question is presumably one that can be resolved along the lines of a relatively straightforward combinatorial survey, and poses no difficulties of a more far-reaching sort.

It is important to note that only a description that is saturated and complete can specify or individuate a particular merely possible individual. Any genuinely particular individual must be property-decisive,[6] and nonexistent possible individuals can obtain this decisiveness only through the route of descriptive saturation. Accordingly, if it is to be an *individual* that is specified descriptively, then this description must be saturated (complete): it cannot be vague or schematic but must issue a committal yea or nay with respect to every property whatsoever.

This second point resolves some of the puzzlements of the Quine passage. The reference to a "(possible) fat man in the doorway" just does not identify any single possible individual; it is a descriptive *schema* to which many such individuals might answer. This plurality is due precisely to the *incompleteness* of the specification: it stems from the fact that we are dealing with incomplete and *schematic* indications. The source of the puzzlement lies not at all in its being *nonexistents* with which we deal but stems solely from the fact that incomplete suppositional specification is at issue. Thus consider the solely actuality-envisaging case "Suppose one of the (perfectly real) coins in my

---

[6] Compare J. M. E. McTaggart, *The Nature of Existence*, Vol. I (Cambridge, 1921), sect. 62. To be sure, one can perhaps contemplate the prospect of schematic quasi-particulars whose status in point of certain properties is nonstandard in that (1) these properties are in principle qualified for application to them (unlike, e.g., color to numbers), but (2) they nevertheless fail to be committed with respect to them—one way or the other. For this issue see Appendix I to Chapter IV (pp. 95–101 below). The present approach does not in the final analysis block the way to introducing this variant prospect at a later stage.

pocket were placed on the table." What shall we say of this coin? Is it of copper (because a penny) or is it not? We cannot say either way. And this is not because a rather mysterious sort of thing is at issue—a coin made not of copper, nor yet not made not of copper. As long as our specification of something remains incomplete, so is what we can say about the thing at issue. Here the fault lies not with the thing but with our specification. Accordingly, we must stipulate that if a *particular* non-existent individual is to be at issue—i.e., if there is to be genuine *individuation* (and not just abstract schematization)—then the (genuine) properties of the nonexistent thing at issue must be detailed with *complete* comprehension.

Finally, the problem of *counting* possibilities—of deciding just how many fat men there are in the doorway—will also find its resolution in the light of these considerations. If descriptions determine possibilities, then there are as many possibilities as can be described (indeed an uncountable infinity of them, given the existence of continuous numerical parameters like weight and height). But, of course, to say that all these possibilities exist in some world or other is not to say that they can all *coexist* in any one selfsame possible world. Given the dimensions of the doorway, it may be able to accommodate no more than one fat man in any one possible world (though this leaves open the prospect of its accommodating a great many different fat men in various different possible worlds).

Such considerations may lead us to regard the idea of possible individuals as representing a prospect that can be rejected straight out of hand. But we are then led to the question: Under what conditions are two possible individuals to be identified with one another? In confronting this knotty problem, let us begin with its formulation by Roderick Chisholm:

> We start with Adam, say; we alter his description slightly and allow him to live for 931 years instead of for only 930; we then accommodate our descriptions of the other entities of the world to fit this possibility (Eve, for example, will now have the property of being married to a man who lives for 931 years instead of that of being married to a man who lives for only 930); and we thus arrive at a description of another possible world.

Let us call our present world 'W^1' and the possible world we have just indicated 'W^2'. Is the Adam of our world W^1 the same person as the Adam of the possible world W^2? In other words, is Adam such that he lives for just 930 years in W^1 and for 931 in W^2? And how are we to decide? . . .

The Adam of this world, we are assuming, is identical with the Adam of that one. In other words, Adam is such that he lives for only 930 years in W^1 and for 931 in W^2. Let us now suppose further that we have arrived at our conception of W^2, not only by introducing alterations in our description of the Adam of W^1, but also by introducing alterations in our description of the Noah of W^1. We say; "Suppose Adam had lived for 931 years instead of 930 and suppose Noah had lived for 949 years instead of 950." We then arrive at our description of W^2 by accommodating our descriptions of the other entities of W^1 in such a way that these entities will be capable of inhabiting the same possible world as the revised Noah and the revised Adam. Both Noah and Adam, then, may be found in W^2 as well as in W^1.

Now let us move from W^2 to still another possible world W^3. Once again, we will start by introducing alterations in Adam and Noah and then accommodate the rest of the world to what we have done. In W^3 Adam lives for 932 years and Noah for 948. Then moving from one possible world to another, but keeping our fingers, so to speak, on the same two entities, we arrive at a world in which Noah lives for 930 years and Adam for 950. In that world, therefore, Noah has the age that Adam has in this one, and Adam has the age that Noah has in this one; the Adam and Noah that we started with might thus be said to have exchanged their ages. Now let us continue on to still other possible worlds and allow them to exchange still other properties. We will imagine a possible world in which they have exchanged the first letters of their names, then one in which they have exchanged the second, then one in which they have exchanged the fourth, with the result that Adam in this new possible world will be called "Noah" and Noah "Adam." Proceeding in this way, we arrive finally at a possible world W^n which would seem to be exactly like our present world W^1, except for the fact that the Adam of W^n may be traced back to the Noah of W^1 and the Noah of W^n may be traced back to the Adam of W^1.

Should we say of the Adam of W^n that he is identical with the Noah of W^1 and should we say of the Noah of W^n that he is identical with the Adam of W^1? In other words, is there an x such that x is Adam in W^1 and x is Noah in W^n, and is there a y such that y is Noah in W^1 and y is Adam in W^n? And how are we to decide?[7]

Once we start to tinker with the properties on an individual, we seem to be putting our foot on the edge of a slippery slope. It becomes difficult if not impossible to say whether or not we are dealing with "the same individual"—and to specify the boundaries where this sameness is to begin and leave off. No doubt some such considerations made Aristotle unwilling to grant individuals any species-internally differential essential properties at all, and led Leibniz to the somewhat opposite—but equally effective—tactic of insisting that *all* of its properties are essential to an individual.

The issue posed by Chisholm's example is to be resolved along the following lines. As long as it is (*ex hypothesi*) *Adam* we're talking about, and *Adam* we're changing by hypothetical alterations, then it will clearly be Adam we're dealing with—no matter how Noah-like we may make him. Once an individual is settled upon as a starting point of hypothetical modification, then it continues at issue throughout, no matter what sort of suppositional changes may be made regarding *it*. The fundamental rule is this, that if one is introducing a series of modificatory suppositions regarding a certain individual, then this individual which is *ex hypothesi* to be at issue, is decisively determinative of the identity of the result. A modificatory assumption made (*ex hypothesi*) about x will necessarily produce a result that is about x as well.[8]

Hypothetical individuals are not to be encountered in experience; they do not somehow mysteriously "confront" us,

[7] R. M. Chisholm, "Identity Through Possible Worlds: Some Questions," *Nous*, vol. 1 (1967), pp. 1–8; see pp. 1–4.

[8] As I interpret him, this is also essentially the view of Saul Kripke. See his "Naming and Necessity" in *Semantics of Natural Language, op. cit.*, pp. 253–355 (see pp. 272–3).

taking us quite unaware. Rather, they have to be introduced as the product of some specificatory process of intellectual indication, proceeding through some suitable complex of hypotheses.

A possible individual is an intellectual artifact: the product of a projective "construction" that proceeds by way of such suppositions as: "Suppose x to be exactly like y except for . . ." "Suppose a thing (not any actual one) that is like y except for . . ." or the like. Possibilia are hypothesis-correlative: they are the termini of such supposition-claims that link them to (or detach them from) the actual individuals of this world. And this suppositional linkage to the actual must prove to be the key factor in settling questions of identity. And when their characterizing construction proceeds by way of the hypothetical alterations of a given thing—a certain "prototype"—then this thing which is (*ex hypothesi*) at issue serves to settle the question of individuation.

One major way of introducing possible individuals within the framework of discussion is exactly that envisioned in Chisholm's example, which proceeds by a linked series of suppositions: Suppose x to be changed in *this* respect, and then in *this*, etc. The thesis is that when one begins with a certain individual, then only one individual—namely itself—is accessible under the transformation introduced by such hypothetical alterations. When we postulate the variant form of some actual individual as doing duty for it, then this actual individual is and remains the source of the identity of the thing at issue, however drastically it might be altered. The key consideration is that on our approach nonactual individuals are (whenever possible) to be individuated on the basis of the real-world prototypes that provide the reference point for their conceptualization.

The view of possible-individual identification we espouse here might be characterized as the *ontogenetic* theory in contrast to the *phylogenetic* theory of the more usual approaches to cross-world identification.[9] It does not proceed to individuate in terms of likeness or similarity, and so avoids at one stroke all of the difficulties that one encounters here.[10] It is not based on

[9] The phylogenetic standpoint is implicit in R. M. Chisholm, *op. cit.*, and is explicit in David Lewis, "Counterpart Theory and Quantified Modal Logic," *The Journal of Philosophy*, vol. 65 (1968), pp. 113–26.

[10] See Appendix II to Chapter IV.

property-similarity at all, but on *tracking*. To say this is to speak somewhat figuratively, for what is at issue is not *physical* tracking, of course, but tracking along lines of thought, or rather along "lines of supposition"—that is the linked series of suppositions by means of which a *given* individual is to be reconstituted.

Just as a physically real individual is standardly to have the question of its identity resolved on the basis of its being "tracked" through positional changes in physical space from the reference-point of a certain physical starting point, so a possible individual is to have the question of its identity settled on the basis of a (conceptual) "tracking" or "tracing back" throughout descriptive changes in "conceptual space" from the reference-point of a certain actual individual as the starting-point.

The central features of our theory of possibility now comes into clear view. An altogether nonexistent (i.e., supernumerary) individual is to be construed as the product of an *hypothesis of incarnation*, postulating the actualization of a descriptive specification that is intrinsically (or "merely logically") possible, albeit not realized in fact—nor perhaps even *realizable* by the things of this actual world (i.e., altogether "actuality detached" in the specified sense of being *ineligible* for actual individuals). This role of an hypothesis of incarnation provides a basis for determining merely possible individuals on a *descriptive* basis, and means that with respect to such mere *possibilia* we assume the stance of an Aristotelian view of individuation, in sharp contradistinction to the situation with respect to *actualia* and their hypothetical transforms. (Since the linguistic machinery of description at issue here may be assumed to include mathematics and to embrace numerical *parameters*, there is no question of the range of available descriptions being limited to a finite or even countably infinite number.)

The assumptive factor introduced by the "incarnation hypothesis" of this discussion is important. The descriptive specification of an individual must be distinguished from the individual itself: its description is a linguistic-conceptual artifact, the individual itself presumably not. The individual is the *thing* that supposedly answers to its descriptive specification. And when nothing *in fact* does so, because a "nonexistent individual" is at issue, then this individual is, at best, the product of an assumption (supposition, hypothesis) that something does so. The descriptive specification does no more than present a possibility *for* an individual, the "possible individual" that answers to this "possibility-for" remains at the assumptive level, and can be realized only through an incarnation hypothesis.

Subject to this line of thought, we define the *fully individualizing characterization* ("*fic*" for short) of an unactualized possible individual x as given by indicating two items:

(i) the full, essentialistically complete description (C.D.S.) of x, and in particular the sets $\mathscr{P}(x)$ and $\mathscr{E}(x)$ that comprise the essentialistically complete descriptive specification of the individual at issue, and

(ii) the actual-prototype (if any) of x—the particular *actual* individual y (if such there be) of which this individual is to be the variant, subject, of course, to the obvious condition that:

$$\mathscr{E}(x) = \mathscr{E}(y).$$

The *fic* of a (nonactual) possible individual thus consists of an ordered pair, the former member of which is its essentialistically complete descriptive specification (C.D.S.), and the latter of which is either the specification of an *actual* individual as prototype, or else a blank—if there is to be such actual (i.e., a "null prototype"). A *fic* thus has the form $\langle d, x \rangle$ or $\langle d, \star \rangle$—where d itself takes the form $[\mathscr{P}, \mathscr{E}]$, the complete descriptive specification (C.D.S.) of an individual, and x is some member of "the real world" ($x \in w^*$), while $\star$ is the "null-individual" whose invocation indicates that no individual at all is at issue. (It should be noted that all the technical terminology introduced here and elsewhere in the chapter is reviewed in the Glossary appended at its end.)

In following this line of approach, we take the issue of the individuation of individuals to be settled on the following basis:

(1) Within *the actual* world an individual is completely specified by the combination of its merely qualitative (nonessentialistic) description (c.d.s.) as given by its property-set $\mathscr{P}$, *plus* its ostensively locative indicator, i.

(2) Other (nonactual) individuals are individuated as follows: (1) by their actual-world prototypes, if they have one, regardless of any descriptive considerations (beyond those of essentialistic qualification), and (2) if they do not have an actual-world prototype, then simply on the basis of their characterizing C.D.S.

Thus actualia (and their variants) have an identity that is *pre-established* from the angle of possibilistic theorizing, while mere possibilia have one that hinges altogether on their descriptive construction. We arrive at a tripartite theory of individuation:

(1) Actuals are individuated on the basis of their A-descriptions (actualistic descriptions = c.d.s.) *together with* some appropriate ostensive indicator: $\langle \mathscr{P}, i \rangle$, with i as effectively identity-decisive. (Recall that any sort of "objective" locational placement becomes a part of $\mathscr{P}$.)

(2) Actuality-attached nonexistent possible-individuals are individuated simply and purely on the basis of their actual-prototypes: $\langle [\mathscr{P}, \mathscr{E}], p \rangle$, with p alone identity-decisive. (Note that the role of i in (1) as an actuality-relator is *in this regard* similar to that of p here.)

(3) Actuality-detached merely possible individuals (supernumeraries) are individuated on the basis of their E-descriptions (essentialistic descriptions $\equiv$ C.D.S.) alone: $\langle [\mathscr{P}, \mathscr{E}], \star \rangle$ with $\mathscr{P}$ and $\mathscr{E}$ as jointly identity-decisive, since $\star$ indicates the "null-prototype" or "the null individual," the Leibnizian *non ens*.

The preceding line of approach leads to two very distinct sorts of unactualized individuals: (i) those which are actual-variants, that is, alternative versions of actual individuals, and (ii) those which are *supernumerary*, i.e., are wholly actuality-detached "new" individuals. The former (actual variants) may be taken to form a set **v**, the latter (supernumeraries) a set **s** of merely possible individuals. A very different principle of individuation obtains in each of these cases. The former, actual-attached individuals are individuated solely on the basis of their actual prototypes (descriptive considerations are in effect irrelevant). The latter, actuality-detached individuals are individuated solely on the basis of descriptive considerations. In this latter case—but only in this latter case—does the Aristotelian theory of individuation reign supreme. (Note that one would, on this approach, arrive at a Meinong-reminiscent theory of *impossible* objects, by dropping in the case of prototypeless individuals the consistency condition that the property sets $\mathscr{P}$ and $\mathscr{E}$ be self-compatible. However, we shall not pursue this prospect here, since our present interest relates to the theory of *possibilia* and not *impossibilia*.)

Thus consider an individual x individuated by a certain *fic*, as follows:

$$x \sim \langle [\mathscr{P}(x), \mathscr{E}(x)], \xi \rangle$$

where ξ is (i) i_x for the actual individuals of w^*, (ii) p_x for the actual-variant individuals of $\mathbf{v}$, and (iii) ☆ (the null individual) for the supernumeraries of $\mathbf{s}$. In case (i) this individual is individuated completely by i_x; in case (ii) by p_x; and in case (iii) by the combination of $\mathscr{P}(x)$ and $\mathscr{E}(x)$. The total *fic* is completely identity-decisive in every case.

By way of notation we shall adopt

(i) ' $\sim$ ' to represent the correlation of an individual with its individuating *fic*

(ii) ' $\doteq$ ' to represent the identity of individuals within one selfsame world (in general the *actual* one)

(iii) ' $\cong$ ' to represent the generalized identity of individuals as operative in the deliberations of the present section. (NOTE: individuals that are not identical in the sense of $\sim$-identity—i.e., answer to different *fic*'s—can be identical in the sense of $\cong$-identity.)

Only with respect to actuality-detached (supernumerary) merely possible individuals do we adopt (in its Aristotelian, essentialistic version) the Leibnizian conception that an individual is to be individuated through its descriptive specification alone. Only here is the principle of the identity of indiscernibles operative (in its strong, essentialistic version) at the level of possible-individuals-in-general. That is, the principle

$$(\Pi x)(\Pi y)[([\mathscr{P}(x) = \mathscr{P}(y)] \, \& \, [\mathscr{E}(x) = \mathscr{E}(y)]) \supset x \cong y]$$

will hold not in general, but only under the supposition that the range of the variables x and y has been confined to the supernumerary sphere. With actual and actuality-attached

individuals we break the connection between descriptive specification and individuation: In this sphere nothing impedes the
identification of individuals with different descriptions (though
they will, of course, be incompossible), or the differentiation of
individuals with the same description. Neither the individuation
of actuals nor that of actual-attached possibles is to be settled
automatically on the basis of solely descriptive considerations.
In abandoning the Leibnizian Identity of Indiscernibles and the
idea that individuals can be individuated on the basis of descriptive information, we in effect abandon also the Scotist theory of
individual essences: essences that completely individuate their
bearers. Descriptive specifications are viewed as of themselves
impotent to effect *individuation* in a way that is adequate *in
principle*—rather than simply *in practice*. (Of course, descriptive
identification might continue operative given the contingent, *de
facto* arrangements that obtain in certain possible worlds.)

One part of this theory of individuation deserves special
attention: its bearing upon supernumeraries. Here the principle
of the identity of indiscernibles is—as just stated—operative
in its strong essentialistic form. But consider now the supernumerary individual x whose fic is as follows

$$x \sim \langle [\mathscr{P}, \mathscr{E}], \; \star \rangle$$

where (let us suppose) there is some property ϕ such that $\phi \in \mathscr{P}$
but $\phi \notin \mathscr{E}$. Then, of course, ϕ is (*ex hypothesi*) not an essential
property of x, since it is not a member of $\mathscr{E}$. But yet there is a
certain sense of "essentiality" in which ϕ *is* indeed "essential"
to ϕ in view of the operative identity of indiscernibles.

In explicating this, one should note that $\mathscr{E}$-membership
indicates *descriptive* essentiality, and that this contrasts with that
sort of "essentiality" that pertains to *individuation* itself, let us
call it I-essentiality (individuative essentiality), which is at
issue in the following definition:

> The feature f is I-essential to an individual x iff anything that
> is to count as (world-indifferently) identical with x will also
> have to possess f.

Clearly in *this* sense "having ϕ" is indeed "essential" (that is, I-
essential) to x, for—in view of the operative principle of individuation—nothing that lacked this feature could be identical
with x. (Indeed—though it sounds paradoxical to say so—it

happens that "having ϕ *accidentally*" is in fact an I-essential feature of x.) Accordingly, we arrive at the result that *all* of the properties of a supernumerary individual (even its accidental ones) represent I-essential features of the item at issue.

The upshot is that every property that is essential (simpliciter) for *any* individual whatever represents an I-essential feature of it, but for supernumeraries (only) the accidental properties *also* turn out to be I-essential, given the applicability of the principle of the identity of indiscernibles in its strong, essentialistic form. I-essentiality eventuates as a necessary but not sufficient condition for essentiality *per se* (although it is both necessary and sufficient with actualia and actual-variants). Thus for actualia and actual-variants we have the principle:

$$\phi!x \text{ iff } (\Pi y)(y \cong x \supset \phi y)$$

But the implication only holds in one direction (left to right) in the case of supernumeraries.

The fact that even the accidental properties of supernumeraries turn out to be I-essential could perhaps be deemed objectionable. For someone might be inclined to argue:

> What real point can there be to maintaining the difference between essential and accidental properties for supernumeraries, given that all the properties of such individuals, even the "accidental" ones are I-essential?

But there is in fact a point, and it is an important one. It relates to *hypothetical* reasoning. We want to be able to discuss what would happen and what would be possible if some other non-actual world were in fact actual. We want to consider not only what is *really* actual and possible, but also what is actual and possible in a "story-relative" sense. And at this point the distinction between I-essentiality and essentiality *per se* comes as crucially into play for supernumeraries as for actuals and their variants.

The following possible objection against the preceding theory of individuation must also be considered:

> You tell us that in the case of actuality-detached individuals individuation must rest solely on *descriptive* considerations.

But why should one be prepared to exclude the prospect that there might be multiple realizations in some possible world of descriptively indistinguishable individuals? In particular, could this not happen when such individuals occupy different spatial "locations" (in a suitably symmetric world).

To deal with this objection we must first of all recall to mind our earlier insistence (see Section 2 above) that any information regarding the placement of individuals in an objective positional framework (rather than one given through egocentric indications of an ostensive type—such as that of "here" and "there") is to count as part of the *descriptive* characterization of individuals. The "description" at issue in the descriptive aspect of individuation is thus to include not only various *qualitative* characterizations, but also (whenever applicable) the *positional* placements of an (*ex hypothesi*) objectively given framework of "positions."[11] This fact, that "descriptively indistinguishable" also includes "in point of placement (location, position)" removes the sting of the objection under consideration. (Some further ramifications of this issue of spatial positioning are dealt with in Section 5 of Chapter IV below.)

Of course, if one wanted to preserve parity in point of the characterization of possible individuals as compared with actual ones, one could detach positional from qualitative description. Then just as an actual individual is given as

$$\langle \mathscr{P}, \mathscr{E}, \pi, i \rangle$$

a possible one would be given as

$$\langle \mathscr{P}, \mathscr{E}, \pi, \not{e} \rangle$$

where π is that part of the *old* $\mathscr{P}$ that deals with locational placement in a framework of objective positions. The remaining discussion could be readjusted, *mutatis mutandis*, to this change of approach. But we shall not pursue the matter here.

---

[11] As mentioned in Section 2 above, all of these positional properties must be excluded from qualifying as essential; they must invariably be regarded as accidental, save in those cases where (as with "the North Pole" they enter *definitionally* into the characterization of the item at issue).

7. THE TAXONOMY OF POSSIBILIA

To make possible the step from the realm of descriptive specifications to that of *things* (or possible things), some postulate of basically *ontological* import is required. Only by stipulating a suitable relationship of correspondence between descriptions (of an appropriate sort) on the one hand, and merely possible unactualized individuals on the other, are we able to implement the conception of possibilia as the products of rational construction (viz., a descriptive construction) from descriptive materials obtained in the scientific study of the real. Leibniz's thesis that every (self-consistent) thing-description is exemplified by some possible individual clearly illustrates the sort of ontological principle at issue. The view that every descriptive possibility can be filled by an individual, if only *in modo potentialitatis*, through the vehicle of an incarnation hypothesis—one by whose means the realization of a certain descriptive specification can be descriptively projected—is the key to the "constructive" theory of possibility we are endeavoring to articulate here. However, the firm foothold of this approach in the analysis of the real should go at least part way towards satisfying those philosophers who have an aversion to possible individuals on grounds that they create an ontological slum that provides "a breeding ground for disorderly elements" (as W. V. Quine has vividly put it[12]).

We are led to a triple-domain theory of individuals, along the following lines:

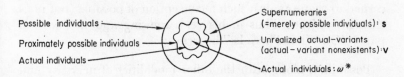

Possible individuals

Proximately possible individuals

Actual individuals

Supernumeraries (=merely possible individuals) : **s**

Unrealized actual–variants (actual – variant nonexistents) : **v**

Actual individuals : ω^*

Such a tripartite division effectively implements Dana Scott's proposal that modal logicians adopt a layered-sandwich universe consisting of actual, potential, and virtual individuals. It parallels closely the distinction drawn in ordinary language between "the really real," "the genuinely possible," and the

[12] In "On What There Is" in *From a Logical Point of View* (Cambridge, Mass., 1953), p. 4.

domain of "mere fiction." Thus there is a certain ambiguity in speaking of "alternatives" for the actual individuals: one might merely mean alternative, hypothetically modified versions *of* them, or one might mean items alternative *to* them by way of hypothetical individuals that are nowise mere revisions of actual things but are altogether absent from the real world.

A quite distinct process of individuation operates in each of the three rings according to our theory, the individuation of actualia involves an ostensive element, that of actual-attached possibilia is parasitic upon the former in requiring the specification of an actual prototype. Only with actuality-detached supernumeraries do we proceed on the "purely conceptual" basis of an abstract description, and so a Leibniz-reminiscent principle of the Identity of Indiscernibles operates in this last realm alone: here but here alone do *individual concepts* and *individuals* stand in a one-to-one correlation.

This recognition of an "outer ring" of supernumeraries requires special comment. The relatively uncontroversial thesis that "things could have been different in countless ways" is ambiguous.[13] It might mean merely that various of the actually existing things might be modified in some ways, or that there could be *new* "foreign" things, altogether different from the actual ones. The former construction envisages merely the domain of unrealized actual variants, the latter moves on to that of outright supernumeraries. Both of the constructions of the thesis thus lie within the horizons of the present theory.

Among modern logicians, Quine especially has been concerned to argue against such a conception of possible (but nonexistent) objects. Thus in his very amusing and well-written paper "On What There Is," he writes:

> Possibility, along with the other modalities of necessity and impossibility and contingency, raises problems. . . . But we can at least limit modalities to whole statements. We may impose the adverb 'possibly' upon a statement as a whole, and we may well worry about the semantical analysis of such usage; but little real advance in such analysis is to be hoped for in expanding our universe to include so-called *possible*

[13] For an interesting discussion of this thesis in the context of an ontology of possible worlds see David Lewis, *Counterfactuals* (Oxford, 1973), p. 84.

entities. I suspect that the main motive for this expansion is simply the old notion that Pegasus, e.g., must be because it would otherwise be nonsense to say even that he is not.[14]

However this line of argument will not do at all, because the doctrine of nonexistent possibles can without difficulty be formulated in sentences with suitable use of *de dicto* modalities. The following statement represents the essential condition under which an object n is a nonexistent possible:

$$(N) \quad \neg(\exists x)(x = n) \;\&\; \Diamond(\exists x)(x =)n.$$

This asserts that there exists (in the sense of existential quantification) nothing identical with n although it is possible that there might. Now we must be careful to refrain from the temptation to infer from (N) that:

$$(N') \quad (\exists y)\,[\neg(\exists x)(x = y) \;\&\; \Diamond(\exists x)(x = y)].$$

For (N') entails $(\exists y)(\forall x)(x \neq y)$ which is flatly incompatible with the thesis $(\forall x)(x = x)$. But this merely goes to show that nonexistent possible cannot be taken to lie within the range of values of our individual variables, 'x', 'y', and so forth, so that Existential Generalization is not valid with respect to such objects as the n of (N). The self-contradictory character of (N') must *not* be construed to show that there "are" no nonexistent possibles, but only that they are not in the standard range of $(\forall/\exists)$-quantification.

We shall thus need to adopt two distinct styles of quantifiers, the orthodox $\forall$ and $\exists$ with respect to the domain of actual individuals w^*, and Π and Σ with respect to the wider domain of possibilia in general. (Henry Leonard employed bracket-quantifiers instead of the familiar parenthesis-quantifiers for this same purpose.[15]) We must develop this theory of quantification in such a way as to obtain equivalences like the following:

$$\Diamond(\exists x)\phi x \text{ iff } (\Sigma y)(\exists x)(y \cong x \;\&\; \phi y)$$
$$\Box(\forall x)\,\phi x \text{ iff } (\Pi y)(\forall x)(y \cong x \supset \phi y).$$

[14] *Review of Metaphysics*, vol. 2 (1948), pp. 21–38 (see p. 24); reprinted in *Semantics and the Philosophy of Language*, ed. by L. Linsky (Urbana, 1952), pp. 189–206.

[15] Henry S. Leonard, "Essences, Attributes, and Predicates," *Proceedings and Addresses of the American Philosophical Association*: 1963–1964 (Yellow Springs, 1964), pp. 25–51 (see pp. 39–41).

The former must obtain iff there is some possible alternative version of a real thing that has ϕ, the latter iff every possible alternative version of every real thing has ϕ.

Now someone might well object as follows:

> It is bad enough that your ontology of possibilia admits unactualized modifications of actual things. What need and what justification is there to admit altogether nonexistent things into one's ontology?

The answer here lies in the requisites of an adequate account of hypothetical reasoning. Consider the supposition: *Suppose an elephant were standing under yonder tree.* This supposition could be realized in various ways, each of which carries further suppositions in its wake:

1. Some actual elephant (say that of the local zoo) might be supposed to be in that spot.
2. Some actual nonelephant (say that boulder) might be assumptively metamorphosed into an elephant, and placed at that spot.
3. An altogether new elephantine item—wholly supplemental to the actual furniture of the universe—might be assumptively introduced.

If one envisages the first avenue to possibility-realization, then the hypothesis at issue immediately opens up the question: "But which actual elephant is one to suppose present under the tree?" And the impropriety of this question suggests—quite rightly—that it is simply not a consequence or presupposition of the original hypothesis that any sort of reshuffling take place among the actual elephants.

Exactly the same situation obtains, *mutatis mutandis*, with respect to the second avenue to hypothesis-realization. The assumption at issue just does not require us to forego the existence of any other item of the furniture of the universe as price for obtaining our hypothetical elephant.

The fact is that the assumption in view proceeds on a plane that is strictly neutral as between all three alternatives, and requires that all of these alternatives be kept open. The closing off of any one of them creates an unacceptable result. But the third alternative requires that recognition of strictly supernumerary "virtual individuals" whose justification is at issue, and these are, accordingly, a needed resource.

It might seem that one can dispense with "nonexistent individuals" in the most emphatic sense, viz., supernumeraries, by some such device as that proposed by Nelson Goodman, who writes:

> Offhand, we might expect to encounter new difficulties when faced with discourse ostensibly pertaining to non-actual enduring things rather than to non-actual happenings to actual things; but even such discourse can readily be interpreted as the application of certain predicates to certain actual things. We can truthfully put fictive mountains in the middle of London simply by applying to London a certain projection of the predicate "mountainous". . . . Thus we begin to perceive the general way in which statements affirming that certain possible so-and-sos are not actual so-and-sos may be reconciled with the doctrine that the only possible entities are actual ones. . . . Possible processes and possible entities vanish. Predicates supposedly pertaining to them are seen to apply to actual things, but to have extensions related in peculiar ways to, and usually broader than, the extensions of certain manifest predicates. A predicate ostensibly of possibles as compared to a correlative manifest predicate, like an open umbrella as compared to a closed one, simply covers more of the same earthly stuff.[16]

Goodman's conclusion that possible entities can be got rid of on this basis is drawn too hastily. To be sure possible changes in real things (the terrain of London or the length of the Prophet's beard) can be accommodated in this way—just precisely because the individuals they envisage are actual-variant, But wholly new, strictly supernumerary possibilities are not to be got rid of so easily.

8. THE CENTRALITY OF THE ACTUAL

One recent Leibniz-commentator has urged the following on behalf of his theory:

[16] *Fact, Fiction and Forecast* (London, 1955), pp. 55–6.

... we interpret the term "possible world" as referring for Leibniz to a set of individual concepts, and not to a set of individuals. In that way he can avoid introducing a shadowy realm of "possible individuals" in addition to the abstract entities (i.e., the attributes and concepts) already involved in his metaphysics.[17]

The present theory of individuation gives up this supposed advantage of relying on concepts alone subject to a purely descriptive route to individuation. But it does not move very far towards establishing a "shadowy realm," since its only extra-descriptive machinery relates to the identification of *actual* individuals.

There is no question that our theory of possibilia gives to the domain of actuals a central and preeminent place. They alone furnish the individuative starting-point for constructing the specifications of possible individuals. Of course, someone may ask:

On your approach a nonexistent possible individual x must answer to a *fic* of the form

$$x \sim \langle d, \xi \rangle$$

where for ξ you permit only
    (i) an actual individual $y \in w^*$
or
    (ii) the "null individual" $\star$.
Now why not allow ξ itself to be a nonexistent possible individual $x \notin w^*$ and let the construction be carried out with respect to a basis of such unactualized individuals?

But, after all, the very object of the exercise is (so to speak) the *introduction* of possible individuals outside w^*. To be told that we already need them in an individuative construction is not very helpful, to say the least. However, a deeper point lies behind this one. In a certain sense we *must* begin the construction from this the actual world—for *us* there is no effective way

[17] Benson Mates, "Leibniz on Possible Worlds" in B. van Roolselaar and J. F. Staal (eds.), *Logic, Mathematics and Philosophy of Science* (Amsterdam, 1968, pp. 507–29 (see p. 510).

of avoiding beginning in the projective construction of possible cases "from where we are" in this actual world of ours. Think here of the simpleton in the old story who accepted the wager of the man who challenged him: "I'll bet you that you can't get to Paris without going there from here [Dresden]!" and returned in due course, hoping to collect by insisting that he had gone to Paris not from here (Dresden), but from Vienna instead.

Notwithstanding this insistence that possibilia are exfoliated with reference to that *actual* world, there is no intrinsic infeasibility—once the exercise of developing possible worlds has got under way—of setting up some "merely possible" world as *hypothetically actual*, and then proceeding to elaborate the processes of individuation and world-construction with reference to *this* actual-world basis. The old inherently distinct supernumeraries might now well become trans-world reidentifiable with other individuals. And a wholly new set of surrogacy-relationships can now be developed. We can, accordingly, articulate a new conception of relative possibility (or "accessibility") with respect to a possible world specified as *hypothetically* actual. And even the *actually* actual world can now be visualized as just another possibility relative to the hypothetically "actual" one.[18] But, of course, the elaboration of such relative possibilities does not abrogate the fundamental distinction of categorical actuality and categorical possibility which underlies the entire process as a whole.

APPENDIX. TERMINOLOGICAL GLOSSARY

1. **C.D.S.**: the (*strongly* or *essentialistically*) *complete descriptive* specification of an individual calls for the indicating of *all* its properties and specifying their essentiality status. This takes the form of an indication of the pair of sets: $[\mathcal{P}(x), \mathcal{E}(x)]$.

[18] Curiously enough, it might turn out on this basis that the real world is *not* possible relative to a given "hypothetically actual" world. For example, suppose that $w^{\#}$ were this (hypothetically) actual world and that the real world w^* contained numerically distinct individuals x_1 and x_2 which were descriptively indistinguishable. Suppose neither of these x_i to be a member of $w^{\#}$ nor a variant of any such member. Then w^* would not be possible relative to w, since it would require conjoining distinct supernumeraries answering to the same description.

2. c.d.s.: (*weakly*) *complete descriptive specification* of an individual. This is that component of the C.D.S. that is "purely" descriptive in content: the "full" description minus any essentiality specifications. This simply takes the form: $\mathscr{P}(x)$.

3. *fic*: *fully individuating characterization* of an individual. This takes the form $\langle d, x \rangle$, where d is a C.D.S. and x is that *real* individual ($x \in w^*$) which serves as the identificatory basis ("prototype") for the individual at issue, or else it takes the form $\langle d, \star \rangle$, where no such actual individual is at issue, so that '$\star$' represents the null individual, as it were. (Note that d must qualify as a variant description for x.)

4. *prototype*: let $\langle d, x \rangle$, with $x \in w^*$, be the *fic* of some possible individual. Then x is said to be the *prototype* of this individual. (A prototype is thus always an actual individual; and every actual individual is its own prototype.)

5. V.D.S.: a *variant descriptive specification* for a given C.D.S. is any one that differs from it solely in inessential respects.

6. *actual variant*: a possible individual whose *fic* takes the form $\langle d, x \rangle$, that is, one which has a prototype.

7. *supernumerary*: a possible individual whose *fic* takes the form $\langle d, \star \rangle$, that is one which lacks a prototype.

8. *surrogate*: possible individuals with the same prototype are said to be *surrogates* for one another.

9. *simulacrum*: two possible individuals are said to be *simulacra* of one another when they share the same C.D.S.

It should be noted that surrogacy and simulacrahood are equivalence relations.

Chapter IV

THE CONSTITUTION OF POSSIBLE WORLDS AND THE PROBLEM OF THE TRANS-WORLD IDENTITY OF INDIVIDUALS

1. INTRODUCTION

The theory of possible worlds and the theory of essentialism are intimately intertwined because possible worlds and essential properties stand in mutually reciprocal coordination. It is very much a matter of which end of the stick one is to pick up. One can start by taking possible worlds as somehow given (never mind how!), and then introduce essentiality on this basis, defining an essential property of a thing as one that it has in every possible world. Or one can approach the issue the other way round. Starting with essentiality-imputations one can proceed to determine possible worlds on this basis. Abstractly speaking, either approach is possible. But, for the reasons already adumbrated, considerable theoretical advantages accrue to the latter, world-derivative rather than world-assumptive tactic. This, at any rate, is the mode of procedure throughout the present discussion. Accordingly, this chapter delineates a *constructive* approach to the elaboration of a theory of possible worlds, systematizing their development on the basis of the essentialistic machinery articulated above.

An important preliminary observation is in order. Two quite different sorts of "possible worlds" can be envisaged: (1) the *proximately* possible ones that include only those individuals belonging to this, the actual world, albeit perhaps in different and in fact "unrealized" variant forms, and (2) the *remotely* possible ones that include also wholly different supernumerary individuals that are not to be found in this world at all. Accordingly, two quite distinct sorts of possible worlds can be envisaged, the one (former) sort much less "unrealistic" than the other (latter) one, since it envisages merely an alternative version *of* the things of this world and does not assume things that are altogether alternative to the things of this present dispensation. It is the plan here definitely to permit *both* sorts of possible worlds, proximate and remote alike, to fall within the purview of our discussion. There are sound reasons for taking this libertarian approach. For—as will be shown below—an adequate account of hypothetical reasoning needs a theory of possibility that can accommodate both of these sectors.

2. COMPOSSIBILITY AND POSSIBLE WORLDS

The population of a possible world will, of course, consist of possible individuals (in a sense which includes the actual): possible worlds simply *are* collections of possible individuals duly combined with one another. Our "constructive" approach proceeds by way of moving first to possible individuals, and then, with these *prefabricated* individuals at our disposal, proceeding to stock the various possible worlds with this population.[1]

Yet the fact that the population of alternative possible worlds will consist of possible individuals—of the fully individuated type—is, while true enough, only the beginning of the long story of how such worlds are constituted. For while every possible world is a set of possible individuals, the converse question arises: Does *any and every* collection of possible individuals constitute a possible world? This question must be answered decisively in the negative: various sorts of considerations can render *individually possible* individuals mutually *incompossible*. In general, for a set of severally possible individuals to be *conjointly admissible* as a "possible world," certain special conditions will have to be satisfied, and only when these conditions are met can the individuals at issue be characterized as systematically "compossible." This important point demands closer scrutiny.

Possible individuals can be logically *incompossible* (L-incompossible) in having individuating specifications that are

---

[1] Regarding this line of approach see Richard Montague, "Pragmatics" in R. Klibansky (ed.), *Contemporary Philosophy: La Philosophie Contemporaire*, vol. I (Florence, 1968), pp. 102–22 as well as Montague's "On the Nature of Some Philosophical Entities," *The Monist*, vol. 53 (1969), pp. 159–94.

logically incompatible with one another, so that their conjoint realization is rendered logically impossible. For example, no individual—and no version of an individual—having (*inter alia*) among its *essential* properties that of existing in a setting in which no individual whatsoever has feature F, that is, no individual to which the property

$$(\lambda x)[\neg Fx \;\&\; \neg(\exists y)Fy]$$

is essential, can possibly exist in a world in which there is an individual having (even though accidentally) the feature F. Thus, once relational properties are admitted, suitably described possible individuals can exclude one another as a matter of logical principle alone, even without appeal to *metaphysical* compossibility conditions—as, for example, when x_1 has the [essential] property of bearing the relation R to every individual and x_2 has the [essential] property that no individual bears R to it. Again, suppose that x_1 essentially has the property $\lambda x(\exists y)(x \neq y \;\&\; Gy)$. Then no set containing x_1 but lacking some other possible individual that has G would represent a possible world. An analogous, and less schematic example is due to Leibniz: We could not stipulate a "possible world" which contains Cain, the son of Adam, did this world not contain Adam as well. Not only can one possible individual exclude certain others from any possible world that contains it, but it may also demand the inclusion of certain others. Sets of individuals which violate those requirements of presence or absence that are built into the individuating descriptions of its individuals cannot qualify as *compossible*.

It deserves note that the defining properties of an individual may well include essential reference to the entire set of individuals—the one in view specifically included—that can comprise a possible-world setting for this individual. Thus the individuating specifications of an individual may be *impredicative* in just the way to which Henri Poincaré took exception in condemning *impredicative definitions*, i.e., "*définitions par . . . une relation entre l'objet à définir et tous les individus d'un genre dont l'objet à définir est supposé faire lui-même partie.*"[2] Thus an individual may, for example have the essential property $(\lambda x)[\neg Fx \;\&\;$

---

[2] Henri Poincaré, "La Logique de l'infini," *Scientia*, vol. 12 (1912), pp. 1–11 (see p. 7); quoted from Alonzo Church, *Introduction to Mathematical Logic*,

$\neg(\exists y)Fy]$ (i.e.,—"nothing has F in my world, myself specifically included") as part of its defining specification. In the present context, this mode of impredicativity produces no mischief. In the final analysis, indeed, *all* of the *fic*'s of individuals will presumably prove impredicative and involve specification of the fact that *all* the individuals of its environing world must meet certain conditions.

In cases of the sort dealt with to this point, the incompossibility of the possible individuals at issue rests in a *purely logical* way on features of their individuating descriptions. A second sort of incompossibility is represented by incompatibility relative to natural laws, viz., *nomic* incompossibility (N-incompossibility). This turns on the issue of preserving, in the possible world in question, some or all of the "laws of nature" of the actual world. For example, if one is to have it that "Copper conducts electricity" then one could not emplace in a possible world a hypothetical "possible object" that is both copper and a nonconductor. Or again, if one is to have the law that "acids redden blue litmus paper," then one cannot emplace in a possible world both a bowl of acid and an unaffectedly blue bit of litmus paper submerged within it. (It merits remark—although the observation is at this point somewhat premature—that the category of N-compossibility can be subsumed within that of L-compossibility by treating laws as universal dispositions essential to the descriptive make-up of all the individuals within the law-governed world.)

Finally, yet another sort of incompossibility must also be recognized, M-*incompossibility* which rests ultimately on *metaphysical* rather than purely *logical* considerations. Such ontological incompossibility is grounded in the following principles:

(I) The Identity of Indiscernibles is to be preserved to the maximum feasible extent in the possibilistic sphere as an *intra-world* principle. No possible world apart from the actual can contain distinct possible individuals with the same description—unless these are mere carryovers of indiscernible actualia. Specifically, no non-actual possible

---

Vol. I (Princeton, 1956), p. 347. See Church's discussion of the ramifications of this idea, its relationship to Bertrand Russell's vicious circle principle, etc.

world can contain two individuals $x \sim \langle d_x, p_x \rangle$ and $y \sim \langle d_y, p_y \rangle$ where $d_x = d_y$ and p_x and p_y represent descriptively distinct individuals in the *real* world.

Thus the Identity of Indiscernibles (in its stronger, Aristotelian —i.e., essentialistic—form) holds as an *intra-world* principle within all merely possible worlds, save for those cases in which qualitatively indiscernible actual individuals have been carried over, bodily (so to speak), into some other possible world.

Consider a situation in which this principle were violated, by supposing a world w which contains two individuals $\langle d, p_x \rangle$ and $\langle d, p_y \rangle$, with $p_x \neq p_y$. Note that when one takes one's standpoint *within w* (drawing no "external" relationship to w^*), these two individuals are by hypothesis wholly indiscernible. Their differentiation proceeds wholly *in terms of an external relationship to another world*. This position seems anomalous, to say the least.

(II) Description-splitting is precluded. No possible world can contain distinct versions of the same prototype: distinct possible individuals can never stand surrogate in any possible world for the same actual individual. That is, no possible world can contain two individuals $x \sim \langle d_x, p_x \rangle$ and $x' \sim \langle d_x, p_x \rangle$ with $d \neq d'$ (i.e., where d and d' are distinct [essentialistically complete] individuating descriptions [C.D.S.], both attributed to one selfsame individual).

To motivate this principle, consider how the variant forms of an individual were determined in the first place. We said that certain features of, say, Caesar were essential to him (e.g., his being a Roman) and other accidental (e.g., his decision to cross the Rubicon). Any of the accidentally variant forms could possibly be realized—a Caesar that crosses and one that does not. Both could be realized, *but not together*. We are prepared to see either one realized, and to contemplate a world where Caesar does not cross, but we are not prepared to see both realized conjointly in a world where Caesar both does and does not cross the Rubicon—where *one selfsame person* (rather than say, two distinct causal successors into which he somehow "splits") both does and does not have some feature.

Principle II is crucially important because it assures that in any world-setting the actual prototype of an individual is a wholly sufficient basis for its individuation: given that one individual of the world has a certain prototype, no other individual *in that world* is in a position to contest this prototype with it. Principle II lays it down that in a possible world there cannot be two distinct surrogates for one and the same actual individual; Principle I has it that there cannot be one and the same surrogate for two distinct actual individuals. This avoidance of collisions smoothes the way for the correlation of the population of other possible worlds with that of the actual.

We may thus introduce the notation

$$S^w_{yx}$$

for "y is the (unique) surrogate of the actual individual x in the possible world w," with the assurance of intra-world uniqueness whenever $y \in w$ has x as its prototype. Thus whenever $x \in w^*$ we have:

$$S^w_{yx} \text{ iff both } y \in w \text{ and } y \cong x.$$

Real-world prototypes serve an essentially naming function with respect to their surrogates in other worlds, and the classical doctrine of names is relevant here. That a name must as a matter of logical principle indicate what is one single thing which must not "split apart" into two or more distinct items capable of laying equal but competing claims to it is part of the scholastic principle of *unum nomen unum nominatum* ("one name, one bearer").

* * *

A possible world is thus not just any set of possible individuals. Only a *compossible* set of possible individuals qualifies as a possible world, and any such world must, accordingly, meet not only the logical conditions of L-compossibility among its members, but also the conditions of metaphysical compossibility (M-compossibility) specified above—and perhaps ultimately those of nomic N-compossibility as well.

Once we know that the possible individual $x \sim \langle d_x, p_x \rangle$ belongs to the possible world w (where $w \neq w^*$), then we have it that for every $y \sim \langle d_y, p_y \rangle \in w$:

(1) Always: $p_x \neq p_y$ unless $d_x = d_y$ (i.e., unless $x \doteq y$)

(2)   Generally: $d_x \neq d_y$ unless $\rho_x = \rho_y$ (i.e., unless $x \doteq y$)[3]

These two theses conjointly yield that in general

$$d_x = d_y \text{ iff } \rho_x = \rho_y$$

whence it follows that

$$d_x = d_y \text{ iff } x \doteq y.$$

The principles of compossibility thus assure that internally, *within* each actuality-remote possible world, the principle of the Identity of Indiscernibles holds in its strong (Aristotelian) form. The rules of compossibility suffice to assure that in the realm of unrealized possibility an "exclusion principle" obtains in such a way that occupancy by an individual of a certain (complete) descriptive compartment will block all *other* individuals from it.

While the preceding version of the Identity of Indiscernibles principle settles the question of the reidentification of individuals *within a given unrealized possible world*, the issue of *transworld* identity remains as fixed by the general principles delineated above:

$$x \cong y \text{ iff } [(\rho_x \doteq \rho_y \neq \star) \lor [(\rho_x \doteq \rho_y = \star) \,\&\, (d_x = d_y)]]]$$

where $\star$ is "the null individual," the having of which as "prototype" simply indicates the absence of any real prototype at all. Accordingly, any individual possesses two sorts of "identity" its *strict* or *specific* identity (S-identity) as determined by its *fic*, and its *generic* identity (G-identity) as determined by the equivalence class of those individuals with which it is cross-world reidentifiable in the sense of $\cong$-identity. And correspondingly, possible worlds are also subject to two distinct sorts of identity conditions: They are S-identical when their members are S-identical (i.e., answers to the same set of *fic*'s) and G-identical when their members are G-identical (i.e., can be cross-world reidentified in the sense of $\cong$). When speaking of "the same" individuals or "the same" worlds we need to bear in mind that very different sorts of sameness can be at issue.

---

[3] Note that this condition can fail to obtain in the actual world or in a nonactual world into which indiscernible real-world individuals ρ_x and ρ_y are simply carried over. However, the principle will always obtain apart from this one exception regarding reals.

3. POSSIBILITY AND COMPOSSIBILITY

Our discussion displays throughout a uniform approach to possibility, based on the principle of construing all the relevant modes of possibility in terms of a compatibility or relative logical possibility with respect to some suitable basis:

possible = L-possible relative to specified conditions.

The theory thus develops a relativistic conception of possibility. Logical possibility is fundamental; other modes of possibility are elaborated in terms of logical possibility relative to certain presuppositions. A "possible individual" is one that is so duly relativized to some characterization of the actual world. A "possible world" is one that not merely consists of possible individuals, but satisfies certain metaphysical considerations as to the "compossibility" of individuals capable of copresence in one common world.

Beginning with the actual world and its characteristics, we stipulate a mode of "essentiality" in terms of which the family of actual individuals can be supplemented by a domain composed of "actual variant" individuals as well as those that are "merely possible." These, in turn, form the potential population of the possible worlds. To be sure, not just any collection of such individuals forms a possible world, but only those which are *compossible* in the way explicited above. The theory of compossibility brings us to the end of our "constructive" process for developing the manifold of possible worlds. The whole approach proceeds from the starting-point afforded by the actual world, for it is the actual world that provides the machinery for the entire constructive process. (The actual world furnishes the inventory of individuals and the taxonomy of properties in whose terms the whole development proceeds.)

Of course, once we have carried out this constructive process, we can take the hypothetically assumptive approach of viewing some "merely possible" world as the *hypothetically* actual one. And we can then say how the whole process of constructing other individuals and other worlds would go "if *this* world were—reality to the contrary—to have been the actual one." But this prospect does not undo the fact that the merely possible (albeit *hypothetically* actual) world in question was itself initially derived with respect to the actual world. The genuinely actual world—in contradistinction to some merely hypothetically actual one—thus plays an indispensably central part in this process, one that prevents it from being viewed as being altogether on the same plane with its "merely possible" alternatives.

4. THE PROBLEM OF TRANS-WORLD IDENTITY

Our "constructive" approach commits us fundamentally to the idea that, *pace* Leibniz, one selfsame thing can recur in a variety of possible worlds—a view adopted by most writers on the subject since Carnap.[4] A great deal of heavy weather has been made in the literature of the subject about "the problem of the trans-world identification of individuals." But on the present proceeding this "problem" simply evaporates—or, if you prefer, is so shifted that it becomes displaced to an altogether different context: that of the initial specification (or individuation) of possible individuals.

Consider a (hypothetically actual) microworld of three individuals answering to the following descriptive specifications:

	F	G	H
x_1	[+]	+	+
x_2	[+]	−	−
x_3	[−]	[+]	+

One arrives here at the following inventory of actual-variant descriptions:

	F	G	H	x_1	x_2	x_3
d_1	+	+	+	@	#	
d_2	+	+	−	#	#	
d_3	+	−	+	#	#	
d_4	+	−	−	#	@	
d_5	−	+	+			@
d_6	−	+	−			#
d_7	−	−	+			
d_8	−	−	−			

---

[4] "Modalities and Quantification," *The Journal of Symbolic Logic*, vol. 11 (1946), pp. 33–46.

On this basis, the nonactual but possible versions of the actuals will answer to the following *fic*'s:

$$\text{For } x_1 = x_1^0 \qquad\qquad \text{For } x_2 = x_2^0$$
$$x_1^1 = \langle [d_2, \{F\}], x_1 \rangle \qquad x_2^1 = \langle [d_1, \{F\}], x_2 \rangle$$
$$x_1^2 = \langle [d_3, \{F\}], x_1 \rangle \qquad x_2^2 = \langle [d_2, \{F\}], x_2 \rangle$$
$$x_1^3 = \langle [d_4, \{F\}], x_1 \rangle \qquad x_2^3 = \langle [d_3, \{F\}], x_2 \rangle$$

$$\text{For } x_3 = x_3^0$$
$$x_3^1 = \langle [d_6, \{\overline{F}, G\}], x_3 \rangle$$

The principles of compossibility now delimit the prospects of combining these individuals in forming possible worlds. For example, they would rule out the placing into one possible world both x_1^1 and x_1^2, or again both x_1^1 and x_2^2.

To be sure, given solely the *purely descriptive* facts about the individuals that make up a possible world, one cannot say which possible world is at issue. Suppose, for example, that all we know is that the following three descriptive specifications are actual variantly instantiated, d_2, d_3, d_5. Then we do not know which of the following two possible worlds is to lie in view:

(1) x_1^1, x_2^3, x_3
(2) x_1^2, x_2^2, x_3.

The descriptive characterization of its population is of itself far from sufficient to determine a possible world completely; descriptions by themselves may leave the matter of just which individuals are at hand grossly undetermined. On the other hand, when possible individuals are "given" as duly individuated by their *fic*, then the question of their identity is settled once and for all. For on our theory the *fic* plays just the role of what Saul Kripke calls a *rigid designator*—i.e., one that inevitably specifies precisely the same individual in the context of *every* possible world.[5] (This concept coincides pretty much with what is traditionally referred to in the literature of philosophical logic as a "logically proper name" for an individual.) The *fic* individuates *world invariantly* because it does so in a *world-neutral* way.

---

[5] Saul Kripke, "Naming and Necessity" in D. Davidson and G. Harman (eds.), *Semantics of Natural Language* (Dordrecht, 1972), pp. 253–355 (see pp. 269–70).

An important lesson regarding the "trans-world identification" of individuals is inherent in this construction-from-individuals line of approach to possible worlds. For according to this perspective one would clearly have an altogether misled and misleading picture of the status of possible worlds in thinking of them as *given* and then, subsequently thereto, being faced with questions of the sort "Is $x \in w_1$ the same as $y \in w_2$?" Now on taking the view that possible worlds are built up from predeterminate and world-neutral possible individuals, questions of this sort cannot arise in baffling form, since we need simply determine those *previously identified* individuals from which these worlds were composed in the first place.

On the constructive approach, the identification of a possible individual is the primary and basic issue; possible worlds simply amount to suitable sets of such individuals. Accordingly, one can, of course, settle whether a given (duly identified) individual of one possible world is identical with one that belongs to another. *Trans*-world identity is resolved in terms of *pre*-world identity. Since possible worlds are stocked with *prefabricated* individuals, the issue of reidentification cannot prove problematic.

The relationship between essentiality and trans-world identity warrants a word of comment. A one-way street leads from identity to essentiality, since one can characterize a property as essential to an individual if this property is shared by all of its surrogates in all worlds, but we cannot go in the reverse direction. Barring a Scotist theory of individual essences, no volume of information about an individual's essential properties will enable us to reidentify it in a different world environment. One sometimes finds it said that "The question of essential properties so-called is supposed to be equivalent (and it is equivalent) to the question of identity across possible worlds."[6] Given an essentialism on which, as on Aristotle's, an individual shares each *and all* its essential properties with many others (viz., those of its "species"), no amount of essentialistic information can enable us to reidentify an individual *vis à vis* its species-congeners in this world, let alone another.

On our approach, the very individuation of the individual provides the key to trans-world identification: its identity follows

[6] *Ibid.*, see p. 266.

an individual as unfailingly through different possible worlds as a person's shadow does in this one. No matter how clever he is in altering his garb and contorting his facial or bodily features (say to resemble Napoleon), Smith's shadow is still *his* shadow; he can assume Napoleon's expression, posture, mannerisms, dress, etc., but there is nothing he can do to assume his shadow and get rid of his own. Identity, on our view, behaves in exactly the same dogged way. Once we take ourselves to be dealing with an individual and hypothetically modifying *it*, then it remains self-identically on our hands throughout. The survival of identity through all (logico-metaphysically admissible) hypothetical alterations is a basic principle of our theory.

In defending his own theory of possible individuals against Quinean strictures David Lewis has written:

> ... well-nigh incorrigibly involved ... mysteries of individuation ... [are posed by] unactualized possibles who lead double lives, lounging in the doorways of two worlds at once. But I do not believe in any of those. The unactualized possibles I do believe in, confined each to his own world and united only by ties of resemblance to their counterparts elsewhere do not pose any special problems of individuation. At least, they pose only such problems of individuation as might arise within a single world.[7]

The merit of the present theory of possibilia lies exactly in this, that while prepared to assume the more liberal stance of admitting one individual into distinct possible worlds, it reduces the problems of individuation and trans-world-reidentification to those with which any theory of individuals must deal—to wit, identification in the real world.

Our theory leads to a position where one selfsame individual can reappear in different descriptive guises in different possible worlds. It accordingly becomes necessary to distinguish between two versions of what it is to be a "single individual": (1) specific individuation (S-individuation) which proceeds in the by now familiar manner of *fic*-specification, and (2) generic individuation (G-individuation) which treats as representative of a single individual the entire equivalence class of those S-

[7] David Lewis, *Counterfactuals* (Oxford, 1973), p. 87.

individuated items that are coidentifiable in the mode of trans-world individuation. From this point forward we shall frequently construe the concept of "individual" in the latter, generic sense, as the context of the discussion will make clear. But we shall adopt the technical term *version* whenever this somewhat loose way of talking will not do, and speak of the various $\cong$-reidentifiable items as "distinct versions of the same individual" in the different world-environments at issue. Accordingly, $x \in w$ will be said to be the w-included *version* of some individual y belonging to $w' \neq w$ whenever this $x \in w$ is such that $x \cong y$. (The *version* of a real-world individual in any world w will always be unique *surrogate* for this actualium in its world.)

Correlative with G/S-distinctness, one must also recognize two distinct constructions of the idea of compossibility, according as the incompatibility obtains between S-individuated items, and individuals in the stronger, generic sense. Individuals are incompossible in this second, stronger sense when *every* version of the one is incompossible with every version of the other. (That is, x is G-incompossible with y if no x-version is compossible with any y-version.) An example of this arises when x *essentially* has the property "no individual in my environing world has ϕ" and y *essentially* has the property ϕ. (Note that this strong mode of incompossibility can arise only in the presence of essential relational properties.)

5. THE CENTRALITY OF THE ACTUAL

If a possible world is to be fully determinate and well-defined, one must not just be able to *describe* its contents taken in isolation, but also, by fully individuating its members, be able to relate them to those of the actual and of other possible worlds. Accordingly, the following two items must be included in the adequate specification of a possible world:

(1) the essentialistically complete descriptive specification (C.D.S.) of the various individuals that constitute the population of the world.

(2) the specification of which individuals are to be surrogates for actual individuals—and just which actual individuals.

In sum, if a possible world is to be well-defined, then its membership must be specified by information sufficient actually to *individuate* its members: one must be in a position to determine the *fic* for every individual comprised in a possible world. (The *fic* of a possible individual—precisely because it is a full and individuationally adequate specification of it, determines a definite individual that remains self-identically the same throughout all of its possible-world contexts.)

In the full characterization of an alternative possible world, it thus does *not* suffice to specify simply the pure descriptions of its individuals. On our constructive approach to possible worlds, it is not enough to specify the merely descriptive phylogeny of their membership; the ontogenesis implicit in their (conceptual) extraction from the actual is also to be taken as an essential aspect of "what makes things the things they are." Thus possible worlds—like the possible individuals that populate them—are defined relative to the actual world as basis (or at any rate relative to a hypothetical actual world—a possible world *assumed* to be actual).

One should not be misled into thinking that we have been presented with a possible world—nor even a possible individual within one—when we are simply given purely descriptive information about its members. Unless and until the question of the relationship of the individuals that bear these descriptions to those of the actual world has been settled, a specific (individuated) individual has not been indicated at all, but merely a descriptive individual-schema to which many particular possible individuals may in principle answer. That such incomplete information does not enable us to resolve the issue of trans-world identity is a matter of course. But once the crucial facts about actuality-relatedness are added to descriptive information (i.e., once we are given the *fic* of the individual, and not merely its C.D.S.), then the process of individuation is complete, and we are actually in a position to settle questions of trans-world identification in a relatively straightforward way.

From this standpoint there is thus something decidedly wrong-headed about the way in which this problem of the trans-world identity of individuals is posed in much of the literature. For the problem is frequently approached as follows:

It is supposed that one is presented with two complete and finished possible worlds (arising in full-blown perfection like Venus from the head of Zeus), and then asked whether certain individuals of these worlds can be identified with one another. From our standpoint, this way of looking at the matter is utterly unrealistic as well as misguided because it poses the problem in unsolvable terms. Unsolvability arises because the problem is about the identity of individuals in circumstances where information crucial to their identification (viz., the issue of relationships to the real world) has deliberately been suppressed. And unrealism arises because the problem envisages possible worlds as arising *ex nihilo*. But possible worlds are never "given" from on high, they are made up, manufactured in assumption-contexts where the issue of the nature of their ingredients must in principle be resolvable and may well actually have to be resolved if certain questions (e.g., those regarding the identity of individuals) are to be answerable. The make-up of possible worlds must not be allowed to baffle us—we enjoy mastery over their descriptive detail precisely because they are products of our own devising.

This position seems closely akin to that of Saul Kripke when he writes that it is a mistake to regard

> a possible world as if it were like a foreign country [already *there* and awaiting our inspection]. . . . Some logicians in their formal treatment of modal logic may encourage this picture. A prominent example, perhaps, is myself. Nevertheless, intuitively speaking, it seems to me not to be the right way of thinking about possible worlds. A possible world isn't a distant country that we are coming across, or viewing through a telescope. Generally speaking, another possible world is too far away. Even if we travel faster than light, we won't get to it. A possible world is given by the descriptive conditions we associate with it. . . . Possible worlds are *stipulated*, not discovered by powerful telescopes.[8]

This position of Kripke's appears from the angle of our theory to be entirely right-minded.

To insist on such a primacy for the actual world may seem

[8] Kripke, *op. cit.*, see pp. 266–7.

unduly parochial. One could certainly contemplate a position prepared to maintain a strict parity among possible worlds along something like the following lines:

> Our actual world is only one world among others. We call it alone actual not because it differs in kind from all the rest but because it is the world we inhabit. The inhabitants of other worlds may truly call their own worlds actual, if they mean by "actual" what we do; for the meaning we give to "actual" is such that it refers at any world i to that world i itself. "Actual" is indexical, like "I" or "here", or "now": it depends for its reference on the circumstances of utterance, to wit the world where the utterance is located.[9]

But this position fails to give due heed to one significant fact: one must "begin from where one is," and WE are placed within this actual world of ours. There is no physical access to other possible worlds from this one. *For us* other possible worlds remain intellectual projections. Doubtless these worlds are (or can be projected to be) such that *from their* perspective our world (*the* actual one, since "the actual" like "the present" place or time has its egocentric aspect) has the status of an intellectual projection from *their* perspective. But this does alter the fact that they are and must be accepted by us as projections from the perspective of *this*, the only perspective in whose terms any discussion of *ours* can proceed. The priority of the actual in any discussion of *ours* is *inevitable*: it is not a matter of overcoming some capriciously adopted and in principle alterable point of departure.

One qualifying concession is in order. Once the constructive projection of a possible world is a matter of *fait accompli*, one can then assume *thereafter* the stance of cutting loose from the actual world, blowing up behind one, so to speak, the bridge by which one has effected one's crossing from the sphere of the actual. Thus individuation within antecedently specified worlds can also proceed ostensively—knowing where its constituents are located relative to one another and whither members of its populace are (*ex hypothesi*) pointing, one can also identify objects

---

[9] David Lewis, *Counterfactuals* (Oxford, 1973), pp. 85–6.

in nonexistent worlds in a quasi-ostensive way. But this concession must not be construed to abate one jot or tittle from the fundamentability of the actual in the over-all possibilistic scheme of things. For while the members we postulate as populating possible worlds can no doubt be stipulated to make ostensive indications of other things, ostension is an inextricably intra-world process, and so *we*, the actual individuals are inherently unable to have any resort to ostensive mechanisms in *our* suppositional constituting of possible worlds.

This point has important implications for our treatment of spatial positions as descriptive. Someone may well object: "In a perfectly symmetrical world, it would seem that a system of objective locations is impossible. How, then, could reference to such a system be invoked legitimately as a basis for the descriptive differentiation of (otherwise) indiscernible objects?" The key question for us is always: How does one get there *from here*? Symmetrical worlds are not given from on high: they are imaginatively projected by us against the background of a positional framework that is already at hand. The fact that the (hypothetical) beings of the symmetric world could not differentiate descriptively between (*ex hypothesi*) indiscernible things—but could only do so by a hypothetical ostension—does not mean that *we* cannot do so (in terms of our preestablished locational machinery)—as indeed we *must* do if we ever intend to entertain the hypothesis at issue.

6. THE INDEPENDENCE OF INDIVIDUALS AND THEIR PRIORITY OVER WORLDS

One aspect of the constructive approach demands explicit consideration. We have first dealt with the specification of individuals and only then—subsequently and with fully individuated items in hand—have proceeded to the specification of worlds in terms of suitable sets of "prefabricated" individuals. This seems to lead to the seemingly unpalatable consequence that individuals cannot reflect their world-environments, that they are, so to speak wholly context-independent *vis à vis* worlds.

This seeming result is not, however, actually forthcoming. Individuals are *not* (or *need* not be) wholly independent of their environing world. We cannot put an individual into any world-environment we please. Thus if, for example, it is essential to Cain to be the son of Adam (to take Leibniz's example), then clearly we cannot emplace Cain in any world from which Adam is absent. Insofar as relational properties are seen as built into the very essence of certain individuals, we face insuperable constraints in the sorts of worlds in which they can be accommodated. They are then *not* independent of their environment, but can demand the presence of some individuals and the absence of others. Exactly this is the crucially operative effect of the principles of compossibility. We shall resume this important theme in the later chapter on the internality of relations. But it must be stressed already at this point that in proceeding from individuals to worlds our theory does not commit us to the view that individuals are "windowless" (to adopt Leibniz's phrase regarding monads to our somewhat different purposes). There is, on our approach, no reason why an individual, though "prefabricated" cannot be so fabricated as to impose restrictive preconditions on any world-environment which it is to be capable of occupying.

This line of approach to possible worlds does, however, commit one to an *aggregative* conception of possible worlds. Possible worlds just *are* certain collections of possible individuals. The features of such worlds are what they are because they consist of certain individuals. Worlds impose no "emergent" features on their individuals, features which could not in principle be determined to hold of these individuals considered in separation, without reference to world environments. (The accidental individual-oriented relational features of individuals are an exception to this rule. See Appendix I below.)

Precisely because possible worlds are artifacts which we create through certain (in principle *complete*) stipulations about their make-up, a possible world cannot surprise us. Of course, exploration and discovery is possible in connection with possible worlds, but only in precisely the same manner as with an axiomatic theory in mathematics, viz., that certain consequences of assumptions may well not be immediately accessible to a finite mind. The sort of *authentic* discovery that is directed towards genuinely "new" facts lying outside the cognitive range of even a perfect reasoner working from the "facts in hand" is not feasible with respect to nonexistent possible worlds: they admit only of *analysis* and not of *exploration*.

APPENDIX I. INCOMPLETE SPECIFICATIONS OF WORLDS: WORLD SCHEMATA

Every incomplete individual-description represents not, to be sure, a possible individual, but a possibility *for* individuals. All of those individuals (actual or possible) whose complete descriptions in fact round out the incomplete description at issue will represent *realizations* (actual or possible, respectively) of this schematic possibility. In this manner, an incomplete description —precisely because it admits of multiple realizations—cannot present an individual, but only a *schema* for individuals.[10]

However, world-contexts within which incompletely described individuals are placed may be such that this indefiniteness is reduced or even eliminated. Suppose, for example, that one is told that the (*ex hypothesi* actual) world has three individuals, answering to the following *incomplete* identifying descriptions (with respect to a descriptive taxonomy based on F, G, H):

$$x_1 =, (\imath x)(Fx \ \& \ Hx)$$
$$x_2 =, (\imath x)\bar{G}x$$
$$x_3 =, (\imath x)\bar{F}x.$$

Given that these definite descriptions are (by assumption) well-defined—that is, actually indicate unique individuals in their world (so that, for example, x_1 is to be the only individual in the world to have both F and H)—we can infer that the C.D.S. of these three individuals must have the following descriptive structure:

	F	G	H
x_1	+	+	+
x_2	+	−	−
x_3	−	+	?

[10] This distinction between actually individuated individuals and individual schemata is closely analogous to Meinong's distinction between complete and incomplete objects (*Gegenstände*). Cf. H. Poser, "Der Möglichkeitsbegriff Meinongs" in R. von Haller (ed.), *Jehnseits von Sein und Nichtsein: Beiträge zur Meinong-Forschung* (Graz, 1973), pp. 187–204; cf. especially p. 196.

We correspondingly obtain several alternative feasible realizations of (fully specified) possible worlds, according as the H-entry for x_3 is to be $+$ or $-$. In an analogous way *any* such incompletely presented actual world admits of different realizations: each is a "superposition" of several alternatives (in something like the quantum-mechanical sense), and every so indicated but not fully individuated individual is a superposition of several distinct possible individuals.

This idea of superposition is an efficient way to clarify the idea of world schemata. Consider for example the hypothesis:

Suppose a world otherwise like our actual one except that there is an elephant in yonder corner of the room.

Contrary to first appearance, this supposition does not introduce a particular (individuated) world, but a world-schema that can be filled out in many alternative ways. For example: Are we to redistribute the actually existing elephants and put one of them into the corner (if so—*which* one)? Are we to take some actual thing—say the chair in the corner—and transmute it into an elephant (given that such a supposition could qualify as feasible)? Are we to keep all the actual things of our world's inventory in existence and somehow "make room" for an additional, supernumerary one—viz., the (hypothetical) elephant at issue? Until questions of this sort have been resolved, the supposition does not introduce a definitely identified world into the framework of discussion—any more than the supposition "Assume there were a red-headed person sitting in that chair" succeeds in introducing a definitely identified person.

Of course, this sort of indetermination or indefiniteness is to be construed as epistemological rather than ontological. It pertains not to what a world is in fact like, but simply to what we can know of it given certain descriptive data. This points towards a characteristically *epistemic* sense of "possible" which we might accordingly characterize as E-possibility, and leads to a new concept of "possible world," namely one defined relatively to an incompletely specified actual world—one that agrees with the actual world insofar as all our information extends. This sort of incompleteness of specification will, of course, also affect any indication of merely possible worlds introduced through reference—implicit or overt—to a pre-supposedly given actual world. Thus, as R. C. Stalnaker cogently puts it:

> There is no mystery to the fact that I can partially define a possible world in such a way that I am ignorant of some of the determinate truths in that world. One way I can do this is to attribute to it features of the actual world which are unknown to me. Thus I can say, "I am thinking of a possible world in which the population of China is just the same, on each day, as it is in the actual world." I am making up this world—it is a pure product of my intentions—but there are already things true in it which I shall never know.[11]

One must, however, be careful here. The reason for my ignorance is simply that the world to be at issue has been characterized only partially, so that in effect no one single definitely identifiable world is in view. It is *not* the case that some one individuated world is before us, only one that is in some respects inherently incomprehensible, so that there are facets about *it* that cannot be known.

A "partially defined" possible individual (or possible world) is in effect a *schema* to which a plurality of definite possible individuals (or worlds) can in principle answer, exactly as a partially described actual individual can (for all we know) turn out to be any one of a plurality of alternatives. Such incomplete specifications of individuals confront us with possible individual world *schemata* rather than *individuated* possible individuals or worlds, and indicate an indeterminacy that is epistemic rather than ontological. A striking fact about schematically identified individuals is that the Law of Excluded Middle—in the form of principle that of a thesis P and its contradictory $\neg P$, one must be true—fails to obtain. Thus in the context of the hypothesis, "Assume there were a red-headed person sitting in that chair" we could neither say that this hypothetical person is male nor that it is not, nor again, neither that it is six feet tall nor that it is not. Indeed this very failure, even in principle, of a complete

---

[11] Robert C. Stalnaker, "A Theory of Conditionals," *Studies in Logical Theory* (Oxford, 1968; *American Philosophical Quarterly* Monograph Series, No. 2), pp. 98–112; see pp. 111–12.

determinateness in point of properties is what marks what is at issue as something schematic. On the other hand, one can indeed infer about schematic individuals more than is explicit in the introducing characterization itself. For example, we do know of our hypothetical person that he is less than twenty feet tall. The incompleteness of the schematically presented information does not abrogate our background information, and the fact that a *part* of our knowledge is put into suspension by a fact-violating assumption (for there is no one in that chair) does not mean that the whole of it is (i.e., we still know that people don't grow to twenty feet).

This line of thought regarding epistemic possibility leads in directions that we need not follow out further here, save in one crucial direction, viz., that of the question: Can one ever in actual fact deal with a *specific* unactualized individual (let alone a specific unactualized world—i.e., collection thereof)?—or must we always deal with possibilia at the level of schematic generalities?

The answer to this question is—somewhat disconcertingly—that we are indeed confined to the level of generalized schemata, and cannot in realistic cases (unlike that of artificial micro-worlds we standardly invoke by way of examples) deal with what I have characterized as a fully individuated nonexistent particular. Given the infinitistic aspects of realistic item-descriptions we finite information-processing mechanisms cannot ever spell out the descriptive sector of the *fic*'s of possibilia. This limitation to the schematic case, however, represents an inherently epistemological aspect of the matter from which we can, in principle, abstract in considerations on the ontological side. The fact remains that it seems plausible to hold that the only realistic possibilities we can ever discuss are in some degree schematic, and that the prospect of dealing with *individuated* possibilities inevitably lies beyond our reach, save in those cases in which, because we deliberately confine ourselves to a limited and incomplete descriptive apparatus, we are—thanks to *this* artificiality—in a position to give complete descriptions relative to such incomplete terms of reference.

One significant exception to the preceding contention should perhaps be made, viz., that of those possible individuals generated wholly by a hypothetical *spatial rearrangement* of actual objects (as, for example, when I postulate the possible but, as such, nonexistent book arrived at by creasing the title page of that one down the middle, or—if you prefer—tearing a corner off it). It seems plausible to say that, given modificatory instructions of a sufficiently specific sort, the schematic aspect can be taken to be absent from these spatial rearrangement cases (except, presumably, insofar as they run afoul of natural laws).

This conception of descriptively schematic individuals actually plays a crucial role in our theory of possibilia. Indeed, possible individuals are (as we have dealt with them) *always descriptively schematic* in one narrow respect—to wit, *in point of their accidental individual-oriented relationships* (let us call them "*i*-relationships"). For we have deliberately excluded *these* relational properties from their C.D.S. (be they specific, such as "bearing R to x_1," or generic, such as "bearing R to some other individual"). The C.D.S. is thus "complete" by courtesy only—it is not actually complete, but only as complete as it can be without specifying an individual's accidental relational properties to others. (Thus, for example, it would *not* be a part of the C.D.S. of Hannibal that he was admired by Count Schlieffen.)

The reason for this policy is simple. If we allowed the accidental *i*-relationship of merely possible individuals (supernumeraries) to figure in their individuating C.D.S., then we would here stand in the posture of the classical idealists who hold that in their case each and every one of the *i*-relationships of an individual is a crucial element in its individuation. (With actuals or actual-variants there would be no difference, to be sure, as their individuation is not descriptively based.) Merely possible individuals would become altogether world-bound: one could not specify such an individual without specifying its whole environing world.

Such a stance would be drastically at variance with our line of approach, as based on the principle "individuals first—worlds later." Our strategy has been to characterize possible individuals in isolation without specifying their possible worlds until a later stage, thus proceeding in their specification in an environment-ignoring manner, save where essential relationships are involved. We treat accidental *i*-relational properties as *supervenient* for *all* individuals (supernumeraries included), in that they are to come about *after* the individual's identity is already established, through the further specification of its environing world. If we did not take this stance, supernumeraries would become world-specifying. (We would then have to resolve the issue of their trans-world identity on a more complicated basis, excluding the accidental *i*-relations of supernumeraries from consideration as an identity-differentiating factor.)

Note that the element of schematism induced for supernumeraries by the exclusion of accidental *i*-relations from their C.D.S. *is always removed in context*—that is, in relation to a specified world-environment. Once a world is specified, these accidental *i*-relational properties all become straightforwardly *derivative* and become a "mere logical consequence" of the world-specification. Such accidental *i*-relations are the *only* "world-emergent" properties of individuals, and they are always *derivable* from the atomistic characterization of the individual world-members (and in this sense conform to the anti-Gestaltist principle that "the whole is no more than the sum of its parts"). Our constructivistic approach to possible individuals and possible worlds has turned its back on that sector of the idealist tradition that adopts a theory of internal relations stipulating that a thing is what it is only because its environment is as it is—a view opposed to the spirit of our "individuals first—worlds later" approach. (On other aspects of this issue see Chapter X below.)

However, it warrants stress that even if one were to class the accidental *i*-relations of a merely possible individual as part of its individuating C.D.S.—insisting that all such individuals are world-bound, and scrapping the "individuals first—worlds later" approach—this would *not* block the fundamental strategy of our conceptualistically constructivistic approach. It would mean only that one could not proceed in the *sequential* manner we have envisaged here, but would have to proceed *coordinately and concurrently* with the constructive specification of possible individuals and their worlds.

* * *

The ontological position assumed throughout the preceding discussion is the orthodox (or *classical*) one according to which the real (or potentially real) is always maximally definite and determinate: regardless of the state of our *knowledge* about it, any possible particular must either actually have or actually lack any specifiable well-defined property, and any possible world must either actually have or actually lack any specifiable well-defined feature. Things and worlds are by their very nature ontologically determinate vis-à-vis descriptive features.

It is possible, however, to contemplate the prospect not just of world-schemata but of *descriptively schematic worlds*: worlds such that certain (perfectly definite) questions about their descriptions are not answerable even in the light of "complete information"—worlds which simply do not "make up their minds" about certain issues (to put it figuratively). Such a world w will admit of certain (well-defined) features f such that neither $f(w)$ nor $\neg f(w)$, but rather w is f-blurred. As in the case of *incomplete information* a world-schematization is a *disjunction* of (perfectly definite and mutually incompatible) worlds, so in the present case of a descriptively *ontological indeterminacy* a schematic world is a *superposition* of (perfectly definite and mutually incompatible) worlds. The two cases of epistemic underdetermination and ontological underdetermination are wholly parallel on the *logical* side. Despite the drastic metaphysical disparity between the two cases, no item of logico-semantical machinery is needed—over and above what is required to deal with the latter issue of ontological indeterminacy.

Thus if we enlarge our ontological imagination to provide for indeterminately schematic *quasi-worlds* (so let us call them), no special machinery supplemental to that introduced above will be needed. The ontological case can be treated in terms of a superposition of definite orthodox worlds, on rigid analogy with the way in which the epistemic case deals with a *disjunction* of such definite, orthodox worlds. And the same mechanisms of conceptual construction operative in the one case can be taken to provide the basis needed for the rational systematization of the other. Our foray into ontological unorthodoxy does not issue in any difficulties which the constructive theory of possibility need regard as insuperable.

APPENDIX II. TRANS-WORLD IDENTITY AND LEWIS' THEORY OF COUNTERPARTS

In a stimulating recent paper David Lewis has advocated the (essentially Leibnizian) program of (1) *abandoning* any prospect of trans-world identity by adopting the view no individual in any world is identical with one in another, and (2) *replacing* the concept of identity across worlds by that of *counterparts* based on similarity:

> The counterpart relation is our substitute for identity between things in different worlds. Where some would say that you are in several worlds, in which you have somewhat different properties and somewhat different things happen to you, I prefer to say that you are in the actual world and no other, but you have counterparts in several other worlds. Your counterparts resemble you closely in content and context in important respects. They resemble you more closely than do the other things in their worlds. But they are not really you. For each of them is in his own world, and only you are here in the actual world. Indeed we might say, speaking casually, that your counterparts are you in other worlds, that they and you are the same; but this sameness is no more a literal identity. . . . It would be better to say that your counterparts are men you *would have been*, had the world been otherwise.[12]

On this theory, $y \in w_2$ is to qualify as a counterpart of $x \in w_1$ iff (1) y shares all of x's essential properties, and moreover (2) y is "sufficiently similar" to x in terms of its resemblance in important regards.

We shall abstract from all of the *practical* difficulties of applying this idea (e.g., how, given that "similarity" splits apart into a multiplicity of respects, is one to tell where sufficient similarity begins and ends?). And we shall also not say much about the cognate perplexities of approaching reidentification through similarity which are implicit in Chisholm's discussion of the

---

[12] David Lewis, "Counterpart Theory and Quantified Modal Logic," *The Journal of Philosophy*, vol. 65 (1968), pp. 113–26; see pp. 114–15.

Adam-Noah example and its implications.[13] Perhaps the most serious of these is that mooted by Saul Kripke. Objecting to Lewis' thesis that "Your counterparts ... resemble you ... more closely than do the other things in their worlds ... weighted by the importance of the various respects and the degrees of the similarities," Kripke complains:

> Surely these notions are incorrect. To me Aristotle's most important properties consist in his philosophical work and Hitler's in his murderous political role; [yet] both, as I have said, might have lacked these properties altogether. Surely there was no logical fate hanging over either Aristotle or Hitler which made it in any sense inevitable that they should have possessed the properties we regard as important to them; they could have had careers completely different from their actual ones. *Important* properties of an object need not be essential, unless 'importance' is used as a synonym for essence; and an object could have had properties very different from its most striking actual properties, or from the properties we use to identify it.[14]

Accordingly, substantial practical difficulties afflict a program of basing an identificatory correlation of individuals on the basis of similarity-considerations.

Moreover, various *theoretical* difficulties of this approach revolve about the fact that similarity is neither transitive nor symmetric. It is difficult to see how any relationship that is proposed as a reasonable substitute for the *identity* relation can fail to have these properties.

This can be brought out in terms of Lewis' own explanation. An individual's counterparts are (as Lewis says) to be those individuals it "*would have been*, had the world been otherwise" in certain respects. Thus, to take a schematic example, consider the claim that if some particular (unrealized) circumstance

---

[13] R. M. Chisholm, "Identity Through Possible Worlds: Some Questions," *Nous*, vol. 1 (1967), pp. 1–8. Also the appeal to similarity in this context is beset by what Goodman calls "the companionship difficulty." See Nelson Goodman, *The Structure of Appearance* (Cambridge, Mass.; 1951).

[14] "Naming and Necessity" in D. Davidson and G. Harman (eds.), *Semantics of Natural Language* (Dordrecht, 1972), pp. 252–355 (see p. 289).

or condition had actually obtained, then x would have been y. But how can we make sense of this? Seemingly, only in such counterfactual terms as:

> If the extant world were w instead of the actual world w^*, then the individual $x \in w^*$ would [or might] have taken a different form, and existed in the version $y \in w$(i.e., if certain circumstances had obtained, then x would [or might] have been y).

But, it is difficult to see how serious sense can be made of this sort of claim within the setting of Lewis' commitments, for such discourse envisages a counterfactual moving from the assumptive realization of certain conditions contrary to fact to a conclusion which depends upon the availability of a *prior* concept of trans-world identity, and consequently is disqualified as a means for *replacing* this conception.

But perhaps the most crucial theoretical difficulty is posed by the question: Just how to understand the issue of "sufficient similarity" central to the explication of counterparthood? When is $y \in w$ to be "sufficiently similar" to something actual, say $x \in w^*$, to qualify as x's counterpart in w? Presumably we could best implement this idea by listing various properties $(F_1, F_2, \ldots, F_n)$ that are to be essential to x, and moreover various other properties $(G_1, G_2, \ldots, G_n)$ that are quasi-essential in the sense that anything purported to represent x would have to have almost all of these (say all but two). Thus y is to qualify as a counterpart to x iff y has *all* of x's essential and *most* of x's quasi-essential properties. Lewis, moreover, appears to suggest that shared essences and "close resemblance" (quasi-essential community) are not enough for counterparts, that a counterpart $y \in w$ to an individual $x \in w^*$ must also resemble x at least as closely as anything else in w does.[15] Thus the conditions of counterparthood would be three: shared essence, close resemblance, and locally maximal resemblance.

But now a crucial problem arises. If counterparthood is to be articulated in some such way of sufficient similarity, how can it possibly do the work it is asked to do as a substitute for trans-

---

[15] David Lewis, "Counterpart Theory," *op. cit.*, p. 116.

world identity and an indication of what a thing would-have-been-if? How can one move from similarity to replacement? Certainly in the *actual* world, the fact that X shares my essential properties (say animality and rationality) and shares a plethora of common properties (is a fellow-businessman and co-religionist with similar tastes and employment, etc.) motivates no inclination in the direction of *identifying* the two of us or towards saying that if one were not there the other would somehow exist in his stead. It is difficult to see how this situation is altered as one moves across world-boundaries. Why should we say of a *merely resembling* individual in another world (even one that is maximally similar) that "had things been otherwise I would have been him"?

It appears as a fatal gap in Lewis' theory that just the theoretical work which he wants counterparthood to do—viz., to serve as a basis for the replacement in other contexts, implementing the idea of what a thing would-have-been-if—is work for which the machinery of "sufficient similarity" is altogether unsuited.[16] For what justification could there possibly be for saying of an individual that some individual in another setting which is in various respects similar to it is the one that IT would have been had matters been different? The theory seems to be caught in a cleft stick: Without replacement one does not get the machinery needed to explicate the claims at issue in counterfactual contentions, and yet with replacement one asks for more than one could securely obtain on the basis of resemblance alone (however elaborate).

To be sure, if possible worlds were *given* us full-grown by some *deus ex machina*, the similarity approach to counterparthood would presumably be the best we can do, and we would then be well advised to abandon claims of reidentification as such. But, given the mechanism of a hypothetico-constructivistic carryover of actual individuals into nonactual worlds, there is no reason for us to feel driven to any such desperate expedient.

---

[16] For other considerations relevant to the role of similarity in reidentification see the monograph by Ernst Mally, A. Meinong's pupil and successor to his chair in Graz: *Studien zur Theorie der Möglichkeit und Ähnlichkeit: Allgemeine Theorie der Verwandtschaft gegenstandlicher Benehmungen* (Vienna, 1922: *Sitzungsberichte der Akademie der Wissenschaften in Wien, Philosophisch-historische Klasse*), vol. 194, fasc. 1, pp. 88ff.

APPENDIX III. DESCRIPTION THEORY

Identification is something vastly weaker than individuation. To individuate an individual is to specify it *vis à vis* all of its *possible* alternatives in a totally decisive way; to identify it is merely to distinguish it from everything in its "immediate environment," to single it out within its given setting in a specific possible world.

Descriptive identification can be massively incomplete. If x is the only green thing in the world, it suffices for descriptive identification to characterize it as such, viz., as "the green thing." Clearly this may leave volumes unspoken.

We shall introduce a citation of the style

$$(\imath x/w)\,dx$$

to stand for "the (one and only) thing in w that answers to the description d (in w)." Such a *description name* can be based on what is, from the abstract logic of the situation, a very incomplete descriptive specification of the item at issue. A description-name is adequate only because of the specific (*contingent*) make-up of the world w: it does not meet the systematic requirements of (logical) adequacy traditionally imposed upon a "logically proper name."

The abbreviated form $(\imath x)\,dx$ will be employed whenever the real world w^* is at issue, so that $(\imath x)\,dx$ is simply short for $(\imath x/w^*)\,dx$. We shall stipulate that the predication-statement "$\psi[(\imath x/w)\,dx]$" is (i) true, (ii) false, or (iii) undefined, according as

    (i) There is exactly one individual $y \in w$ such that dy, and for this individual y we have $\psi \in \mathscr{P}(y)$

    (ii) There is exactly one individual $y \in w$ such that dy, and for this individual y we have $\psi \notin \mathscr{P}(y)$

    (iii) otherwise (i.e., in all other cases)

The description d may be called a *rigid descriptor* if every world w in which $d[(\imath x/w)\,dx]$ is true—i.e., every world in which this item exists at all—is such that $(\imath x/w)\,dx$ identifies the same individual (with "the same" construed in our usual sense of trans-world reidentification):

$$(Aw)(Aw')[(d[(\imath x/w)\,dx] \;\&\; d[(\imath x/w')\,dx]) \supset (\imath x/w)\,dx \cong$$
$$(\imath x/w')\,dx].$$

The fact that

$$(\imath x/w)\,dx \cong (\imath x/w')\,d'x$$

will in general lack any aura of "necessity": only if d and d' happen to be rigid descriptions for the same item will this relationship qualify as inevitable. (It seems worth noting that adjectives like *contingent* and *necessary* do not apply in the usual way to cross-world "facts"—an entirely new set of categories must be deployed in operating at this level.)

APPENDIX IV. PARTS AND WHOLES

With respect to *composite* things, wholes made up of parts, three theses governing the essentiality of part-possession are possible:

(1) the possession of all and exactly those parts it actually has is an essential facet of the thing.
(2) the possession of a given part is never essential to the thing
(3) the possession of some (but not necessarily all) of its parts can be essential to a thing.

Our own policy is to opt for (3). Accordingly, the position is maintained that the operative criteria of item-identity permit a thing to maintain its identity in the face of an hypothesis of part-replacement in some cases (e.g., a kidney transplant in the case of a person), but not in others (e.g., a brain transplant). The key point is that, looking on "possession of a certain specified part" *as simply yet another property* of a thing, one can apply to these mereological properties the same general conditions of essentiality that were set out in Chapter II for properties in general.

APPENDIX V. THE TRANS-WORLD IDENTITY OF PROPERTIES

The trans-world reidentification of properties is in general an issue that poses little difficulty on the present world-constructivistic approach. This is so because on such an approach the properties of *this*, the actual world, are (given a few ramifications) to be taken as operative throughout the manifold of possibility. Accordingly, the reference-framework of *this* world provides the operative standard of property-identity. This point of procedural simplicity is indeed one of the real merits of the present theory vis à vis other alternatives which would have to envisage some sort of hyperworlds within which the properties of different possible worlds could be compared. Thus on a "realistic" approach to possible worlds, the issue of the relative similarity of worlds—which our constructivistic theory can handle on the basis of their descriptive make-up relative to the reference-taxonomy of the *real* world—becomes a problem whose resolution poses seemingly insuperable obstacles. For in the absence of a common and conjointly operative standard, no basis of similarity-comparison can be forthcoming.

The centrality of the real world in providing a common standard is particularly clear in the case of *metrical* properties, with respect to which not merely qualities but even *things* must be present in common across the frontiers of this world and one of its merely possible alternatives.

To be sure, the *relative* size of "possible" physical objects with respect to one another is an issue of their respective relationships to one another within *their* possible world. It need have nothing to do with *this* world. This holds good for their mensurational comparison in general. But the specifically *metrical* concepts of the usual sort—which proceed with respect to meters and kilograms and hours—are inherently actual-world oriented. They are *defined* in terms of comparisons with *standardized* objects or object-families in *this*, the actual world w^*, namely the standardized implements of mensuration, weighing, and chronometry. By their very conceptual nature, the units of kilograms and hours envisage a reference to the things and processes *of this world*.

How, for example, could one proceed to construe the following thesis so as to make sense of it:

(T) The (nonactual) world w contains an object x that is r meters long = If a meter-stick were applied to x in w it would fit r times.

There are clearly only two avenues open to the interpretation of such a claim.

(i) x in fact a *real* thing—a member of the actual world w^*—which has been introduced into w by hypothesis. (For example if I emplace Napoleon in another possible world—one, say, where he won at Waterloo—he will (barring explicit hypotheses to the contrary) take along his various properties, his actual metric length included.)

(ii) x is an actually unrealized thing (a "nonexistent possible"). And now EITHER (A) w contains one of the meter rods M of this actual world w^* and application in w of M to x does (or would) reveal that M fits x exactly r times, OR (B) w contains no actual-world meter rods, but if one of them, say M were introduced into w, then it would transpire that application of M to x in this duly modified world w' does (or would) reveal that M fits x exactly r times.

Case (ii/B) can be eliminated from further consideration. Hypothetical modifications of *possible* worlds simply take us to further cases where these possible relations are realized. Thus (ii/B) carries back to a case of (ii/A) type.

Note, then, that in both cases (i) and (ii) the measurement of the x at issue is to proceed with reference to an actual-world standard. To be sure, in a type (i) case we can certainly get metrically determinate objects even in worlds without any meter-sticks, but we do so *only* because the metric relations have been *pre-arranged* with reference to *this*, the actual world with its actual meter-sticks.

The upshot is that we obtain *metrically* mensurable objects in a possible world only by either (1) supposing it to contain an object whose metric properties are predetermined because it is itself a real-world object, or (2) supposing it to contain a real-world meter-rod by reference to which length determinations can then be made "locally" in the possible world. If neither of these conditions are met, there can be no *co*-mensurability with the metric standards of a real-world mensuration process. And in either case a real-world object is recruited to bear the burden of metrization, viz., one or more of those items which provide the metrical standard. Moreover, on both sides, some community of membership between the actual world and its merely possible alternative is an indispensable requisite as a basis for applying metrical concepts in the latter case.[17]

---

[17] To be sure, the worlds w and w' can admit of metrical comparison without any overlapping membership *with one another*, provided only that each is duly membership-connected with objects of w^*.

As this case of metrical properties with real-world *standards* shows, not only will the *qualities* of the real world figure crucially in the descriptive make-up of other possible worlds, but even its *things* may prove indispensable to the descriptive enterprise.

Chapter V

THE SYSTEMATIZATION OF QUANTIFIED MODAL LOGIC

1. THE Rw-CALCULUS

The present chapter will consider how systems of quantified modal logic of the standard sort can be erected on the foundations of the theory of possible individuals and worlds developed in the preceding discussion.[1] Let it be that the formulas of quantified modal logic are articulated in the usual way, based on the standard connectives $\neg$, &, $\vee$, $\supset$, and $\equiv$, with $\forall$ and $\exists$ for universal and existential quantifiers *over the individuals of the actual world* (or a hypothetically actual one).[2]

We shall proceed by relating such a quantified modal logic to a logical system designed to serve as a realization-in-worlds calculus (Rw-calculus). A brief review of the *modus operandi* of such an Rw-calculus is in order.[3] This is based upon adding to a basic system of (standard) quantification logic the operator Rw (for variable w) with "$Rw(P)$" to be construed as saying "the proposition that P is realized in world w."

The following equivalences are stipulated as axioms governing the Rw-operator:

(R1) $Rw(\neg P) \equiv \neg Rw(P)$

(R2) $Rw(P \ \& \ Q) \equiv [Rw(P) \ \& \ Rw(Q)]$

(R3) $(Aw)[Rw'(Rw(P))] \equiv Rw'[(Aw)Rw(P)]$

(R4) $P \equiv Rw^*(P)$

(R5) $Rw'(Rw(P)) \equiv R\langle w' \star w \rangle(P)$ for some suitable (but for the moment unspecified) $\star$-function that is subject only to the stipulation that $\langle w \star w^* \rangle = w$

---

[1] For background information on modal logic see G. E. Hughes and M. J. Cresswell, *Introduction to Modal Logic* (London, 1968).

[2] For the systematization of quantified modal logic see Hughes and Cresswell, *op. cit.*, Chap. 8.

[3] For a more detailed picture of the workings of such a calculus see Chaps. XII–XIII of N. Rescher, *Topics in Philosophical Logic* (Dordrecht, 1968).

Here A and E are to be the universal and existential quantifiers over possible worlds, respectively, and 'w^*' is a distinguished constant which represents "the actual world."

The $\star$-function is to operate in the following way: Given any pair of possible worlds w and w', it is to yield some world $\langle w' \star w \rangle$ which is, so to speak, "the image one sees when looking at w from w'." Presumably, if our "vision" is reliable, this would be w itself, and so the special case of $\langle w' \star w \rangle \equiv w$ (i.e., identically for all w and w' provided $w \neq w^*$) is of special interest, but we need not make this restrictive assumption.[4] The stipulation that $\langle w \star w^* \rangle = w$ means, so to speak, that the real world is, as it were, a mirror in which all worlds manage to see themselves. The cognate relationship that $\langle w^* \star w \rangle = w$ follows from (R4) and (R5). The real perspective always manages to portray other worlds as they are. The $\star$-function implements the notion of "accessibility" as familiar from recent discussions of the semantics of modal logic. We may regard the accessibility relation $\alpha(w', w)$—read "w' is accessible from w"—as given by the equivalence:

$$\alpha(w', w) \text{ iff } (Ew'') \, [\langle w'' \star w \rangle = w']$$

The $\star$-function represents the mechanism by which "accessibility" must be understood in the context of an Rw-calculus.[5]

The axioms (R1) and (R2) ensure than the Rw-operator distributes over all truth-functional connectives. Moreover, these equivalences allow us to prove

$$[Rw'(Rw_1(P)) \& \ldots \& Rw' \, (Rw_n \, (P))] \equiv Rw'[Rw_1(P) \& \ldots \& Rw_n(P)]$$

which is just what (R3) amounts to for an n-membered—i.e., *finite*—domain of worlds. Thus (R3) might be viewed simply as an unrestricted generalization of this thesis. According to (R4), there is a distinguished world—the actual one—such that the absolute proposition making the unqualified claim that P amounts to the thesis that P is realized relative to this

---

[4] For the workings of this $\star$-function in an Rw-calculus see the chapter on "Topological Logic" in N. Rescher, *op. cit.*

[5] For further development of this idea of accessibility and its role in the semantics of modal logic see G. E. Hughes and M. J. Cresswell, *op. cit.*, pp. 77–80.

special world. Absolute propositions, then, are to be construed with respect to the actual world. The significance of (R5) is implicit in the preceding discussion of the ★-function.

The following rule of inference is also stipulated:

(R)   If ⊢ P, then ⊢Rw(P)

The intuition behind the rule (R) is that logical truths are realized in *every* world. It is an immediate consequence of (R) that:

If ⊢ P, then ⊢Rw(P), for arbitrary w.

Hence the addition of (R) enables us to obtain such results as:

If ⊢P ≡ Q, then ⊢Rw(P) ≡ Rw(Q).

The preceding collection of rules establishes the basic mechanism for operating with the conception of "the realization of propositions with respect to a diversified manifold of possible worlds." Such a mechanism is the beginning—but only the beginning—of a body of machinery adequate to our present needs.

This Rw-calculus provides a framework for speaking of the realization of certain relatively simple relationships (truth-functional compounds) in the case of closed propositions. Let us next extend this machinery to open propositions (propositional functions). The basis here will be the rule:

(R†) $Rw(\phi x) \equiv (\Sigma y) [y \in w \ \& \ y \cong x \ \& \ \phi \in \mathscr{P}(y)]$

Note that the right-hand side of this equivalence yields the following specifications:

(i) when $x \in w^*$: $(\Sigma y) [S_{yx}^w \ \& \ \phi \in \mathscr{P}(y)]$
(ii) when $x \in \mathbf{v}$: $(\Sigma y) [y \in w^* \ \& \ y \cong x \ \& \ Rw(\phi y)]$
(iii) when $x \in \mathbf{s}$: $x \in w \ \& \ \phi \in \mathscr{P}(x)$.

It is significant that (R†) yields:

$\neg Rw (\phi x) \equiv (\Pi y) [y \in w \ \& \ y \cong x \supset \phi \notin \mathscr{P}(y)]$
$Rw(\neg \phi x) \equiv (\Sigma y) [y \in w \ \& \ y \cong x \ \& \ \phi \notin \mathscr{P}(y)]$

Because worlds contain at most one single version of an individual, the right-hand side of the second equivalence entails that of the former. Thus $Rw(\neg \phi x)$ entails $\neg Rw(\phi x)$. But the converse entailment holds only subject to the proviso that $(\Sigma y)[y \in w \ \& \ y \cong x]$, i.e., that some version of x belongs to w. Thus the analogue of rule (R1) holds for *open* formulas only under restrictive conditions regarding the representation of the relevant individuals in the specified world.

We now have a framework for speaking of the realization of certain relatively simple contentions (truth-functional compounds) in possible worlds. What is still wanting is a method for dealing with the additional complexity of quantifiers and modality. We shall now amplify the Rw-calculus further to provide for these resources.

2. THE INTRODUCTION OF QUANTIFIERS AND MODALITIES

To obtain the formulas of the extended Rw-calculus at issue, one relates the symbolic machinery of quantified modal logic (QML) to formulas built up by applying the standard machinery of truth-functional logic to the special operators of world-membership $(x \in w)$, trans-world generalized individual-identity $(x \cong y)$, and individual-surrogacy (S_{yx}^{w}), together with the Rw-operator (for each world-term w), and the quantifiers Π and Σ ranging over the totality of all possible individuals (without regard to their setting in some specific world-contexts). Note that the following relationship will obtain in view of the theory of trans-world identity developed in the preceding chapter:

$$(x \in w^* \ \& \ y \in w \ \& \ x \cong y) \equiv S_{yx}^{w}.$$

Let us first relate the actuality-restricted quantifiers of QML to our synoptic quantifiers Π and Σ of the extended Rw-calculus. In developing an extended theory of quantification within the scope of the Rw-operator, we shall adopt the further axiom:

$$(R6) \quad Rw[(\forall x)\phi x] \equiv (\Pi x)[x \in w \supset Rw(\phi x)].$$

This has as an immediate consequence:

$$Rw[(\exists x)\phi x] \equiv (\Sigma x) [x \in w \ \& \ Rw(\phi x)].$$

Further, (R4) yields the following results when we set the w of the above relationships at w^*:

$$(\forall x)\phi x \equiv (\Pi x)[x \in w^* \supset \phi \in \mathscr{P}(x)],$$
$$(\exists x)\phi x \equiv (\Sigma x)[x \in w^* \ \& \ \phi \in \mathscr{P}(x)].$$

Thus the quantifiers $\forall$ and $\exists$ of QML are to be taken as restricted versions of the more comprehensively oriented quantifiers Σ and Π. In effect, the former are a more myopic version of the latter, with a vision limited to the boundaries of the actual world.[6]

Note that there is a crucial difference in import between

(1) $(\forall x) Rw(\phi x) \equiv (\forall x)(\Sigma y)[S_{yx}^w \ \& \ Rw(\phi y)]$,

that is, "All *actualia* have w-surrogates that have ϕ (in w)," and

(2) $Rw[(\forall x)\phi x] \equiv (\Pi x)[x \in w \supset Rw(\phi x)]$

that is, "All w-members have ϕ (in w)." These are altogether independent—neither entails the other.

It follows from the way in which possible worlds have been constructed that the following principles must obtain:

$(\Pi x)\phi \in \mathscr{P}(x)$ iff for every w: $(\Pi x)[x \in w \supset Rw(\phi x)]$
$(\Sigma x)\phi \in \mathscr{P}(x)$ iff for some w: $(\Sigma x)[x \in w \ \& \ Rw(\phi x)]$

In view of these equivalences, one might as well adopt the useful convention that an *explicit* world-placement indication should always govern the variables bound by a Σ-operator (so that an R-operator and a world-placement indicator [$\in$ or S] should always occur inside the scope of $[\Pi/\Sigma]$-quantifier).

Let us now turn to the modal dimension of our logical system. Here again we need the quantifiers A and E to operate with respect to the range of possible worlds. The basis for handling modalities is given by the following specification:

(R7) $Rw(\square \, \phi x) \equiv (\Pi y)[y \cong x \supset \phi \in \mathscr{P}(y)]$[7]

This is equivalent with

(R7) $Rw(\square \, \phi x) \equiv (Aw')(\Pi y)[(y \in w' \ \& \ y \cong x) \supset Rw'(\phi y)]$

The fact that the w of the left-hand side of this equivalence does not recur on the right-hand side reflects the fact that necessity-theses are world-independent.

---

[6] It thus becomes clear that if one sets the difference between $\forall$ and Π at naught by the stipulation that w^* exhausts the domain of individuals—that the actual individuals as they actually are exhaust the sphere of possibility—then all modal distinctions collapse, and the enterprise we are about to launch upon is blocked, or rather rendered pointless.

[7] We suppose also the obvious generalization of this relationship when the ϕ at issue is a propositional function of not one but many variables.

In the special case where x occurs vacuously in ϕ, so that ϕx is simply a closed formula P, (R7) comes to: $Rw(\Box P) \equiv (Aw')\ Rw'(P)$. Consequently in the special case when the w at issue is w^*, we obtain via (R4) that: $\Box P \equiv (Aw)Rw(P)$. The present theory thus holds, with Leibniz, that a necessary truth is one that obtains in all possible worlds. We shall characterize this pivotal equivalence as *Leibniz's principle*.

One further point merits discussion. In principle, the relationship between a modal logic and a quantified Rw-calculus could be elaborated in two distinct ways: (1) by articulating the Rw-calculus first and separately, and then stipulating *translation-rules* that make it possible to reconstrue modal theses specifically in the Rw-calculus, or (2) by developing both modalities and Rw-principles within one single comprehensive system, and then stipulating *equivalence-theses* that make it possible to *relocate* modal theses in another, modal-free sector of the over-all system. Our present approach deliberately espouses the second, unisystematic equivalency route rather than the duosystematic, translational one, and enables us to embed the modal fragment of the over-all system within a modal-free sector of it. The basic reason for choosing this route is to facilitate the handling of iterative modalities.

In view of the rules of the Rw-calculus, and the negation-duality of necessity and possibility ($\Diamond \equiv \neg\Box\neg$), (R7) leads to

$$Rw(\Diamond \phi x) \equiv (Ew')(\Sigma y)[y \in w' \ \& \ y \simeq x \ \& \ Rw'(\phi y)]$$

In consequence, a property is possible for an individual if it is exhibited by some of its versions in some possible worlds. As with necessity, so possibility is world-independent. Again, note that we shall have: $\Diamond(P) \equiv (Ew)Rw(P)$.

3. MODALITY IN THE ACTUAL WORLD

The central role of the *actual* world lends special importance to the form that (R7) takes when the w at issue is w^*

$$\Box \phi x \equiv (Aw)(\Pi y)[y \in w \ \& \ y \simeq x \supset Rw(\phi y)].$$

Accordingly, a property characterizes an individual of necessity iff it characterizes all its versions in all those possible worlds that do indeed contain versions of this individual.

This thesis has an important consequence. Given our specification of what it is for a possible individual to qualify as the surrogate for an actual individual in a possible world, it follows that: those properties of an actual individual that characterize *all* of its surrogates in *all* possible worlds that have surrogates for it *will be exactly its essential properties*. In view of the specified relationship between essentiality and surrogacy in possible worlds we have it that for any *actual x*:

$$\phi!x \text{ iff } \phi x \ \& \ (Aw)(\Pi y)[S_{yx}^w \supset Rw(\phi y)]$$

The constructive processes at issue thus guarantee the equivalence:

$$\Box \phi x \text{ iff } \phi!x.$$

The properties that necessarily characterize an (actual) individual are just exactly its essential properties. Accordingly, the equivalence now in view assures a perfect correspondence between the *de re* necessity of an individual's essential possession of a property, $\phi!x$, and the *de dicto* necessity of the modal thesis that the attribution of this property represents a necessary fact: $\Box \phi x$. Note, however, that this correspondence turns crucially on the fact that our construction process for possible individuals was deliberately designed to exhaust the entire logical spectrum.

Now turning to possibility we observe that (R7) leads to:

$$Rw(\Diamond \phi x) \equiv (Ew)(\Sigma y)[y \in w \ \& \ y \cong x \ \& \ Rw(\phi y)].$$

In view of (R4) this yields:

$$\Diamond \phi x \equiv (Ew)(\Sigma y)[y \in w \ \& \ y \cong x \ \& \ Rw(\phi y)].$$

This thesis has the consequence that—given our stipulation regarding the surrogates of actuals in other worlds—the possible-properties of actuals are exactly those the attribution of which to the individual at issue result in a possibly true assertion:

$$\Diamond(\phi x) \text{ iff } \phi?x.$$

Again, as regards possibility too, the desired correlation between *de dicto* and *de re* modality is seen to obtain.

It is worthwhile to contrast the equivalence

$$(\exists x)\Diamond \phi x \equiv (\exists x)(Ew)(\Sigma y)[S_{yx}^w \ \& \ Rw(\phi y)]$$

which obtains in view of the preceding principles, with the analogous, but crucially different equivalence:

$$\Diamond (\exists x)\phi x \equiv (Ew)Rw[(\exists x)\phi x] \equiv (Ew)(\Sigma y)[y \in w \ \& \ Rw(\phi y)] \equiv$$
$$(\Sigma y)\phi y.$$

Thus $(\exists x)\Diamond \phi x$ says that "the surrogate in some possible world w of some actual individual has ϕ in this world" while $\Diamond (\exists x)\phi x$ merely says that "some possible individual—actual surrogate or not—has ϕ." The "Barcan Formula" stipulating the implication from $\Diamond (\exists x)\phi x$ to $(\exists x)\Diamond \phi x$ consequently fails to obtain in the setting of the present theory. And an analogous difference obtains between $\Box (\forall x)\phi x$ and $(\forall x)\Box \phi x$ (see p. 120).

4. PROPOSITIONAL MODAL LOGIC

Since no deductive structure has been imposed upon QML directly, but only indirectly, through mediation of the Rw-calculus from which our system of QML has been developed by means of embedding equivalences, it is of some interest to note which strictly modal theses "fall out" of this approach by way of derivative consequence. It is readily seen that, in its *purely propositional* part (i.e., where the modal operators are followed only by *closed* formulas), the modal logic as issue has an **S5** structure.

For **S5** is based on the following axiomatization as supplemental to the standard system of propositional logic:

Rule of Necessitation: If $\vdash P$, then $\vdash \Box P$
  Axioms: 1. $\Box p \supset p$
      2. $\Box (p \supset q) \supset (\Box p \supset \Box q)$
      3. $\Diamond \Box p \supset \Box p$

Let us verify their applicability to our modal system.

(i) *The Rule of Necessitation*
    Assume $\vdash P$, where P is a closed formula not containing w^*. Then by rule (R) we have $\vdash Rw(P)$ for any w. Thus $\vdash (Aw)Rw(P)$. And by Leibniz's principle this leads to $\vdash \Box P$.

(ii) *Axiom 1*
    (a) $\Box p \equiv (Aw)Rw(p)$ by Leibniz's
                                                        principle

    (b) $(Aw)Rw(p) \supset Rw^*(p)$ by quantificational logic

    (c) $Rw^*(p) \equiv p$ by (R4)

    (d) $\Box p \supset p$ from (a)–(c)

(iii) *Axiom 2*

    (a) $\Box(p \supset q)$ hypothesis

    (b) $\Box p$ hypothesis

    (c) $(Aw)Rw(p \supset q)$ from (a) by Leibniz's principle

    (d) $(Aw)[Rw(p) \supset Rw(q)]$ from (c) by (R1), (R2)

    (e) $(Aw)Rw(p) \supset (Aw)Rw(q)$ from (d) by quantificational logic

    (f) $(Aw)Rw(p)$ from (b) by Leibniz's principle

    (g) $(Aw)Rw(q)$ from (e), (f)

    (h) $\Box q$ from (g) by Leibniz's principle

    (i) $\Box(p \supset q) \supset (\Box p \supset \Box q)$ from (a)–(h)

(iv) *Axiom 3*

    (a) $\Box p \equiv (Aw)(Rw(p)$ by Leibniz's principle

    (b) $\Diamond\Box p \equiv$ $(Ew')Rw'[(Aw')Rw'(p)]$ from (a) from Leibniz's principle

    (c) $\Diamond\Box p \equiv (Ew')(Aw)Rw(p)) \equiv (Ew')(Aw)R$ $\langle w' \star w\rangle(p)$ from (b) by (R3), (R5)

    (d) $\Diamond\Box p \equiv$ $(Aw)R\langle w^* \star w\rangle(p)$ from (c) since $w' = w^{*8}$

    (e) $\Diamond\Box p \equiv (Aw)Rw(p) \equiv \Box p$ from (d) by (R4), (R5), (a)

This completes the verification that the modal logic of the closed formulas of our system includes all of the system **S5**. And, indeed, it can be shown that **S5** represents just exactly the modal logic of the purely propositional fragment of our system of QML.

---

[8] It is clear that for (d) to obtain it is necessary and sufficient for w^* to serve as the requisite w'

5. QUANTIFIED MODAL LOGIC

The question of how the modal operators and the quantifier interact is of somewhat more interest. We list the possible combinations of one of each, together with their nonmodal equivalents. (It is crucial to these explications that they relate to the operation of modalities in the context of real-world oriented quantifiers.)

	Modal Thesis	*Nonmodalized Equivalent*
(1)	$\Box(\forall x)\phi x$	$(Aw)(\Pi x)[x \in w \supset Rw(\phi x)]$
(2)	$(\forall x)\Box\phi x$	$(\Pi x)[x \in w^* \supset (Aw)(\Pi y)[y \in w \,\&\, S^w_{yx} \supset Rw(\phi y)]]$
(3)	$(\exists x)\Box\phi x$	$(\Sigma x)[x \in w^* \,\&\, (Aw)(\Pi y)[y \in w \,\&\, S^w_{yx} \supset Rw(\phi y)]]$
(4)	$\Box(\exists x)\phi x$	$(Aw)(\Sigma x)[x \in w \,\&\, Rw(\phi x)]$
(5)	$\Diamond(\forall x)\phi x$	$(Ew)(\Pi x)[x \in w \supset Rw(\phi x)]$
(6)	$(\forall x)\Diamond\phi x$	$(\Pi x)[x \in w^* \supset (Ew)(\Sigma y)[y \in w \,\&\, S^w_{yx} \,\&\, Rw(\phi y)]]$
(7)	$(\exists x)\Diamond\phi x$	$(\Sigma x)[x \in w^* \,\&\, (Ew)(\Sigma y)[y \in w \,\&\, S^w_{yx} \,\&\, Rw(\phi y)]]$
(8)	$\Diamond(\exists x)\phi x$	$(Ew)(\Sigma x)[x \in w \,\&\, Rw(\phi x)]$

If we make the near-trivial supposition of assuming that the actual world w^* is non-empty

(i) $(\Sigma x)[x \in w^*]$,

then we obtain the following implications

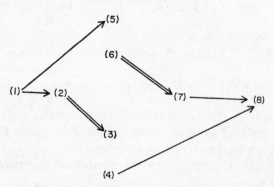

where $\Rightarrow$ indicates dependence upon (i). If we move on to the essentially trivial—because stipulatively true—assumption that *every* possible world is non-empty,

(ii) $(Aw)(\Sigma x)[x \in w]$,

which, of course, implies (i), then we will have

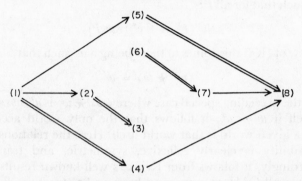

where $\Rightarrow$ now indicates dependence upon (i) or (ii). Finally, if we assume in addition to (ii) that every actual individual is represented by some surrogate in some other possible world

(iii) $(\Pi x)[x \in w^* \supset (Ew)(\Sigma y)[y \in w \,\&\, S^w_{yx}]]$

then we will have

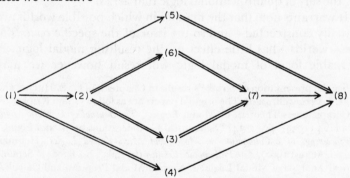

where $\Rightarrow$ indicates dependence upon (i) or (ii) or (iii). This assumption too is virtually trivial because of our supposition that every actual individual is a surrogate of itself

(iv) $(\Pi x)(x \in w^* \supset S^w_{yx})$

which yields (iii).

It is necessary also to consider at least briefly the logical structure of the over-all quantified modal logic to which our approach has led us. The decisive question here is that of the *accessibility* of possible worlds to one another. We adopt the position that the possible world w' is accessible from w iff there is a w'' such that for all P:

$$Rw'(P) \equiv Rw''\,(Rw(P))$$

In view of (R5) this comes to there being a w'' such that

$$\langle w'' \star w \rangle = w'$$

In the preceding special case where $\langle w'' \star w \rangle$ is *always* simply w itself if $w \neq w^*$, it follows that the only world accessible from a given world is that world itself. Here the relationship of accessibility is clearly reflexive, symmetric, and transitive. Accordingly, it follows from Kripke's well-known results[9] that the over-all QML at issue must have an **S5**-structure. But it is clear that very different sorts of modal structures must arise when (R5) assumes various different guises. Since modal iteration always crucially involves the iteration of Rw-operators, it follows that the exact form of (R5) will play a crucial role in determining the nature of accessibility and hence in determining the sort of quantificational logic that arises.

It warrants note that the manner in which possible worlds are actually constructed—and so the issue of the specific *contents* of these worlds—has little effect on the resulting modal logic. A workable form of modal logic will result however we may

[9] See the presentation of Kripke's results in Chapter 4 of G. E. Hughes and M. J. Cresswell, *op. cit.* The original papers are as follows: Saul Kripke, "A Completeness Theorem in Modal Logic," *The Journal of Symbolic Logic*, vol. 24 (1959), pp. 1–14; "Semantical Considerations on Modal Logic," *Proceedings of a Colloquium on Modal and Many-Valued Logics* (Helsinki, 23–6 August 1962), *Acta Philosophica Fennica* 16 (1963), pp. 83–94; "Semantical Analysis of Modal Logic: I. Normal Modal Propositional Calculi," *Zeitschrift für mathematische Logik und Grundlagen der Mathematik*, vol. 9 (1963), pp. 67–96; "Semantical Analysis of Modal Logic: II. Non-Normal Modal Propositional Calculi" in *The Theory of Models* (Proceedings of the 1963 International Symposium at Berkeley, ed. by J. W. Addison, L. Henkin, and A. Tarski [Amsterdam, 1965]), pp. 206–20; "The Undecidability of Monadic Modal Quantification Theory," *Zeitschrift für mathematische Logik und Grundlagen der Mathematik*, vol. 8 (1962), pp. 113–16.

carry out the world-construction procedure; although, as noted above, it does make a decided difference whether or not the actual—or any other—world is empty.

6. CONCLUSION

The present approach to the semantical foundations of modal logic has taken a constructivistic line, seeking to construct the realm of the possible on the basis of an initial inquiry regarding the nature of the real. We have tried to show that this constructivistic approach is in fact adequate to provide an appropriate semantical foundation for quantified modal logic. A development of possible-world machinery along such constructivist lines is advantageous precisely in order to avoid pulling the possible-world rabbit out of an unrationalized postulational hat.

This constructivist line of procedure does, however, require that we presuppose a system of (non-modal) logic as given to serve as the guiding mechanism of the construction. We must, therefore, avoid taking the view that *this* logic is determined on the basis of a survey of principles holding in all possible worlds in line with some *prior* development of possible worlds machinery. We cannot develop our basic logic from possible worlds if we choose to *construct* our possible worlds by the use of this logic.

Of course, one must insist upon a *systematic conformity* between the "system of possible worlds" and the logical system at issue: The logical principles we derive *retrospectively* from a consideration of the theses obtaining "in all possible worlds" must square with the principles of the base-logic that was our guide in devising the framework of *possible* individuals with *possible* worlds. The logic we would obtain derivatively from an analysis of the manifold of possible worlds must be commensurate with the logic we use to construct them. But this requirement will, on our approach, be satisfied *automatically* (or, if you prefer, trivially) by the nature of the construction process. Indeed, this process was designed precisely to guarantee this sort of systematic conformity. Accordingly, two principles must obtain:

(I) If a thesis is (logically) possible, then it will hold in some (logically) possible world.

(II) If a thesis holds in some (logically) possible world, then it is (logically) possible.

The first of these obtains because we have deliberately elaborated the manifold of possible worlds to ensure coverage of the entire spectrum of (logical) possibilities: this manifold is *designed* to sweep out the full range of feasible variations. The second principle obtains thanks to exactly that factor which determines a putatively possible world as actually possible—namely, a screening that assures that whatever holds in a world admitted as "possible" is actually possible in terms of the basic logic that is our guide. A rigid correspondence between a thesis' being logically possible on the one hand, and its holding in some possible world on the other is thus guaranteed.

Moreover, when everything is said and done, this way of proceeding does indeed validate the principle that logical truths are to be identified with those theses that obtain in all possible worlds. But this is now seen simply to reflect the fact that the development of the machinery of possible worlds is such as to guarantee the principle, because our determination of what sorts of putative worlds are indeed *possible* is decisively guided by the logical system with which we began. The crucial fact is that on our constructivist approach we extract the manifold of possible worlds from an actually given logic, rather than proceeding conversely to extract our logic from an allegedly given manifold of possible worlds.

Interestingly enough, the significant fact has emerged that the construction-process for possible worlds does *not* determine in any sensitive way the modal logic that can be articulated on this basis. Within (broadly speaking) minimal assumptions about world-construction, virtually *any* construction-process suffices to give the modal logician a semantical basis for all the various formal systems with which he wishes to deal. (This affords an excuse for the profession's disinterest in the epistemo-logico/metaphysical dimension of possible individuals and worlds.) At any rate, the logicians' demands upon possibilia are not great, and are readily met by the present constructional approach.

But while the logician does not make great demands upon the theory of the possible-worlds, the reverse circumstance is quite different. On our constructive approach, the possible world theorist does most emphatically require a logical mechanism for his productive efforts. And the important thing here is that, having begun with a logic, we have proceeded thence to the exfoliation of possibilia, and thence to the revalidation of logic as correlative with the sphere of what is true in all possible worlds. It is clearly crucial that this cyclic route should close smoothly upon itself. That is, the logic obtained with reference to possible worlds must conform to the initial logic from which the construction set out, and thus *revalidate* it. Just this in fact is the crucial test of adequacy which the possibility-constructive process *must* (and in the case of our own theory demonstrably *does*) pass.

Chapter VI

EXISTENCE STIPULATIONS

1. CLAIMS OF EXISTENCE AND NONEXISTENCE

Why endorse the idea of nonexistent possibles; why not just hold that everything, every *genuine* thing exists? Various quite serious considerations militate against accepting the thesis that all things exists: $(\Pi x)Ex$ (where 'E' is a special existential qualifier). Two fundamental factors necessitate this rejection, the one stemming from modal logic, the other deriving from the theory of counterfactual statements. These considerations— both drawn from different branches of logical theory that are seemingly removed from the problem area at issue—must be considered in detail.

It cannot reasonably be gainsaid that there are true statements to the effect that certain things are possible, though not in fact actual or extant. An example of a statement of this kind is the statement that, while unicorns do not exist, it is perfectly possible that they might. There are surely true statements which say that certain possible states of affairs might have obtained, or things might possibly have been, though these are not in fact realized or actual. Indeed, to maintain the actuality of all alternative possibilities is logically untenable in view of the fact that these will mutually exclude one another. For reasons such as these one wants to affirm the proposition:

$$(1) \quad (\Sigma x)(\Diamond Ex \,\&\, \neg Ex)$$

which in turn entails

$$(2) \quad (\Sigma x)\neg Ex.$$

But (2) clearly contradicts

$$(3) \quad (\Pi x)Ex.$$

We are thus brought to a choice between (1) and (3). Now there is—to my mind—simply no gainsaying the fact that an adequate logic of modality requires acceptance of (1); and there is thus little recourse but to reject (3).

A second objection to acceptance of the thesis that $(\Pi x)Ex$ is based upon the consideration that there are true but counterfactual existential statements. The following is surely an instance of this kind: "If Hamlet had actually existed, he could not have been a more complex personality than the protagonist of Shakespeare's play." Now the analysis of counterfactual statements is a complex and difficult matter into whose technical intricacies I have no desire to enter here.[1] But fortunately the sole feature of these statements that is required for our purpose is virtually the only point on which general agreement among all the diverse accounts obtains. If a *counterfactual* statement of the form "If X were to have been realized, then Y would also have been realized" is true, this requires that the claim X involved in the protasis or antecedent of the counterfactual statement must be false. But consider now any counterfactual statement with an existential protasis, such as that given above. Such a statement P has an antecedent of the form "Ex_1." By the very nature of counterfactuals, we therefore at once have:

(4) $\quad P \supset \neg Ex_1$.

Now this entails:

(5) $\quad Ex_1 \supset \neg P$.

Since one cannot very well avoid having

(6) $\quad (\Pi x)Ex \supset Ex_1$

it follows at once that:

(7) $\quad (\Pi x)Ex \supset \neg P$.

Thus the maintenance of $(\Pi x)Ex$ precludes *ab initio* the truth of any counterfactual existential statement whatsoever. Since this consequence cannot be regarded as acceptable, we have here yet another line of argument for rejecting $(\Pi x)Ex$. If we are

---

[1] The pioneer studies are: R. Chisholm, "The Contrary-to-Fact Conditional," *Mind*, vol. 55 (1946), pp. 289–307; and N. Goodman, "The Problem of Counterfactual Conditionals, "*The Journal of Philosophy*, vol. 44 (1947), pp. 113–28. A particular helpful survey of the extended literature is: E. F. Schneider, "Recent Discussions of Subjunctive Conditionals," *The Review of Metaphysics*, vol. 6 (1952), pp. 623–47. See also N. Rescher, *Hypothetical Reasoning* (Amsterdam, 1964).

seriously interested in having an adequate theory of hypothetical reasoning, we do well to take seriously the prospects of a theory of nonexistent possibilia.

2. IS EXISTENCE A PREDICATE?

It is fitting to give at least some brief consideration to the historic and much-disputed issue of whether *to exist* qualifies as a property of things. In the traditional terminology: Is existence a predicate?[2] There is, of course, no question that a *grammatical* predicate is at issue, and nobody wants to deny the merely verbal point that one can broach the issue by adopting the rule:

Ex iff $x \in w^*$ (i.e., iff x is a member of the actual world w^*).

But is this feature E to count as a *predicate* in the logico-conceptual sense of the term? That is, are we entitled to take E as lying within the range of our predicate variables ϕ, ψ, χ, etc.?

Presumably this is not a question to which a simple *yes* or *no* answer can be given. The matter just is not one of answering correctly or incorrectly here. It is, in the final analysis, a question of *policy*: Is our systematization to be such that E can legitimately be *treated* as a predicate or not? Is the analogy between E and the unproblematically qualified predicates sufficiently close and the disanalogies sufficiently minor that it makes sense to assimilate E to the orthodox predicates, or are there decisive grounds for excluding it?

From our standpoint, the issue is best viewed from the following perspective. We know that every individual x has an associated c.d.s.: $\mathscr{P}(x) = \{\phi : \phi x\}$. The problem now becomes: should one inevitably include E or its contradictory $\bar{E}$ in this set, and so qualify this feature of existence to represent a genuinely descriptive aspect of the individual?

Two alternative lines of approach are possible here:

(1) *Essence precedes Existence.* Take the historic view, whose most emphatic spokesman was Leibniz, that one can (completely) settle the issue of description first and independently, before mooting the issue of existence. Thus one can in principle (and indeed—if one is God—in prac-

---

[2] See the Bibliography regarding the literature of this subject.

tice) resolve the issue of description wholly without thereby settling that of existence, adopting the precept: *Description first, existence later.* (This indicates the "creators' eye-view" inherent in Leibniz's approach of viewing a particular in its full descriptive panoply, only subsequently and superveniently settling the issue of whether it *deserves* to exist.) On this approach, existence is disqualified as a descriptive feature, so that it makes good sense to exclude existence as a property and not to count "exists" as a predicate.

(2) *Existence Precedes Essence.* The existence or nonexistence of individuals is a pivotal and crucial aspect of them—and so why not a *descriptive* aspect? Existence represents a fundamentally descriptive fact, something that must be dealt with from the very first. One must assume an emphatically "man's eye view" of the matter: a purported "description" of something that omits to indicate whether or not this thing exists leaves out of account something crucial to an adequate characterization of the sort of thing at issue. The (descriptive) essence of an individual must be recognized as itself hinging on a prior determination of its existence.

Now if any one thing is clear at this stage, it is that our own approach to possibilities has systematically granted precedence and priority to the actual. Accordingly, the present theory is predicated upon a commitment to the *second* alternative.

It is, of course, no valid objection to this view that it leads to the conclusion that an individual may possess a property in one world (viz., its *existence* in this *actual* world) that it lacks in others. For this just illustrates in a special case what is, for us, a commonplace circumstance that arises generally with respect to other properties as well.

From the aspect of our general theory, there is, in the final analysis, no persuasive reason against classing E as a predicate, and indeed, quite to the contrary, there is considerable warrant in favor of this policy. Existence simply happens to represent that predicate which can be predicated truly *only* of members of the real world w^*, though it applies universally and trivially throughout *this* particular domain.

The introduction of this predicate produces certain advantages of convenience on the side of formalism. For example, it can be utilized to enable us to get by with merely one set of quantifiers as fundamental, viz., Π and Σ. For $\forall$ and $\exists$ can now be reduced definitionally, as follows:

$$(\forall x)\phi x = (\Pi x)(Ex \supset \phi x)$$
$$(\exists x)\phi x = (\Sigma x)(Ex \,\&\, \phi x).$$

That is, the "property" of existing serves to pick out exactly those individuals belonging to the intended domains of $\forall$ and $\exists$, viz., the actual world.

3. FORMULATING EXISTENCE-CLAIMS

The basic formulation of the thesis that x exists "Ex," simply affirms, by definition as it were, that x is a member of the actual world ($x \in w^*$), which gives us the basic stipulation

$$Ex \text{ iff } x \in w^*.$$

Existence *simpliciter* is existence in the real world, and "x exists" simply amounts to "x belongs to w^*". But how are we to treat "existence in w," whenever w is different from w^*? Note that $x \in w$ is *not* tantamount to $Rw(Ex)$. For by (R†) on p. 113 we have

$$Rw(Ex) \text{ iff } (\Sigma y)\,[y \in w \,\&\, y \cong x \,\&\, E \in \mathscr{P}(y)]$$

and the right-hand side of this equivalence is automatically *false* whenever $w \neq w^*$ (since y then belongs to a world different from w^*, whereas E can only belong to the $\mathscr{P}$-sets of w^*-members). There is, of course, nothing to prevent one from introducing a generalized existence-operator

$$E^w x \text{ iff } x \in w$$

where $E^w x$ is to mean "x exists in w" (rather than exists *per se*), with the result that E becomes tantamount to E^{w^*}, and so represents a special case of this more generalized idea. But the fact remains that a claim that $Rw(Ex)$ is very different from a claim that $E^w x$.

4. EXISTENCE AND NECESSITY

It is of interest to consider the question: Under what conditions can one assert of something that it exists necessarily? From the present perspective, note that

$$\Box Ex$$

amounts to

$$(\Pi y) \; [y \cong x \supset E \in \mathscr{P}(y)]$$

which in turn yields:

$$x \in w^* \; \& \; \neg (\Sigma y) \; [y \notin w^* \; \& \; y \cong x].$$

Accordingly, to say of something that it exists necessarily *in this sense* is to say of it that it is something actual and moreover that the actual world is the *only* one to which it can possibly belong—that "it has no alternative but to exist" to speak somewhat figuratively. Interestingly enough, the claim of necessary existence *now* says that the item at issue can in principle belong only to *this actual world*; it does *not* say that *whatever world* might be actual, this item must belong to it.

To sum up: There is, in the framework of our theory, no need to abstain from classing "exists" as a predicate. But it becomes clear that this predicate is a somewhat special one; in that its operation is not readily transposible from one world to another, since it is by design and by function inherently real-world bound. And it makes no sense, on this approach, to consider (non-relativized) existence as eligible to qualify among the *essential* properties of things. For these essential properties are exactly the ones they must be able to carry with them into the environment of *other* possible worlds, whereas (real) existence is inherently relativized to the actual world.

Chapter VII

DISPOSITIONS

1. DISPOSITIONAL PROPERTIES

The dispositional properties of things—such as fragility or electrical conductivity—are amphibious in character; they have one foot in the realm of the actual, another in that of the possible. They describe the real, but do so in ways that go beyond what really happens.

Dispositional theses (and laws) always make their claims about the actual world in language whose purport transcends it in envisaging a wider context of possibility—much as inherently comparative theses like "x is taller than average" makes a claim about one item through a form of language that implicitly refers to others, placing the item at issue against the background of a wider context of reality. Dispositions inevitably describe the real in terms of reference to the possible, and possibilistic commitments are always implicit in dispositional language. For this reason, the dispositions of a thing cannot ever manifest themselves totally to our inspection. No doubt, dispositional attributions are the product of empirical enquiry, but they must lie wholly on the side of theory rather than that of observation. A disposition represents a feature that a thing does in reality have, yet which relates not only to how it *does* comport itself in the actual circumstances, but also to how it *would* comport itself in other, strictly hypothetical ones. In talking of the (actual) dispositions of (real) things, we thus characterize the real in a way that is inherently possibility-referring. This possibility-referring aspect endows dispositions with particular interest from the aspect of a theory of possibility.

Precisely because their bearing is actuality-transcending, dispositions are never determinable in terms of observation alone (observation is, of course, an inherently reality-restricted process—one cannot observe the nonactual). Rather, dispositions are *imputed* to things on the basis of *theoretical* considerations. When dispositions are at issue, a reference to actualities alone is never sufficient, because dispositional claims *transcend* the boundaries of the actual.

The conception of a dispositional property is exemplified by the paradigm

(D)   Given x's having F, it must have G.

This is to be understood in a double-edged sense: Not only

(i) *Counterfactually* (when x lacks F): If x were to have F (which it doesn't), it would have to have G

but also

(ii) *Actuality-constrainingly* (when x has F): Since x does have F, it must (in consequence) have G.

The dispositional relation embraces both of these modes. We are thus to construe such property-relating dispositions of things in the following terms:

$(\phi/\psi)x$ that is, ϕ is a *dispositional* property of x relative to ψ (or alternatively: "x has the disposition from ψ to ϕ)": x would have ϕ if it had ψ (in the case that x lacks ψ), or else (in case x does have ψ) *must* have ϕ since it actually has ψ.

Other sorts of dispositions distinct from such *property-relating dispositions* can also be envisaged—for example, those which are *transactional* and relate the properties of *different* individuals (as with mutual attraction or repulsion), or those which are *developmental* and relate the properties of individuals at certain temporal stages with those of other stages (as with the disposition of an acorn to grow into an oak). But we shall focus here upon dispositions of the straightforwardly property-relating sort. This limitation is perhaps not as restrictive as it might first appear, since many other, seemingly different cases of transactional and developmental dispositions can be reduced to this one by introducing suitable complications in terms of *relational* properties in the former example and time-specifying properties in the other. (Thus we could treat the disposition from ϕx to ψy by first introducing the special conjunctive relation R such that Rvu iff ϕv & ψu. This would enable us to treat the disposition from ϕx to ψy as $((\lambda v)Rvy/\phi)x$, which authorizes the inference of

ψy given ϕx. Again, the disposition from ϕ-at-t to ψ-at-t' could be accommodated along analogous lines.)

Note that if the property-relating disposition $(\phi/\psi)x$ is to obtain, then ϕ is a property that x *must* also have *when or if* it has ψ. This would certainly include any logical consequence of ψ itself. Yet presumably it is not only such logically trivial "dispositions" that are to be at issue, but *natural* (physical or empirical) dispositions as well—in terms of those consequences which do not follow from the principles of logic alone, demanding adjunction of certain appropriate constraints of the merely factual sort.

Again, if $(\phi/\psi)x$ is to obtain—i.e., if x is to have the disposition from ψ to ϕ—then ψ must at any rate be a *possible* property of x; i.e., we must have $\psi ? x$. Thus the "logically trivial" disposition ϕ/ϕ will not be strictly speaking universal; it will not characterize everything but only those individuals that may possibly have ϕ—whose lack thereof, if lack there is, is inessential. Such a disposition, which may not belong to everything, but will at any rate belong to everything for which its operative conditional is feasible, will be characterized as *quasi-universal*.

When ψ is not actually a property of x, then adding the hypothesis that ψx to what we in fact know regarding x may lead to inconsistencies for whose resolution special—and to some extent, extralogical—devices are required. The dispositional properties can be looked upon as providing such a resource. Thus if we know that both $\neg \phi x$ and $(\phi/\psi)x$, then in the face of an *ex hypothesi* introduction of the assumption that ψx we must yield up $\neg \phi x$. From a strictly logical point of view, we have a *choice* between abandoning $\neg \phi x$ and $(\phi/\psi)x$, but in the standard range of assumptive contexts, dispositions must clearly take precedence over absolute (nondispositional) properties,[1] and this convention represents the "extralogical device" at issue.

2. SOME FORMAL CHARACTERISTICS OF DISPOSITIONAL PROPERTIES

We must stipulate that the conceptions at issue operate in such a way that various formal principles obtain:

[1] Compare N. Rescher, *The Coherence Theory of Truth* (Oxford, 1973), Chap. XI.

(1) Whenever $(\phi/\psi)x$, then both $\phi?x$ and $\psi?x$.

$$(\psi/\phi)x \vdash [\phi?x \ \& \ \psi?x]$$

(2) Whenever $(\phi/\psi)x$ and ψx then ϕx:

$$[(\phi/\psi)x \ \& \ \psi x] \vdash \phi x$$

(3) If ψ is essential to x, then $(\psi/\phi)x$ holds for all properties ϕ that x can possibly have:

$$[\psi!x \ \& \ \phi?x] \vdash (\psi/\phi)x$$

(4) The dispositional relationship (ϕ/ψ) is reflexive and transitive, i.e., whenever $\phi?x$ then $(\phi/\phi)x$ obtains trivially, and whenever both $(\phi/\psi)x$ and $(\psi/\chi)x$, then $(\phi/\chi)x$:

$$\phi?x \vdash (\phi/\phi)x$$
$$[(\phi/\psi)x \ \& \ (\psi/\chi)x] \vdash (\phi/\chi)x$$

(5) Need (ϕ/ψ) also be symmetric? Clearly not. Let x be such that it must be ϕ whether or not it is a ψ. This is clearly a conceivable circumstance. But if we stipulate the symmetry thesis, then $(\phi/\psi)x \ \& \ (\phi/\bar{\psi})x$ yields $(\psi/\phi)x \ \& \ (\bar{\psi}/\phi)x$ which leads *ad absurdum*.

(6) Dispositional properties can be differential (non-universal) properties of individuals. Thus (ϕ/ψ) could characterize x but not y. In general, we would expect that for the general run of dispositional properties (ϕ/ψ):

$$(\exists x)(\phi/\psi)x \ \& \ (\exists x)\neg(\phi/\psi)x$$

Are we to have

$$(\psi/\phi)x \equiv [\phi?x \ \& \ (\psi x \lor \neg\phi x)]?$$

The answer is negative. An implication relation certainly holds from left to right. But it can fail from right to left: For the right-hand side will be true whenever both ϕx and ψx. But this fact—that x has both ψ and ϕ—fails to assure the proper sort of relationship intended in the dispositional statement, viz., that x has ψ *because* it possesses ϕ.

So much, then, for a review of the formal (and, as it were, "logical") principles that govern the attribution of dispositions. These are necessary, though not, of course, sufficient to characterize the conception at issue.

3. CAN DISPOSITIONS BE ACCIDENTAL?

Can a thing have essential dispositions? Clearly yes—for whenever $\phi?x$, then ϕ/ϕ, for example, will surely (and trivially!) be an essential dispositional property of x:

$$(\forall x)[\phi?x \supset (\phi/\phi)!x].$$

But let us put such trivial (because *logically* constrained) dispositions aside. Can things have nontrivial dispositions essentially? That they can do so seems clear on "general principles." For why should one's disposition (e.g.) to bleed when cut, be any less essential than such categorical properties as one's shape or pigmentation of skin? Moreover, and more decisively, we just are no longer free at this stage to gainsay prospects of essentiality: the considerations of Chapter II preempt a free decision. What's sauce for the goose of categorical properties is sauce for the gander of dispositional ones, and the sorts of considerations that initially led us there to class certain of the properties of individuals as essential must now clearly be applied to dispositional properties as well. So far as the issue of essentiality is concerned, dispositions are simply to be brought within the generic purview of properties in general, and the considerations applied earlier on must be deployed upon them as well.

But does it make sense to view a dispositional property of a thing as characterizing it accidentally? Consider the individual of some (hypothetically real) microworld answering to the following C.D.S.

	F	G	H	G/F
x_1	$+$	$+$	$[-]$	$+$

Viewing G/F as an accidental property of x_1 we obtain the following inventory of actual-variant (partial) descriptions, over and above that of $x_1 = x_1^0$.

	F	G	H	G/F	Comments
x_1^1	$+$	$-$	$[-]$	$+$	case impossible
x_1^2	$-$	$+$	$[-]$	$+$	
x_1^3	$-$	$-$	$[-]$	$+$	
x_1^4	$+$	$+$	$[-]$	$-$	
x_1^5	$+$	$-$	$[-]$	$-$	
x_1^6	$-$	$+$	$[-]$	$-$	
x_1^7	$-$	$-$	$[-]$		

Let our attention now focus on the qualifications of the descriptive form x_1^5 to serve as an x_1-variant description. The question is: What is the point of saying of the original x_1 that it has the feature that it possesses the disposition G/F, if we are prepared to recognize as its variant an individual that has F and lacks G? Considerations of this sort might motivate us towards taking all of the (property-relating) dispositions that a thing has as essential to it. But contrary considerations also press upon us. Why should a disposition be more sacred than any other property—the fragility or malleability of the glass figurine more essential than its shape or its weight? Why should some of an individual person's dispositions—to speak French, say, or eat hurriedly—be any less accidental to him than various other properties? We must clearly find a halfway house between holding (1) that an individual's disposition need hold in the actual world alone (dispositions have a possibilistic—and so actuality-transcending aspect that prevents their being *that* sort of thing), and holding (2) that dispositions are *always* essential and must necessarily hold of the thing in *every* alternative dispensation.

Moving in this direction, let us adopt the idea of a family of individuals that exhibits a dispositionally-based similarity to a given real individual $x \in w^*$:

$$D_x = \{y: (Ew)S_{yx}^w \ \& \ (Aw)(A\phi)(A\psi)(\Pi z)[(\psi/\phi)x \ \& \ S_{zx}^w \supset Rw(\phi z \supset \psi z)]\}$$

The set D_x includes exactly those x-surrogates that exhibit $\phi \supset \psi$ (in their respective worlds) in each case when x has the property-relating disposition ψ/ϕ. We shall thus say that the elements of D_x are D-*similar* (dispositionally similar) to x in that every $y \in D_x$ shares with x at least the "virtual disposition" $\phi \supset \psi$ whenever x has the disposition ψ/ϕ. The given definition of D_x has the consequence that for any $x \in w^*$:

$$(\psi/\phi)x \text{ iff } (\Pi y)[y \in D_x \supset (\phi \supset \psi) \in \mathscr{P}(y)].$$

Whenever a (real) individual has a disposition, the virtual counterpart of this disposition characterizes all possible individuals that are D-similar to it.

Following out this line of ideas somewhat further we may introduce the idea of a property's being D-essential to an individual ($\phi\P x$ for "ϕ is D-essential to x"), subject to the definition:

$$\phi\P x \text{ iff } (\Pi y)[y \in D_x \supset \phi \in \mathscr{P}(y)].$$

That is, ϕ is D-essential to x if it characterizes every possible individual that is D-similar to x. This leads to the consequence that the disposition ψ/ϕ characterizes a real individual iff the property that is its virtual counterpart, $\phi \supset \psi$, is D-essential to this individual:

$$(\psi/\phi)x \text{ iff } \phi?x \And (\phi \supset \psi)\P x.$$

The given definition entails that $\phi\P x$ amounts to:

Every "suitably similar" x-surrogate has ϕ.

It is thus clear that $\phi!x$ entails $\phi\P x$ so that D-essentiality is a mode of essentiality *per se*. Moreover, it is clear that whenever $x \in w^*$ and $\phi?x$, the essentiality of $\phi \supset \psi$ for x would entail its possession of the disposition ψ/ϕ.

It is also useful to introduce the idea of the dispositional similarity of worlds. A world whose surrogate for $x \in w^*$ is D-similar to its real-world prototype will be said to be $\varDelta$-similar to the actual world as regards this individual x. Letting $\varDelta_x$ be the set of all worlds $\varDelta$-similar to the actual one as regards x, we have:

$$\varDelta_x = \{w: (\varSigma y) [S_{yx}^{w} \And y \in D_x]\}.$$

This leads to the consequence

$$(\psi/\phi)x \text{ iff } (\text{A}w)(\Pi y)[w \in \varDelta_x \And S_{yx}^{w} \supset \text{R}w(\phi y \supset \psi y)].$$

A disposition ψ/ϕ characterizes an actual individual iff its virtual counterpart $\phi \supset \psi$ characterizes all surrogates for this individual in all $\varDelta$-possible worlds. Thus the D-essentiality of a property and its obtaining throughout the manifold of $\varDelta$-possible worlds are correlative. We are accordingly able to cash in the idea that dispositional relationships represent a limited essentiality correlative with obtaining throughout a duly limited manifold of possible worlds. But this fact that we are able to move from possible worlds to real-world dispositions must not be allowed to obscure the fundamentality of the reverse direction of movement. *Au fond* one is not in an advantageous-seeming position to infer real-world dispositions from information about possible worlds—and, at that, information which involves no dispositional claims—because our constructive approach in the first instance *extracted* the relevant range of possible worlds on the basis of real-world dispositions.

One can further introduce the idea of certain properties of individuals as "essential" to them not absolutely but in a dispositionally qualified sense: A property ϕ is D-relatively essential to an individual x (symbolically "$\phi!!x$") iff ϕ is dispositionally linked to some essential property of x (even though that disposition itself is not essential):

$$\phi!!x \text{ iff } (E\psi)[\psi!x \ \& \ (\phi/\psi)x]$$

Unlike its essential properties as such, the D-relatively essential properties of an individual can change from one possible world to another, according as its dispositions may be altered. D-relative essentiality is a sort of quasi-essentiality that obtains over a merely restricted range—that of the D-possible worlds.[2] It is readily shown that this presently envisaged D-relative essentiality is tantamount to D-essentiality as introduced above:

$$\phi!!x \text{ iff } \phi\P x$$

The equivalence may be demonstrated as follows: Suppose $\phi!!x$. Then there is a ψ such that (1) all x-surrogates in all Δ_x-possible worlds have $\psi \supset \phi$, and (2) all x-surrogates in all possible worlds have ψ. Hence all x-surrogates in all Δ_x-possible worlds have ϕ, i.e., $\phi\P x$. Conversely, suppose $\phi\P x$. Then clearly (1) all x-surrogates in all possible worlds have $\phi \vee \bar{\phi}$ (i.e., $(\phi \vee \bar{\phi})!x$, and (2) all x-surrogates in all Δ_x-possible worlds have ϕ, so that $([\phi \vee \bar{\phi}] \supset \phi$)holds of all x-surrogates in all Δ_x-possible worlds (i.e., $(\phi/\phi \vee \bar{\phi})x$). Hence $\phi!!x$. Q.E.D.

It warrants note that not every D-possible world is equally proximate to this actual world—the realization of some dispositional potentialities is much less far-fetched than others (e.g., my speaking German, which I know well, in contrast with my speaking Chinese, which I don't know at all, though

[2] For a discussion of philosophical ramifications of this qualified mode of essentiality see A. O. Rorty, "Essential Possibilities in the Actual World," *Review of Metaphysics*, vol. 25 (1972), pp. 607–24, as well as D. Parfit, "Personal Identity," *The Philosophical Review*, vol. 80 (1971), pp. 3–27.

I *could* learn it).[3] In a rather straightforward sense, those merely possible worlds that differ from the actual only in the realization of relatively realistic possibilities are "closer" to the actual world than those that require more far-fetched sorts of possibilities to be realized.[4] (The relevance of this sort of proximity to our present purposes will become clear in the Appendix to Chapter IX.)

4. CAN DISPOSITIONAL PROPERTIES SERVE TO INDIVIDUATE?

We must come to grips with the question of whether dispositions alone could ever individuate distinct but otherwise descriptively indistinguishable individuals. The answer to this question may seem to be a trivial *yes*. For clearly, if two individuals are alike in all quality-descriptive respects (relational differences being admitted, descriptively spatial ones included), except (say) for the one dispositional difference that one of them glows in the moonlight, then we can, of course, simply identify the one descriptively by adding to its almost identifying residual description that "It's the one which glows in the moonlight." But this is clearly cheating. For if we assume that the course of history is such that this disposition ever comes into operative effect, then there will simply be a *manifest* qualitative difference between the individuals, and so we do not at all need to make reference to the disposition in individuating. But on the other hand, if we suppose the disposition never comes into actual effect, then what grounds can there possibly be for attributing the disposition in the one case but not the other? As concerns individuation, dispositional properties seem snagged in a dilemma between superfluity and impotence.

How could it happen that two (actual) individuals differ in point of description *only* in their dispositional properties? For example, would it be possible to include in some (by hypothesis actual) microworld two individuals answering to the following C.D.S.:

---

[3] Cf. A. O. Rorty, "Essential Possibilities in the Actual World," *op. cit.*, see pp. 616–17.

[4] The sort of "comparative possibility" is developed interestingly in the framework of his similarity-theory in David Lewis, *Counterfactuals* (Oxford, 1973), pp. 52–6.

	F	G	H	H/F
x_1	$-$	$[+]$	$+$	$+$
x_2	$-$	$[+]$	$+$	$-$

No simple and superficial means to resolve this issue seem to be available on sole grounds of general principle. But let us examine the situation from a somewhat variant, epistemological perspective. In scrutinizing the *actual* world, one can surely have only manifest properties to go on. As far as any *observational* procedures are concerned, we could not differentiate things that are alike in all respects save dispositional ones. But, of course, the scientific study of the real is a matter of theory as well as of observation. To be sure, the entire nomic aspect of things— dispositions and laws preeminently included—has to do with what is imputed rather than observed. And this theoretical factor might perhaps be held to play a differentiating role in distinguishing between otherwise undifferentiated actuals. But there must—of course—always be a "sufficient reason" for differentiating theoretically between manifestly or observationally indiscernible things, and this reason must in the final analysis itself lie somehow in the sphere of the observable, given our adherence to a strictly naturalistic approach.

There is thus good reason why, with respect to the actual and observationally manifest world, we must not apply the Principle of the Identity of Indiscernibles in such a way that purely dispositional properties are ever allowed to provide the sole and solitary differentiating factors in individuation. Though this is not theoretically or in principle infeasible, it represents a procedure that is evidentially impracticable in relation to the actual world. Even if nothing else impeded, our naturalism would of itself suffice to block the prospect that two *actual* things might differ only in their dispositional properties.

Now someone might object as follows:

This "naturalistic" denial of a differentiating role of dispositions in regard to actual objects is based in the final analysis on an *epistemic* foundation (a Principle of Insufficient Reason). The prospect in view thus cannot count as excluded at the *ontological* level.

There is not, in fact, any reason to deny the tenability of this objection. But even if correct, it remains without force or effect.

For we have said from the outset that the starting-point of our possibilistic construction will be an empirically based world-perspective, the "picture" of the real world as painted in the course of a scientific exploration of the nature of the real. Accordingly, a circumstance that can be excluded at this level on epistemic grounds cannot come into play in any application of the theory at the level of ontological deliberations. So much, then, for the situation of the *actual* world.

With merely possible worlds the case is quite different. In *unactualized* worlds—worlds whose very nature lies at our postulational beck and call—whose make-up is at our control and does not hinge on naturalistic considerations regarding the empirically given—there is no good reason why the case of differentiation by dispositions alone should not arise. For with respect to unactualized individuals, we are not at the mercy of the manifest actualities of the case: we ourselves are masters of the situation and are free to construct such individuals as we please and to combine them (within the limits of compossibility) to form entire possible worlds. There is thus no reason of principle why we should not here countenance as distinct certain individuals whose manifest properties are identical and whose sole points of difference lie in the dispositional range. Once we recognize that they may represent a point of difference in characterization, there is no reason why they should not form the basis of a difference in individuality.

Here, then, the *epistemic* difference between the actual and other merely possible worlds is decisive. For the actual world is *given* and can only be explored by certain actuality-oriented cognitive procedures that are in principle impotent to discern what are (by hypothesis) *merely* dispositional differences. But with merely possible worlds the situation is altogether different. Here the present conceptualistic approach has it that *we* are the masters, and that our intellectual construction of them is decisive. And there is thus no impediment here to any differentiation on the basis of "merely dispositional" features; one is free to *suppose* the difference, and, given its supposed presence, there is no obstacle to allowing it to *make* a difference thereafter.

5. IDIOSYNCRATIC VS. GENERIC DISPOSITIONS: LAWS

The preceding discussion has throughout viewed property-relating dispositions from the standpoint of the over-all descriptive constitution of *particular individuals*. But such a relationship of properties might well in some cases be a *universal* one that is applicable *everywhere*, rather than one restricted to the particular (and conceivably idiosyncratic) make-up of specific individuals. In such universalized cases, the inferential step from a thing's possession of ϕ to its possession of ψ operates independently of any differentiating reference to some particular individual; it is automatically warranted with an appropriate sort of universality and necessity. The property-relationship would then represent an *inevitable* coordination of properties that is truly universal and abstracts altogether from the nature of individuals. In such a case, we would have it that the disposition ψ/ϕ obtains for all x in the possible world at issue —a universality that transmutes into an appropriate sort of necessity, viz., *nomic* necessity. The relationship of ϕ to ψ is nomically necessary in a world when we have it that in this world: $(\forall x)(\phi/\psi)x$.

These lawful relations of universally essential dispositions are the most fundamental sorts of dispositional relationships. Here we no longer have to do with item-pertaining or idiosyncratic dispositions of possibly contingent bearing, but enter into the sphere of generic and inevitable dispositions, that is to say of "general *laws* of nature" with respect to the possible world at issue. With this step one moves from the sphere of the individual and the accidental to that of (nomically) necessary and universal. We shall devote to this important theme the separate chapter it deserves.

But first one final reminder is in order. As was observed at the outset, dispositions represent in a particularly sharp way the relationship maintained in our conceptual scheme between the actual and the possible. They exhibit the tendency implicit in many of our concepts to characterize the actual in possibility-referring terms. This feature of dispositions obtains also and all the more emphatically with respect to laws.[5]

---

[5] Parts of this chapter draws upon my paper "Counterfactual Hypotheses, Laws, and Dispositions," *Nous*, vol. 5 (1971), pp. 157–78.

Chapter VIII

LAWS AND LAWFULNESS

1. LAWFULNESS

A consideration of the "laws of nature" is indispensable to any theory of possibility, because laws and dispositions establish a dividing line between the *genuinely* possible (that which is *really* possible) and the *merely* possible (the sphere of purely speculative possibility), serving to separate proximate from remote possibility, as it were. This acorn might possible develop into an oak tree (it might not, too, for it might be eaten by a squirrel). Here we have a real possibility. One might also contemplate the "possibility" that the acorn develop into a pear tree; but this is clearly no *real* possibility—it is a *purely hypothetical* possibility, and a very far-fetched one at that. In the former case, things run in their lawful channel, while the latter case plainly requires us to abrogate or modify the laws of nature. This important amplification of the distinction between *real*, physical or natural possibility, and *strictly hypothetical* (or "merely logical") possibility—the former of which calls for preserving not only logical and conceptual principles, but the laws of nature as well—is one of the fundamental ideas of our subject.[1]

[1] The idea of a special mode of *real* possibility, different from mere freedom from contradiction, goes back at least to Kant's insistence (against the rationalists) that possibility is not a matter of conformity to logic alone but also of conformity to the formal conditions of experience, both on the side of sensibility and understanding (cf. C.P.R., B 284). A conception of real (objective) possibility is defined with explicit relativization to the laws of nature in J. von Kries "Ueber den Begriff der objectiven Möglichkeit und einige Anwendungen desselben," *Vierteljahrschrift für wissenschaftliche Philosophie*, vol. 12 (1888), pp. 179–240, 287–323, and 393–428. Such real possibilities are given emphasis in A. Meinong's massive treatise on *Ueber Möglichheit und Wahrscheinlichkeit: Beiträge zur Gegenstandstheorie und Erkenntnistheorie* (Leipzig, 1915). The historical background of Meinong's views regarding possibility is examined in David Baumgardt, *Das Moglichkeitsproblem der Kritik der reinen Vernunft, der modernen Phänomenologie und der Gegenstandstheorie* (Berlin, 1920; Kant-Studien Ergänzungshefte Nr. 51). An illuminating recent discussion of Meinong's position is Hans Poser, "Der Möglichkeitsbegriff Meinongs" in R. von Haller (ed.), *Jenseits von Sein und Nichstein: Beiträge zur Meinong-Forschung* (Graz, 1972), pp. 187–204.

The particular importance of laws and dispositions lies in their providing the boundary-marks by reference to which this crucial division of the realm of possibility is effected.

The thesis "All ϕ's are ψ's" offers what is clearly a simply *de facto* contention about the actual arrangements of the (real) world:

$$\text{All } \phi\text{'s are (in fact) } \psi\text{'s} = (\forall x)(\phi x \supset \psi x) = [\phi]_A \subseteq [\psi]_A.$$

There is nothing in this claim as such to prevent its truth from obtaining only as a matter of contingent happenstance: the thesis could very well represent a (merely) "accidental generalization" which, while holding in the actual world, is not "necessary" in any more far-reaching sense of the term. As such, this claim must be contradistinguished from that of the thesis "All ϕ's *must* be ψ's," which claims that there is something in the nature of the ϕ's that means that they have of necessity to be ψ's. But just how is one to construe such a claim of relative necessitation to the effect that

$$\text{All } \phi\text{'s are } \textit{lawfully } \psi\text{'s} = \text{All } \phi\text{'s "must" be } \psi\text{'s} = \phi \Rightarrow \psi$$

for example, that elms must be deciduous or all acids corrosive.

The element of *must* introduces the crucial *nomic* element which goes beyond considerations of what is in fact the case to make claims regarding the realm of possibility. This claim transcends the contention that all the *actual* ϕ's are ψ's to stipulate the correlation of ψ with ϕ in certain possibilistic cases as well. The thesis "All ϕ's are (lawfully) ψ's" requires something far stronger than the merely *factual* relationship $(\forall x)(\phi x \supset \psi x)$ to obtain, something that excedes reference merely to the actual alone. For taken as a law, "All ϕ is ψ" says that not only are all the actual ϕ's in fact ψ's, but that—as indicated above—a sort of hypothetical necessity is so operative that whatever one may assume to be a ϕ *must also* be assumed to be a ψ. That is, one has to rule out as a "genuinely possible" individual anything whose description combines ϕ with $\bar{\psi}$. But to say that an individual so described is not "possible" is not to say that it is (logically) impossible in an absolute or categorical sense, but merely that it is (logically) impossible *relative to laws*, in short, that it is *nomically* impossible.

In accepting laws, we thus revise our concept of a *possible individual*, now reconstruing the "possible" in a nomic (law-relativized) sense which at least on first view moves beyond the essentialistic considerations introduced to this point. Laws are correlative with special and to this point unconsidered ranges of possibility. *To accept a law is to exclude possibilities*—it is to introduce a characteristic restriction on the sphere of "possible individuals." For to recognize "All ϕ's are ψ's" as a law is to expel from the arena of what is "genuinely possible" those putatively possible individuals that have ϕ but lack ψ, so that ψ/ϕ is now in effect cast in the role of a generalized (nomically) essential property-relating disposition.

Moreover, to accept a thesis as a law calls for our also applying it to what is only "possible"; but it is now crucial to distinguish between *genuine or real* possibilities as contrasted with "purely speculative" or "merely logical" possibilities. If we are going to have it that "All ϕ is ψ" is a law, then, *relative to this stipulation*, anything (be it real or not) that is a ϕ must be a ψ. And accordingly, while other sorts of worlds with other sorts of relationships are certainly *possible* in some more far-reaching sense of the term, the only sorts of "genuine" possibilities— possibilities that are *nomically* viable in the sense of being law-conforming—are those that do indeed associate ψ with ϕ whenever ϕ obtains. We shall characterize this nomic or law-relativized mode of possibility as N-possibility. Accordingly, an individual is to be nomically possible if its *fic* involves no conflicts with the law-structure of the actual world.

We arrive at yet another three-fold classification of individuals:

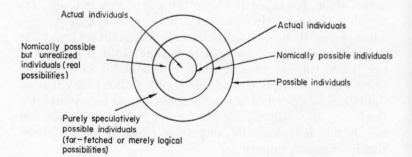

Such a nomically relativized revision of the concept of a possible individual, of course, has immediate implications for the nature of possible worlds. A possible world will be characterized as "nomically possible" if all its members are nomically possible individuals. (The set of all such N-possible worlds will be represented by Ξ.) We thus have:

$$\Xi = \{w: (\Pi x)(x \in w \supset x \in \mathcal{N})\}.$$

However much a world may differ from the actual one in point of its membership, it at any rate preserves the law-structure of the real world. Once a range of possible individuals is fixed by restriction to those that are law-conforming, it follows that the law-correlative possible worlds can contain only law-conforming individuals.

A *law* being a relationship that holds not only for actual, but for all "nomically possible" individuals as well, we obtain the validation of the traditional dictum: *A law is a generalization that obtains in every (nomically) possible world.*—i.e., every possible world populated solely by nomically possible individuals.

The point at issue can be put more precisely as follows. On the proposed construction of lawfulness, "All ϕ is *lawfully* ψ" ($\phi \Rightarrow \psi$) holds iff:

For *all* N-possible individuals (actuals of course included), we have it that if the individual has ϕ, then it will also have ψ:

(1) $(\Pi x)[x \in \mathcal{N} \supset (\phi x \supset \psi x)] \equiv (\Pi x)[x \in \mathcal{N} \supset (\psi/\phi)x].$

(Here $\mathcal{N}$ is the set of all *nomically* possible individuals. Note that $\phi x \supset \psi x$ is not *in general* equivalent with $(\psi/\phi)x$; the equivalence (1) obtains solely because of the special role of $\mathcal{N}$.)

This thesis should be construed as to obtain irrespectively of whatever world may be at issue in providing a world-environment for the individuals:

$$(Aw)(\Pi x)[(x \in \mathcal{N} \ \& \ x \in w) \supset Rw[(\psi/\phi)x]].$$

Accordingly, the nomic or lawful construction of "All ϕ's are ψ's" does not simply say that the *actual* ϕ's are ψ's, but that even if—(practically) *per impossibile*—we changed our minds about the boundaries of reality, and left the sphere of the actual behind, then the ψ-hood of the ϕ's would still have to continue as an abiding fact (as long as we remain within the domain of nomic possibilities).

Now it warrants remark that "All ϕ is ψ" holds *de facto* within the nomically possible world w iff $Rw[(\forall x)(\phi x \supset \psi x)]$, and so iff $(\Pi x)[x \in w \supset Rw(\phi x \supset \psi x)]$. Accordingly, (1) is in effect equivalent with

(2) For *every* nomically possible (N-possible) world w:

$$(\Pi x)[x \in w \supset Rw(\phi x \supset \psi x)]$$

or equivalently

$$(Aw)(\Pi x)[w \in \varXi \ \& \ x \in w) \supset Rw(\phi x \supset \psi x)].$$

This equivalence obtains specifically because every N-possible individual—every element of $\mathcal{N}$, the nomically admissible sector of the over-all domain for the Π-quantifier—belongs to some N-possible world or other (given the principles according to which such worlds are constructed). The "genuinely possible" worlds are exactly those that exhibit the same pattern of laws as the actual: they are nomically conformal to the actual world. (The next section will expose in greater detail just what this involves.) Thus an alternative approach, fully equivalent with our previous explication of lawfulness, is to construe a law as a generalization that obtains in all *suitably* possible worlds. But here possible, of course, means *genuinely* possible, i.e. *nomically* possible, and not just *logically* (or *metaphysically*) possible.

It is again necessary to bear in mind the *direction* in which the reasoning proceeds. If it were the case—which it is not!—that possible worlds (and specifically nomically possible worlds) were somehow given us *ex nihilo*, then we could proceed on this basis to discover what laws obtain by their means. We could—in theory—proceed along such a route from possible worlds to laws. But realism dictates the indicated mode of procedure, which is the very reverse of this. Beginning with the scientific exploration of the real, one determines the laws that govern it; from this one proceeds to specify what sorts of things are nomically possible; and one goes on thence to determine what the N-possible worlds are like. As is standard throughout our theory of possibility, we begin with a scrutiny of the actual and —having arrived at laws for this point of departure—then proceed to move from this law-oriented starting-point towards the imputational elaboration of nomically possible worlds. As usual on our approach, the construction of possibilities sets out from an actualistic point of departure.

It is important to note that a universal thesis which obtains only vacuously with respect to the actual world is *not* thereby rendered lawful. A thesis like

$$(\forall x)(Fx \supset Gx)$$

may well be realized (in the actual world) on grounds that there just are no actual F's, yet this does not establish a *lawful* relation between F's and G's. The fact that there are no actual F's may suffice to assure the preceding thesis or its equivalent

$$(\Pi x)[x \in w^* \supset Rw^*(Fx \supset Gx)]$$

but this plainly does *not* suffice to assure that for every N-possible world w we must have

$$(\Pi x)[x \in w \supset Rw(Fx \supset Gx)].$$

But what of the case of *total* vacuity rather than mere vacuity in the actual world? That is, what if there simply is no possible individual x whatever such that Fx obtains, so that one has:

$$\neg(\Sigma x)\ (Ew)\ Rw(Fx).$$

Clearly this would happen only if anything's having F is impossible; only if F is an intrinsically unrealizable property. Since this case is utterly without practical import, we may as well resolve it in whatever way is simplest and least cumbersome from the angle of theoretical considerations. And this is simply to apply our general formula that no dispositions issue from impossible conditions.[2]

2. LAWS AND DISPOSITIONS

We have adopted an analysis of laws in terms of possible worlds *via* the formula that a law is a generalization that obtains in every *nomically possible* world. But just when is a possible world to count as specifically *nomically*-possible (N-possible)? Infor-

[2] On this issue of conditionals with impossible antecedents see David Lewis, *Counterfactuals* (Oxford, 1973), pp. 24–6.

mally we might offer the (blatently circular) reply: A world is N-possible if all the "laws of nature" hold in it. The problematial aspect must now be removed by suitably cashing in the circularity-generating reference to "laws of nature." This is to be done in dispositional terms.

A *law of nature* represents a *quasi-universal property-relating disposition of the real*, that is, a disposition that characterizes anything in the (actual) world which can possible satisfy its operative condition. To say that the disposition ψ/ϕ is a "quasi-universal disposition of the real" is to say that this disposition holds for *every* $x \in w^*$ for which $\phi?x$. (This amounts to the thesis that ϕ & $\bar{\psi}$ cannot [N-possibly] be a property of any real individual.)

The qualification expressed by the "quasi" in the preceding formula is important. For suppose the following circumstance: (1) that every (actual) individual x for which $\phi?x$ is such that ψ/ϕ, and (2) that for some individual ϕ is simply *not* a possible property. Then one would still want to consider "All ϕ is ψ" as obtaining lawfully. We thus propose to construe a law that not as an *unqualifiedly* universal disposition, but one that is universally present among all those individuals for which this disposition can come into question at all, in that they could possibly satisfy the operative condition at issue.

We thus arrive at the following position. The thesis "All ϕ's are lawfully ψ's"—or symbolically: $\phi \Rightarrow \psi$—is to hold (in the actual world) iff

$$(\forall x)[\phi?x \supset (\psi/\phi)x].$$

We can now define the set $\mathscr{N}$ of N-possible individuals as follows:

$$\mathscr{N} = \{x: (A\phi)(A\psi)[(\phi \Rightarrow \psi) \supset \psi/\phi \in \mathscr{P}(x)]\}.$$

That is, an individual is N-possible if it exemplifies *all* (real-world) laws in its own dispositions. In consequence given the definition of the set $\varXi$ of N-possible worlds, it follows that if $\phi \Rightarrow \psi$, then

$$(Aw)[w \in \varXi \supset (\varPi x)(x \in w \supset Rw\,[(\psi/\phi)x])].$$

Every N-possible world preserves for all its individuals the dispositions corresponding to real-world laws.

It is useful to introduce the idea of N-essentiality, a property being N-*essential* to an individual if it characterizes all its versions throughout the range of N-possible worlds (a qualification that has N-essentiality stop well short of essentiality per se). We shall indicate *this* mode of essentiality by a dagger (†) in place of the exclamation-mark (!), and so obtain the equivalence:

$$\phi\dagger x \text{ iff } (Aw)[(w \in \varXi \supset (\varPi y)[(y \in w \ \& \ y \cong x) \supset Rw(\phi y)]].$$

Thanks to the make up of $\varXi$, this means that in the special case of dispositions we have it that for any actual individual x:

$$(\forall x)(\psi/\phi)\dagger x \text{ iff } (\forall y)[\phi?y \supset (\psi/\phi)y].$$

And accordingly we have:

$$\phi \Rightarrow \psi \text{ iff } (\forall x)(\psi/\phi)\dagger x.$$

In Chapter IV we have specified a conception of a metaphysically possible world (M-possible world) which supplements the purely logical requirements regarding possible individuals with logical and metaphysical constraints on their compossibility. We now move beyond this purely logico-metaphysical basis in also considering physical or *nomic* constraints on possible worlds. These are to be based on the principle that: A *nomically* possible world—on our approach—is one which (however it may otherwise differ from the actual world) is such that *all property-relating dispositions that are quasi-universally present throughout the actual world continue to be quasi-universally operative.* The determination of whether a certain possible world is N-possible is a straightforward matter of checking whether or not its individuals exhibit all those property-relating dispositions that characterize all eligible *actual* individuals.

Lawfulness is, accordingly, construed as operative with respect to the range of N-feasible actual-variation, and *given* this range we can, in general, *deduce* the laws in operation. This point must be considered in somewhat closer detail.

Consider a microworld of the following description:

	F	G	F/G
x_1	+	+	+
x_2	−	−	[+]
x_3	+	[−]	[−]

The descriptive basis of this world gives rise to the following inventory of actual-variant descriptions:[3]

Descriptive Specification No.	F	G	F/G	x_1	x_2	x_3
1.	+	+	+	@	#	
2.	+	−	+	#	#	
3.	−	+	+	L-infeasible		
4.	−	−	+	#	@	
5.	+	+	−	N-infeasible (relative to the actual world)		
6.	+	−	−			@
7.	−	+	−	N-infeasible (relative to the actual world)		
8.	−	−	−			#

Note that specification No. 3 is *logically* infeasible (no individual can possible have both F/G and G, and yet lack F). However, specifications No.'s 5 and 7 are both *nomically* infeasible. No individuals answering to these (partial) descriptions can figure in any nomically possible worlds. For F/G is a quasi-universally operative disposition in the actual world, and so any N-possible individual for which G obtains must also exhibit this disposition. Note incidentally that while F/G is *not* an essential property of x_1 (unlike x_2), it is nevertheless N-essential to x_1, thanks to its quasi-universal presence among the reals. (Thus worlds containing the $F \& G \& \neg(F/G)$ variant version of x_1, while indeed possible *per se*, will not be N-possible.) As this illustrates, the N-essential features of things can in fact root in their inessential dispositions, provided these dispositions are law-correlative (i.e., quasi-universal).

To remain in the sphere of the "genuinely possible" in proceeding on this basis, we must confine ourselves to possible worlds populated by actual-surrogates and/or supernumeraries answering to descriptions that are N-feasible for actual things. And as long as we do so, it is clear that we shall maintain all of the laws (i.e., quasi-universally present dispositions) that are operative in the actual world.

[3] It should be noted that these descriptive specifications are *incomplete*, because they are indeterminate regarding various dispositional properties, e.g., $G/F, F/\bar{G}$, etc. They are, to this extent, schematic.

The "nomically possible" worlds are, accordingly, subject to three categories of constraints:

1. the logico-conceptual constraints operative upon possible individuals in general
2. the metaphysical constraints on compossibility operative with respect to all M-possible worlds
3. the special constraints attaching to the idea of nomic necessity as built into the requirement of maintaining in operation all of the quasi-universal property-relating dispositions of the actual world.

The critical consideration is that nomic possibility is defined relative to the (essentialistically construed) constitution of the actual world.

3. MODES OF POSSIBILITY: A SUMMARY

It may be useful at this stage to review in summarized form the various modes of "possibility" that have been introduced in the course of our discussion:

1. *L-possibility*: an item (e.g., individual, world, state of affairs) is L-possible (*logically* possible) if its introducing characterization does not contravene the "laws of logic" (i.e., the logical organon that serves as basis for the discussion).
2. *E-possibility*: a *prima facie* possible individual (L-possible individual) is E-possible (*essentialistically* possible) if its introducing characterization also satisfies the essentialistic conditions for individuation (and, in particular, if this item does not lack any of the essential properties of its prototype).
3. *M-possibility*: a *prima facie* possible world (i.e., set of possible individuals) is M-possible (metaphysically possible) if the individuals of its population are not only separately E-possible, but also *conjointly compossible* in meeting the various appropriate logical and metaphysical conditions for mutual coexistence within a single possible world.
4. *D-possibility*: an M-possible world is D-possible (dispositionally possible), relative to some specified actual individual x, if x's surrogate in this world has *all* of the

dispositional properties of its real-world prototype x (even its inessential ones). An M-possible world is D-possible simpliciter if it is D-possible with respect to *all* actual individuals.

5. *N-possibility*: an E-possible individual is N-possible (nomically possible) if its specifying description does not violate any "law of nature" (= disposition quasi-universal throughout the actual world). An M-possible world is N-possible if all of its individuals are N-possible, i.e., if *all* the "laws of nature" of the actual world obtain in it as well.

It warrants note that under certain assumptions the machinery of M-, D-, and N-possibility can all be reduced to that of E-possibility, and thus the mechanism of essentiality is the only concept we need adopt as primitive if we so choose. The case of metaphysical possibility will be considered in detail in Section 8 of Chapter X below; at present our attention will be confined to the cases of dispositional and nomic possibility.

Note first the basic uniformity of approach:

$$\phi x \text{ is to be } \begin{cases} \text{E-possible} \\ \text{D-possible} \\ \text{N-possible} \end{cases} \text{ according as there is some}$$

$$\begin{cases} \text{E-possible} \\ \text{D-possible} \\ \text{N-possible} \end{cases} \text{ world whose } x\text{-surrogate has } \phi.$$

To reduce these D- and N-cases to the E-case we need simply adopt the following conventions:

(D) To restrict the range of available (i.e., E-available) x-surrogates to those which are D-possible, we need simply stipulate that *all* of the dispositional properties of an individual are to be taken as essential to it.

(N) To restrict the range of available (i.e., E-available) x-surrogates to those which are N-possible, we need simply stipulate that all of those dispositional properties of x that represent quasi-universal dispositions of all actuals are to be taken as essential to x.

By means of such (admittedly somewhat drastic) assumptions

the various other modes of "real possibility" can be subsumed (at the level of formal machinery) under the case of E-possibility, facilitating a useful economy at the theoretical level in the items of apparatus needed for the handling of "real possibility."

4. LAW-MODIFYING POSSIBILITIES

One important refinement must be introduced. Once *laws* are brought upon the stage of consideration, the notion of an "alternative possible world" can be developed in a rather different direction from that we have been taking so far. For the discussion thus far has been oriented wholly towards changes in the descriptive make-up of individuals. But we can now introduce another distinctive sort of hypothetical alteration of reality, namely a *change of laws*. An "alternative possible world" would on this basis be one in which some altogether different laws obtain, a world governed not by the actual laws of the real world, by "other possible laws." Thus a world endowed with such things as ideal gasses, perfectly elastic bodies, totally efficient engines, and the like would have to be looked upon as law-modifying.

The fact that natural laws (and quasi-universally essential dispositions) are preserved intact in all N-possible worlds means that in analyzing *contrary-to-law* assumptions that envisage worlds whose laws differ from those of the actual one, we cannot confine our purview to N-possible worlds—as we can do when dealing with those *contrary-to-fact* assumptions that merely vary the descriptive make-up of actual individuals. With law-contravening assumptions we must return to the entire range of M-possible worlds and introduce new and different law-modifying constraints, dropping certain laws and (presumably) also adding new ones.

In cases of hypothetical law-modification one cannot carry any of the actual individuals of the real world over into a law-modified world—or at any rate, none of those individuals that can possibly fall within the purview of one of the changed laws. Presumably, the issue is not just the individual's own atomistic disposition to conform to the law, but also its existing within a world-environment where this law obtains. Thus we cannot change the law, given the existence of *this* individual with its essentialistic endowment.

However, such law-modificatory reasonings can also be accommodated by means of the machinery already introduced. To see this, let us begin with the (hypothetically actual) microworld:

	F	G	H	F/G
x_1	+	+	[−]	[+]
x_2	[+]	[+]	+	[+]
x_3	−	−	[+]	[+]

On this basis we would obtain the following inventory of variant descriptions for individuals within the "neighborhood of feasible variation" of the actuals:

F	G	H	F/G	x_1	x_2	x_3
+	+	+	[+]		@	#
+	+	−	[+]	@	#	
+	−	+	[+]			{#}
+	−	−	[+]	{#}		
−	+	+	[+]	L-infeasible		
−	+	−	[+]	L-infeasible		
−	−	+	[+]			@
−	−	−	[+]	#		

The two indicated descriptions are blocked for all nomically possible individuals (i.e., as N-infeasible) by the fact that F/G is a universally operative disposition to which all actual individuals conform, so that F/G must hold of all nomically possible individuals and "All G is F" must obtain in all nomically possible worlds. But now if we take the step of introducing the law-altering hypothesis to the effect that F/G is to be *deleted* as an essential feature of the individuals, and that the converse law "All F is G" is to obtain instead, then, in abandoning our commitment to the essentiality of F/G, we reintroduce certain formerly eliminated cases. But we must now abandon the two brace-bracketed ones. Accordingly, we would, of course, be involved in a change of mind about the sorts of alternative possibilities that qualify for inclusion in "possible worlds."

This example illustrates the (rather obvious) point that when one approaches the issue of alternative possible worlds in this *law*-altering sense, one is involved in a change of mind as to what sorts of things are *nomically* possible. To change laws about is, in effect, to alter the boundaries of the (nomically) possible.[4]

The fact remains that the direction of our standard approach —based on a consideration of what is *nomically* possible, relative to the actual laws of nature—contemplates the variation of individuals within a framework of *fixed* laws. Here the "fixity" at issue is determined in the study of real, and "nomic possibility" is *relative* possibility—defined against this background of the laws that are operative within the "real world."

5. LAWS AND "NOVEL" SUPERNUMERARIES: THE INTERDEPENDENCE OF LAWS AND POSSIBLE INDIVIDUALS

Consider a microworld consisting of three actuals answering to the following C.D.S.:

	F	G	H
x_1	$[-]$	$+$	$-$
x_2	$[-]$	$-$	$+$
x_3	$[+]$	$[+]$	$-$

This leads to the following inventory of actual-variant descriptions (c.d.s.):

	F	G	H	x_1	x_2	x_3
1.	$+$	$+$	$+$			#
2.	$+$	$+$	$-$			@
3.	$+$	$-$	$+$			
4.	$+$	$-$	$-$			
5.	$-$	$+$	$+$	#	#	
6.	$-$	$+$	$-$	@	#	
7.	$-$	$-$	$+$	#	@	
8.	$-$	$-$	$-$	#	#	

Now, clearly, the fact that descriptive compartments No. 3 and 4 are blank means that the disposition G/F is quasi-universal throughout the actual world, since possession of F precludes

---

[4] From this point of view, laws, dispositions, and essentiality-imputations are all comparable—they in effect represent conditions that serve to fix "the limits of the possible" (in various senses of that term) on the side of the "genuinely possible"—in contradistinction to that of the "purely logically possible."

also having $\bar{G}$ as a possibility for any actual individual. The following thesis will thus have lawful force with respect to the actual world:

Whatever has F must also have G

The decision to introduce into a possible world a supernumerary possible individual answering to c.d.s. of the form of No's 3 or 4 would be to abrogate the law-structure of the initial actual world.

This circumstance is perfectly general. The emptiness of a descriptive compartment in such an inventory of actual-variant descriptions *always* entails the obtaining of a certain law. Thus if, for example, we assume the emptiness of the descriptive compartment

$$
\begin{array}{ccc}
F & G & H \\
- & + & -
\end{array}
$$

this means that no actual-surrogate can possibly have G and lack both F and H, so that the following family of laws will obtain:

$$
\text{If something} \begin{cases} \text{lacks } F \text{ and has } G \\ \text{lacks } F \text{ and } H \\ \text{has } G \text{ and lacks } H \end{cases} \text{it must} \begin{cases} \text{have } H \\ \text{lack } G \\ \text{have } F \end{cases}
$$

And conversely, the obtaining of a law always dictates the emptiness of certain descriptive compartments. The inventory of actual-variants, itself determined by the *full* descriptive constitution of the actual world (i.e., a description that encorporates also the essentialistic aspects), serves to determine the law-structure of the world, just as—and indeed because—it determines the dispositional facets of things.

The law-fabric of the (actual) world is altogether determined by the constitution of its nomically possible actual-variants, and indeed this law-structure is such as to eliminate all other descriptive forms from the manifold of the nomically possible worlds penumbral to a given actual world. The law-structure at issue has the consequence that the manifold of nomically possible worlds is "saturated" in that no further totally non-standard and "novel" descriptive individual specifications could be added. Any introduction into the manifold of possible worlds spawned from a given actual world of supernumerary individuals with c.d.s. of a descriptive composition that is totally "novel" (in terms of the real-world possibilities) forces the abrogation of at least some of the actual laws. Wholly new descriptive species require new "laws of nature" to accommodate them. We are led to a form of Leibniz's contention that any possible world—with its given laws—will be such that no altogether new species (or *types*) of individuals could possibly be added to it: that every possible world is descriptively "saturated" relative to its laws and their definition of nomically possible descriptive forms.[5]

When a law obtains, does it obtain necessarily?[6] In one sense, certainly not. Thus consider the hypothetically actual micro-world

	F	G	H	G/F
x_1	[+]	[+]	+	[+]
x_2	−	[+]	−	[+]
x_3	−	−	+	+

Since G/F is a universally present dispositional property, the law-thesis $F \Rightarrow G$ obtains here. But if we suppose yet another

---

[5] Leibniz, to be sure, presses this position even further—from maintaining the correlativity of laws with *types* of individuals to the correlativity of laws with individuals *per se*. But of course, for Leibniz there is, in the final analysis, a coordination of types with particular individuals *via* the Principle of the Identity of Indiscernibles. Thus Leibniz's conclusion could be looked upon as extracted from two premisses:

    1. Laws are correlative with descriptive species
    2. Descriptive species stand in a one-one relationship with individuals

    ∴ Laws are correlative with individuals

Of the three theses operative in this Leibnizian syllogism, we can accept only the first.

[6] This too is a Leibnizian question, and our answer is the same as his:

For since it is contingent . . . that this particular series of things exists, its laws will be themselves indeed absolutely contingent, although hypothetically necessary and as it were essential once the series is given. (*Opuscules et fragments inédits de Leibniz*, ed. by C. Couturat [Paris, 1903], pp. 19–20. Cf. the discussion in E. M. Curley, "The Root of Contingency," in H. Frankfurt [ed.], *Leibniz: A Collection of Critical Essays* [New York, 1972], pp. 69–98.)

possible world, one obtained from the preceding one by the *addition* of an (actual) individual x_4 answering to the C.D.S.

	F	G	H	G/F
x_4	−	−	[+]	−

then it is clear that the augmented world can no longer accommodate the law "All F is G" (even though "All F is G" is true in this world as a matter of "general accident"), since G/F is no longer a universally (or better, quasi-universally) essential disposition. The sorts of individuals that exist play a decisive role in delimiting the sorts of laws that obtain.

All this is not to deny that from the standpoint of the *initial* world as (*ex hypothesi*) actual—and accordingly as determinative of its own characteristic law-structure—the individual x_4 is simply not (nomically) possible. But to say this is to say no more than the obvious point that x_4 violates the law-structure obtaining in the initial (actual) world—it certainly does *not* mean that x_4 is "impossible" *per se*, in some more deep-rooted way. The point is that x_4 is not excluded from *every* possible world as such, but merely from every world that is nomically possible relative to the actual world. To introduce this individual is to alter the law-structure of the world.

The preceding example also shows the potentially covert nature of laws. The dispositions they represent need not always be manifest; they can remain latent (exactly as G/F is not overtly manifest with respect to x_3 above). An element of *imputation* that goes beyond the overt evidence is generally present in attributions of dispositionality and lawfulness.[7]

Can one and the same family of laws survive despite alterations in the descriptive make-up of individuals? Clearly yes, within limits. Thus let the actual world be a microworld constituted as follows:

	F	G	G/F	$F/\bar{G}$
x_1	+	[+]	[+]	−
x_2	−	+	[+]	[+]

Given that "All F is G" has the status of a natural law, the only

---

[7] See Chapter V, "The Imputational Theory of Laws" of N. Rescher, *Conceptual Idealism* (Oxford, 1973).

nomically feasible descriptions for actual-variants will be as follows:

	F	G	G/F	$F/\bar{G}$	x_1	x_2
(1)	+	+	+	+	#	#
(2)	+	−	+	+		
(3)	−	+	+	+	#	@
(4)	−	−	+	+		#
(5)	+	+	+	−	@	
(6)	+	−	+	−		
(7)	−	+	+	−	#	
(8)	−	−	+	−		

The following possible individuals will now be available as actual-surrogates:

$$x_1^0 = \langle(5), x_1\rangle \qquad x_2^0 = \langle(3), x_2\rangle$$
$$x_1^1 = \langle(1), x_1\rangle \qquad x_2^1 = \langle(1), x_2\rangle$$
$$x_1^2 = \langle(3), x_1\rangle \qquad x_2^2 = \langle(4), x_2\rangle$$
$$x_1^3 = \langle(7), x_1\rangle$$

Note now that if the actual world $\{x_1^0, x_2^0\}$ were by hypothesis replaced by $\{x_1^3, x_2^2\}$, as actual (*ex hypothesi*), with both actual individuals thus changed in property make-up, the same descriptive compartments remain empty in the construction of a possibility-inventory, and the laws would continue unchanged, notwithstanding the assumed alterations in the descriptive constitution of individuals. This example shows that one can in suitable circumstances keep the same laws and just change the descriptive make-up of individuals.

The converse question also arises: Can we keep the same, descriptively unchanged actual individuals and just change the laws? On the present approach to lawfulness, the answer is clearly negative. A given law obtains iff every actual individual (that can possibly do so) has a certain dispositional property. To keep the individuals the same and unchanged is to retain *all* of their properties, dispositional ones included, and thus commits us to retaining the "laws of nature" as well.

6. WORLDS AND PROPERTIES

It is useful to supplement these considerations about the nomic interdependence of worlds and individuals with some observations regarding the relations between worlds and properties. Unlike the problem of the cross-world reidentification of *individuals*, whose complexities were recognized and grappled with at length in the preceding discussion, the issue of the cross-world reidentification of *properties* has thus far been treated as altogether unproblematic. An at least brief consideration of this bit of unrealism is mandatory. What a property *is*, of course, hinges on its lawful relations with others that lie in its categorial neighborhood—represented by such "dimensional" groupings as color, size, shape, etc. Its placement within the functional order represented by such a family is part of what makes a property what it is. The sameness of properties is thus fundamentally connected with the sameness of laws: change the laws sufficiently and you destroy the properties, and conversely. The reidentification of properties is inextricably correlated with fundamental constancies of lawfulness. Thus the problems of property-reidentification are inevitably bound up with the question of nomically possible worlds.

But the issue has another, perhaps more fundamental aspect. In the final analysis, the crossworld identification of properties can present no serious problems in the context of the present theory, thanks to the very nature of the constructive approach at work in our theory. Our whole line of approach envisages a constructive process that begins with in-hand nomic and taxonomic machinery as derived from the theoretically informed study of the actual. One is then to carry such a property framework over into the constituting of other possible worlds. The very fact that their descriptive constituting proceeds by use of *given* properties means that those properties we will encounter in the context of "other possible worlds" can pose no serious problems in point of their reidentification. (Compare pp. 107–10 above.)

Chapter IX

CONTRARY–TO–FACT SUPPOSITIONS AND COUNTERFACTUAL CONDITIONALS

1. INADMISSIBLE HYPOTHESES

Clearly, not every conceivable fact-contravening hypothesis can qualify as admissible (legitimate, viable, tenable), but specifically only those which stipulate something that is *possible* under the circumstances.[1] When the antecedent thesis P is in the very nature of things impossible, then a counterfactual conditional of the form "If it were the case that P, then Q" simply becomes nonsensical (meaningless), and it does so precisely for the reason that the antecedent that-P supposition is simply infeasible. A supposition can qualify as legitimately admissible only when its *suppositum*—the thesis whose supposition it stipulates—is a possible one. Thus the admissibility of ϕx as an hypothesis calls for the tenability, and indeed the truth of $\Diamond \phi x$, and so presupposes that of $\phi ? x$.

We thus arrive at a general rule to govern the legitimacy or admissibility of hypotheses:

The supposition that P is to be looked upon as *blocked* (inadmissible, improper) whenever P is, in effect, *impossible*.

This is actually a schema for several rules, rather than a single rule, because different sorts of possibility/impossibility can be at issue, each leading to a correspondingly characteristic basis for the blockage of suppositions (E-blockage, N-blockage, etc.).

Applying this principle in the present context, one is led to the rule:

---

[1] This seems to rule out the introduction of inconsistent hypotheses for the sake of establishing their negations by *reductio ad absurdum* reasoning. But, of course, one way of interpreting the case is simply as argumentation to show that the hypothesis was *not* tenable in the first place. This view of the issue is developed at greater length in N. Rescher, *Hypothetical Reasoning* (Amsterdam, 1964).

The supposition that ϕx is *blocked* (untenable, improper) *simpliciter* whenever it is not the case that $\phi?x$.[2] Moreover, this supposition is D-blocked or N-blocked according as ϕx is dispositionally or nomically impossible.

Accordingly, one is to discountenance as untenable (improper) assumptions to the effect that individuals have (or lack) properties which in principle it is simply not possible for them to have (or lack). And, in particular, one is to regard as blocked the assumptive attribution (or denial) to an individual of any property whose lack (or presence) is actually essential to it.

Consider an illustration of this process. Let it be supposed that Julius Casear, the Roman general and statesman, is under consideration. Then certain suppositions might well be classed as admissible e.g.

—Suppose Julius Caesar had not decided to cross the Rubicon.
—Suppose Julius Caesar had not been assassinated.

These suppositions might well be treated as perfectly proper and legitimate from the point of view of historical speculation. On the other hand consider such hypotheses as

—Suppose Julius Caesar had been born a female.
—Suppose Julius Caesar had lived in the third century A.D.

These distinctly more "far-fetched" hypotheses might well be ruled out as *just too unrealistic* to be admissible. In taking this stance we are, in effect, implementing a (generally tacit) decision *to treat certain properties as essential to Julius Caesar*, as we are prepared to consider him within a given context of inquiry. Given that we are prepared to count a certain property ϕ as *essential* to an individual x, we cannot but preclude the prospect that x lacks ϕ—i.e. of assuming that something which (*ex hypothesi*) lacks ϕ could possibly qualify as x. In the case of Caesar, this might well include such properties as being the child of the persons who were actually his parents, being a male, growing to adulthood, etc. In any event, one would insist that the possible alternative versions of an actual individual continue

[2] Of course, this also embraces the negative form for ϕ.

to maintain some of its real-world footing (some part of its actual history, some facets of its causal origins, or the like).

Moreover, due recognition must be given to the *systematic* character of fact-modificatory hypotheses—that if one postulates a change in one thing (e.g., Caesar's crossing of the Rubicon) one must make due hypothetical revisions in the history of others (Cassius, Brutus, etc.), and effect these changes so that essentialistic requirements are honored throughout. Item-revisions entail world-revisions—modificatory changes in things come not as single spies but in battalions. These systematic ramifications too are a critical facet of admissibility.[3] This facet of networked interrelationships makes nonsense of hypotheses like "Assume a world *exactly like* this one *except for* Napoleon's loosing at Leipzig." If we want to make assumptions of this sort, we had better trade in "exactly" for "very much" and let the assumption itself be our guide—at best it can—in the elimination of possibilities.

On this approach, it eventuates that whenever the thesis that ϕx qualifies as a tenable (admissible) hypothesis, then there is *some* hypothetically modified version of x that does indeed have ϕ. That is, if the assumption that ϕx is not to be blocked, then, since it must be the case that $\phi ? x$, there must be a (suitably) possible world where x—or rather the x-surrogate of that possible world—does indeed have ϕ:

For some [essentialistically, dispositionally, nomically] possible world w:

$$(\Sigma y)[S_{yz}^w \ \& \ Rw(\phi y)].$$

The admissible assumptions—in the various modes of admissibility—are just those which are in fact realized in *some* possible world of the corresponding type (E-possibility, D-possibility, N-possibility). We accordingly arrive at the following explications:

The assumption that ϕx is . . .	*If ϕ holds of x in some . . .*
E-admissible	E-possible world
D-admissible	world that is D-possible with respect to x
N-admissible	N-possible world

[3] For a further treatment of relevant issues see N. Rescher, *The Coherence Theory of Truth* (Oxford, 1973).

And, by parallelism, a supposition is blocked in one of the modes if its suppositum fails to hold in some one of the relevant set of possible worlds. (E-inadmissible assumptions are, of course, blocked altogether.) Now it deserves note again that one can convert the other modes of admissibility into E-admissibility by embedding the relevant sorts of dispositional and nomic features within the essential properties of things. When this is done, all the various modes of admissibility are simply reduced to becoming so many versions of E-admissibility, and the only constraints on the tenability of assumptions are now seen in terms of *logical* constraints.

The three preceding modes of possibility/admissibility are in close parallelism with analogous conceptions introduced by the medieval scholastics, who distinguished three species of possibility/impossibility: moral, physical, and metaphysical. They held that a state of affairs is *morally* impossible if its realization contravenes the normal, ordinary or customary (hence *moral*) course of events—i.e., violates the dispositions of things in the manner of our D-impossibility. A state of affairs is *physically* impossible if, as with a miracle, it contravenes the "laws of nature" (hence *physical*)—i.e., violates the lawful order of things in the manner of our N-impossibility. Finally, they characterized a state of affairs as *metaphysically* impossible if it is impossible in the strict logico-metaphysical sense, so that it cannot be realized even by the omnipotent power of God (*neque per omnipotentiam divinam*). Our own threefold division does little more than clothe these distinctions of the subtle schoolmen in a modern dress.

We must not shirk altogether broaching the theme of "strictly impossible" suppositions and "utterly impossible" objects of discourse in the manner of such Meinongian impossibilia as round squares. About these it must be said:

1. That they take one (*ex hypothesi*) outside the realm of *possible* individuals.
2. To say this is not to deny that orderly discourse and logically appropriate reasoning can be carried on regarding them (e.g., in *reductio ad absurdum* argumentation).
3. While they cannot be dealt with in *ordinary* assumptive reasoning, they can be handled by an as it were extra-

ordinary mode of *per impossibile* assumptive reasoning (as in the counterfactual "If Meinong had found a round square object, he would have treasured it"). But *this* sort of assumptive reasoning is parasitic, in complex ways we need not pursue here, upon ordinary assumptive reasoning. (Cf. p. 65 above.)

The crucial fact about the *impossibilia* at issue is that while they do figure within the pale of rational discourse and argumentation, they (1) lie wholly outside the sphere of possibility (and thus outside the scope of any concern with possible worlds and possible individuals, and (2) they lack any sort of (extra-linguistic) *ontological* ramifications, since it is (*ex hypothesi*) impossible *in principle* for them to exist under any conditions or circumstances whatosever.

2. THE POSSIBLE-WORLDS APPROACH TO COUNTERFACTUALS

For the moment, let us confine our attention to counterfactual conditionals of the property-modificatory sort, that is, those of the form:

If the individual x had ϕ—where x is actual (i.e., $x \in w^*$) and moreover x in fact has $\bar{\phi}$ (i.e., $\neg\phi x$)—then x would have ψ.

The propriety of such a thesis is predicated on the admissibility of the supposition presented by its antecedent, so that ϕ must be a *possible* property of x if the counterfactual at issue is to be legitimate and proper.

It deserves remark that the counterfactual thesis

If x had ϕ, then it would have ψ

which certainly implies that x lacks ϕ, does *not* imply that x does not have ψ. For example, if ψ were an essential property of x (and so one possessed by *all* of its surrogates), then the conditional thesis would be true regardless of which of the nonactual but possible properties ϕ of x were at issue in its antecedent clause.

Accordingly, the mode of counterfactual supposition that is of primary relevance to our present concerns is that which ascribes to an actual (i.e., real) individual a property it does not have or denies of it a property that it does have. Such suppositions take the form:

—Assume x had ϕ (though it doesn't)
—Assume x lacked ψ (though it doesn't).

Counterfactuals are thus viewed as conditionals that specify the resut of an *inference* drawn from such a *suppositio falsi*. These property-modificatory counterfactuals are of the form:

—If x had ϕ (which it doesn't), then ...
—If x lacked ψ (which it doesn't), then ...

This approach represents an inferential conception of property-modificatory counterfactuals, according to which they have a suppositional starting-point, presenting consequences drawn from a hypothesis that is (or purports to be) contrary-to-fact. The resulting view of counterfactual conditionals might be characterized as the natural-deduction theory of contrary-to-fact inferences.

How, then, is the import of such a property-modificatory counterfactual conditional to be construed? Surely along the following lines: that if we make the (not in principle infeasible) assumption that x has ϕ then the circumstances of the case are such that we *cannot avoid* obtaining the result that x has ψ. Accordingly, the truth-condition for the counterfactual will be that *every* ϕ-endowed surrogate for x, in any and every (suitably) possible world, exhibits ψ (in that possible world):

For all w (of the relevant sort): $(\Pi y)[(S_{yx}^w \,\&\, Rw(\phi y)) \supset Rw(\psi y)]$.

The thesis "If x had ϕ, then x would have ψ" is, accordingly, construed in a necessitarian sense: "If x had ϕ, then x would have to have ψ under all (feasible) conditions or circumstances."

But how are we to interpret the crucial phrase "feasible" in this formula? Clearly in this way, that w must be a D-possible world with respect to x, i.e., one that is dispositionally feasible relative to x, in that the x-surrogate of this world continues to bear those dispositional properties that x possesses in the actual world. In short, ψ/ϕ must be classifiable as a property of x in that it obtains throughout a suitably comprehensive range of possible worlds. This brings us to the following upshot of the analysis on the side of "truth conditions," that "If x had ϕ

then x would have ψ" is true iff all of the ϕ-endowed x-surrogates in every world w that is D-possible with respect to x also has ψ (in w). In this way, property-modificatory counterfactuals are in effect grounded in the dispositions of things.

Of course, yet another—and perhaps very natural—way to validate the move from x's having ϕ (*contra actualitate*) to x's having ψ would be for the link of ψ to ϕ to be not merely x-relativized but universal, i.e., lawful. And in this case the "relevant sort" of worlds at issue in the preceding formula would simply be the range of all nomically possible ones, with the disposition at issue effectively universalized.

On both the dispositional and nomic sides, the proposed analyses of property-modificatory counterfactuals proceeds in dispositional terms, and view such a counterfactual as maintaining (from somewhat different perspectives) a "necessary" connection of essentially dispositional (or even lawful) type between the properties of an individual.

This approach, in effect, construes the counterfactual relationship at issue in such a way that

"If x had ϕ (which it doesn't), then x would have ψ" is to count as true just in case three conditions are met

  (i)   the condition at issue is indeed contrary to fact:
        x in fact lacks ϕ—i.e., $\bar{\phi}x$
  (ii) the antecedent envisages a feasible supposition:
        x might have ϕ—i.e., $\phi?x$
  (iii) the linkage from ϕ to ψ is at least of the strength of an ordinary disposition for x—i.e., $(\psi/\phi)x$.

The tendency of the preceding account leads straightway to a generalized possible-worlds analysis of counterfactual condionals. We are led to construe "If x had ϕ then P would be the case" as:

In every (suitably) possible world in which x does have ϕ (or more accurately, in which it has a surrogate that does), P obtains.

Accordingly, the fact-contravening supposition on which the conditional turns determines the delimited range of those possible worlds to which we are to address ourselves. And in constituting these possible worlds, it is clear that "possible" is here to embrace the *genuinely* possible—i.e., possible relative to *given* dispositions or laws, all of which are to be maintained. For example, it is the reality of the law "All copper conducts electricity" that underwrites the correctness of the counterfactual "If this rubber disc were made of copper, it would conduct electricity."

Let us inspect the workings of this analysis somewhat more closely. Consider that paradigm-counterfactual, "If the match *M* had been struck, it would have lit." Analyzing this from the suppositional approach we note, first of all, that we are asking to make a supposition in the background of certain established beliefs:

Beliefs: (1) All dry matches located in an oxygen-containing medium light when struck. [Covering Law]

(2) M is a dry match. [Dispositional Fact]

(3) M is located in an oxygen-containing medium [Dispositional Fact]

(4) M has not been struck [Contingent Fact]

(5) M has not lit [Contingent Fact]

Assumption: ($\overline{4}$) Assume M has been struck.

The assumption instructs us explicitly to drop (4). But we cannot simply subjoin it to the rest—i.e., to (1), (2), (3), and (5) —for a contradiction still ensues. We must also drop one of these, that is, we must choose between the following four "possible worlds":

$$w_1 = \{(\overline{4}), (1), (2), (3), (5)\} - \{(1)\}$$
$$w_2 = \{(\overline{4}), (1), (2), (3), (5)\} - \{(2)\}$$
$$w_3 = \{(\overline{4}), (1), (2), (3), (5)\} - \{(3)\}$$
$$w_4 = \{(\overline{4}), (1), (2), (3), (5)\} - \{(5)\}$$

Clearly the most "acceptable" possible world will result when we retain (insofar as possible) the laws and dispositional facts of *this*, the actual world, and "readjust" the contingent facts, insofar as necessary. And this means dropping (5) to arrive at: "If the match M had been struck, it would have lit." (Rather than, say, dropping (2) to arrive at "If the match M had been struck, it would not have been dry.") It is thus w_4 that this conditional puts before us.

This process typifies the analysis of counterfactual conditionals in terms of the possible-worlds approach. Hypothetical changes in the real permit of different sorts of readjustments, readjustments that will (due to *compossibility* considerations) have to be accommodated in *different* possible worlds. Beginning with a survey of the manifold of "possible worlds" which arise when a counterfactual supposition is introduced, one utilizes plausibility considerations to reduce the remaining alternatives as much as possible, in order to arrive at a set of "consequences" that is as definite (and as plausible) as the circumstances of the case admit of. Those counterfactual "consequences" will then obtain that hold throughout *all* of the noneliminated possible worlds.[4]

Consider now the analogous case of a specifically *possibilistic* counterfactual conditional:

"If x had ϕ (which it doesn't), then x *might* have ψ"

In such cases we must replace condition (iii) above by one that is related but different. For this condition (iii), which comes to

All ϕ-endowed x-surrogates have ψ (in all suitably possible worlds): $(Aw)(\Pi y)[(w \in \Gamma \;\&\; S^w_{yx} \;\&\; \phi y) \supset \psi y]$

must now be weakened to

Some ϕ-endowed x-surrogates have ψ (in some suitably possible worlds): $(Ew)(\Sigma y)[w \in \Gamma \;\&\; S^w_{yx} \;\&\; \phi y \;\&\; \psi y]$.

A comparable—but considerably more complex—sort of analysis would be needed to accommodate probabilistic counterfactuals of the type "If x had ϕ (which it doesn't), then x would *probably* have ψ."

This account of property-modificatory contrary-to-fact conditionals highlights the central rule that a theory of possibility is bound to play in their analysis. On the one hand, the assumption inherent in the antecedent of the conditional must be a possible one (in one of those senses of possibility whose

---

[4] For further details regarding this treatment of counterfactuals see N. Rescher, *The Coherence Theory of Truth* (Oxford, 1973), Chap. XI.

clarification is a central task of the theory). On the other hand, the linkage from suppositional antecedent to the elicited consequent must be mediated by one of those dispositional linkages (be they idiosyncratically particularized or generically lawful) that are also central to our theory in that they represent the sort of *relative* necessity through which "the limits of the possible" are in significant measure determined.

3. VARIANT CASES

The analysis given above for counterfactuals of the property-modificatory type will not apply where the circumstances are sufficiently different. The main departures will be of two sorts.

Variant Case (1): "Purely Factual" Counterfactuals

Counterfactuals may rest on purely factual considerations in which laws and dispositions are not involved at all. Two paradigm examples are:

—If his firstborn had been a boy then all five of Smith's children (born to date) would be boys [all the others being boys].

—If this book had a green cover, then one of the books on the table would have red covers [it being the only red-covered one].

Such counterfactuals clearly do not conform to the essentially dispositional pattern of those upon which the previous discussion was focused.

With such suppositions one not only keeps all laws the same, but also insofar as possible all of the (nonrelational) facts about everything other than the item in view in the antecedent hypothesis (and its logical commitments).

Thus, while our standard case envisages a sameness-of-laws supposition, in the present situation one envisages also a sameness-of-facts-about-other-things, when determining the range of worlds with respect to which the truth or correctness of the counterfactual is to be evaluated.[5]

Variant Case (2): Contrary-to-Law Counterfactuals

Consider the following examples:

—If maples were evergreens, then ...
—If gravity operated on an inverse cube (rather than inverse square) principle, then ...

Examples of this sort envisage a range of cases entirely different from the property-modificatory ones considered earlier in the chapter. These law-contravening counterfactuals call for an altogether different approach. The basic stratagem here is to make reference to a (presumably) given hierarchy of laws. A possible world would then *not* be one where *all* of the laws the same, but only (1) the "higher" laws than the one being modified, and (2) the irrelevant ones, with relevance to be decided with reference to considerations dealt with in these higher-order. In its generic structure this approach calls for the same conceptualization as before: one constructs a suitable range of possible worlds in terms of certain basic ground-rules. And the counterfactual conditional is then to count as true if its consequent obtains in *all* of those possible worlds in which its antecedent does. To be sure, the determination of the relevant range of possible worlds now proceeds on principles different from those of the preceding case, but there remains a *structural* uniformity (isomorphism) in the analysis of all these reality-abrogating conditionals in terms of the possible worlds approach.

4. THE RESTRICTED NATURE OF COUNTERFACTUAL REASONING

In reasoning counter*factually*, we address the issue of *what would happen if something or other were different from what it actually is.* Such

---

[5] Compare the discussion in Robert Stalnaker, "A Theory of Conditionals," *American Philosophical Quarterly*, Monograph No. 2 (Oxford, 1968). Stalnaker takes it to be a *pragmatic* question (i.e., purposive-context-relative issue) in which possible worlds a counterfactual conditional is to be evaluated. It is here viewed as a fundamentally *semantical* question that hinges on the meaning-content of the counterfactual supposition at issue.

considerations never require us to move outside the realm of hypothetical variations in the make-up of the actual. Throughout the counterfactual arena, our horizons are limited to the domain of feasible actual-surrogates; hypothetical reasoning of the markedly *remote* variety, involving utterly nonexistent things ("supernumeraries"), does not enter in the arena of counter-*fact*. By the very nature of what is involved in a fact-altering assumption of the type

> "If such-and-such a thing were so-and-so (which it isn't), then it would have these-or-those features."

only actual-variant items will be at issue. What one deals with here is some alternative possibility for the real, the locution

> "if x were a ϕ, then . . ."

being predicated on the feasibility of the basic supposition at issue, that is, on ϕ's being (minimally) an E-possibility for x. (While one can certainly be asked to assume the false, one cannot reasonably be asked to assume the impossible.) Thus, when contemplating fact-violating possibilities, we remain in the realm of actual-variants. In consequence, counterfactual inference involves only the mildest form of hypothetical reasoning, that concerned with the possible variations of the actual: it does not venture into the sphere of what is utterly nonactual and *merely* possible, that of the outright supernumeraries. *Counterfactual* supposition never takes us beyond the sphere of the *proximately* possible, where one is dealing throughout with possible alterations in the history of this actual world of ours. The same things, the same cast of characters, is at issue here, albeit with a different descriptive make-up. To be sure, such a world with a different history must be a world different from the actual one, but it is, at any rate, a world with the just same individuals. Napoleon would have been the same person had he won at Waterloo (or—for that matter had he died of a childhood disease in Ajacio).

Substantial complications do, however, revolve about these "*possible* variations of the actual," due to the fact that quite distinct modes of "possibility" may be at issue, as we have seen

(E-possibility, D-possibility, N-possibility). One thus arrives at various strata of possibility, depending on just how far we go in making changes that lead away from the bedrock of actuality. The descriptions of individuals (in their nonessentialistic aspect) are readily changeable, the laws of nature far less so, the laws of logic and their conceptual ramifications (especially on the essentialistic side) may be looked at as invariant, inert, and effectively unchangeable. All fact-contravening suppositions produce *some* tremors in the terrain of the actual, but some of these epistemic disturbances involve significantly more violent earthquakes than others.

APPENDIX: TOPOLOGICAL VARIATIONS ON COUNTERFACTUALITY

The existence of certain variant approaches to counterfactuality deserves mention. Suppose that one supplemented the conception of a manifold of possible worlds by a suitable means for determining whether one possible world lies in the "neighborhood" of another. (Thus w_1 might be said to be in w_2's neighborhood if w_1 contains all [or, alternatively, *most*] of the individuals contained in w_2.) Accordingly one could introduce the idea of topological accessibility (T-accessibility) by the convention that:

w_1 is T-accessible from w_2 (symbolically, Tw_1w_2) whenever w_1 lies in the neighborhood of w_2.

And now one could explicate a counterfactual relationship as follows:

The thesis "If p were so, then q would be so" (symbolically, $p > q$) obtains in a possible world w (supposing p itself to be possible) iff for every possible world w' that is T-accessible from w, we have it that q obtains whenever p does:

$$Rw(p > q) \text{ iff } (Aw')(Tw'w \supset [Rw'(p) \supset Rw'(q)]).$$

Thus relativizing to the real world we obtain

$$p > q \text{ iff } Rw^*(p > q) \text{ iff } (Aw)(Tww^* \supset [Rw(p) \supset Rw(q)]).$$

Accordingly, the truth-condition for a counterfactual is simply that in the corresponding (materially) conditional relationship obtains in all reality-accessible worlds.[6]

Applying this machinery requires cashing in the idea of "neighboring" possible worlds in a satisfactory way, a project that is not without its difficulties. Just how is the requisite sort of "proximity" to be determined—in terms of the qualitative similarity of individuals,[7] or in terms of shared or analogous laws, etc.? Each of these possibilities engenders characteristic problems of its own. After all, one wants to have not just a workable formal semantics but a plausible mode of interpretation as well. But, of course, the difficulties at work here do not impede an analysis of counterfactuals that takes its mission to be simply the explications of *truth-conditions* (on the strictly hypothetical side). However, any *categorical* application of these ideas requires the specific determination of suitable proximity criteria. (And just this—viz., the *direct* search for criterion—is what afforded the basis of our own analysis.) The reader interested in pursuing variations on this theme is referred to the journal literature.[8] It is mentioned at this point only by way of comparison and contrast to the approach adopted in this chapter.

[6] Analogous ideas could be developed along more powerful lines if the "manifold of possible worlds" were not just a *topological space*, but actually a *metric* space, or an even more richly endowed mathematical object. But we shall not pursue these possibilities here, except to note that in the tenselogical case of temporal possibility the ideas of Minkowski can be brought into operation.

[7] But see pp. 102–5 above.

[8] See R. C. Stalnaker, "A Theory of Conditionals" in *Studies in Logical Theory, American Philosophical Quarterly* Monograph Series, No. 2 (Oxford, 1968). R. H. Thomason, "A Semantic Analysis of Conditional Logic," *Theoria*, vol. 36 (1970), pp. 23–42.

Chapter X

THE DOCTRINE OF INTERNAL RELATIONS

1. FORMULATION

In its traditional form, the guise in which it was accepted by Leibniz among others, the doctrine of the internality of relations maintains that each of its relations to other things is "internal" to the nature of a thing. But, as A. C. Ewing has shown in detail, the slogan that "all relations are internal to their terms" summarizes a confusing variety of assertions.[1] The most important of these, and the one of preeminent concern here, is that relations "make a difference" to their terms, so that "where terms are related in some specific way, it is always true that they could not have been what they are without the relation being present."[2] It is held that a thing would not be the thing it is, if any of its relationships to others were actually (or even possibly) different.

This contention is presumably to be construed in the following sense, that—independently of the specific relationship R that may be at issue—the thesis inevitably obtains that whenever a (real) individual x is related to R to y, anything that *can* fail to bear this relation to y *cannot* possibly be identified with x:

$$\text{If } xRy, \text{ then } (\forall z)[\Diamond \neg zRy \to \neg \Diamond (x = z)].[3]$$

[1] A. C. Ewing, *Idealism* (London, 1934; 3rd ed., 1961), chap. IV. Here "term" does not have verbalistic or *terminological* connotations, but occurs in the old sense in which the items related by a relation are thought of as placed by it in extreme or *terminal* positions—as in "*X* is the father of *Y.*"

[2] *Ibid.*, p. 131.

[3] The doctrine also admits of a stronger "in-principled" version according to which every relation is internal with respect to every possible world. The traditional internality theorists plied both sides of the street, sometimes advancing internality as an aspect of the very *logic* of relations, sometimes supporting it with reference to the causal interrelationships operative as a *de facto* arrangement in this world. For most of these idealists thinkers the problem was simplified by taking the actual world to be the only possible one.

(Here $\rightarrow$ represents an otherwise unspecified implication relationship; the question as to whether this is material implication or something stronger may at present be left open.) This thesis can be simplified (by contraposition within its consequent) to the equivalent version:

If xRy, then $(\forall z)[\Diamond(x = z) \rightarrow \Box zRy]$ (Internality Principle)

Since, regardless of what x may be, we surely have it that $x = x$ actually, and hence possibly, this leads at once to:

If xRy, then $\Box xRy$ (Essentiality of Relations Principle).

Moreover, let us also explore the converse inference. Note the fact—inherent in the essentialistic aspect of our theory of individuation—that when x bears some property essentially, and y is to qualify as possibly identical with x, then y also must have this property essentially (i.e., that to be possibly identical with something requires possession of its essential properties):

$$[\phi!x \,\&\, \Diamond(x = y)] \rightarrow \phi!y.$$

We now argue for the Internality Principle as follows:

1.	xRy	assumption
2.	$\mathscr{R}x$ where $\mathscr{R} = (\lambda z)zRy$	from 1 by definition of $\mathscr{R}$
3.	$\Box xRy$	from 2 by the principle at issue
4.	$\mathscr{R}!x$	from 3
5.	$\Diamond(x = z)$	assumption (z otherwise arbitrary)
6.	$\mathscr{R}!z$	from 4, 5 by the above principle
7.	If xRy, then $(\forall z)[\Diamond(x = z) \rightarrow \Box zRy]$	from 1–6

Accordingly, the internality thesis and the essentiality-of-relations principle are interdeducible with one another, and are consequently effectively equivalent.

This argument vividly clarifies how the thesis at issue proposes to construe "the internality" of a relation in the nature of a thing. To say that a relation is *internal* to a thing comes down to saying that the corresponding relational property is *essential* to this item, that it is a necessary aspect of what makes the thing into the thing it is. The operative question is that debated between idealists like Bradley and their opponents (especially W. James, G. E. Moore, and B. Russell) as to whether "the same thing" could, without losing its identity, enter into a variety of different relations—"different", that is, from its actual ones. The pivotal issue is accordingly related to hypothetical reasoning: could we meaningfully suppose of a given thing that *it*, this selfsame individual, might be related to others in ways different from those that actually obtain.

According to G. E. Moore,[4] the adherents to the "dogma" of internal relations (as he terms it) confuse two constructions of the basic thesis that "If R be a relational property and A a term which has it ... then anything which had not had R would necessarily have been different from A."[5] The two alternatives include both the construction (R being any relational property):

$$(1) \quad (\forall x)\,\square[Rx \to (\forall y)(\neg Ry \to y \neq x)]$$

and also its very different cognate

$$(2) \quad (\forall x)[Rx \to (\forall y)\,\square(\neg Ry \to y \neq x)].$$

The sole—but crucial—difference here is that of the variant internal placement of the necessity operator. For (1) is an altogether harmless consequence of the standard rules of identity, while (2) has the striking (and eminently debatable) consequence:

$$(\forall x)\,(Rx \to \square Rx).$$

The "dogma" of internal relations arose, so Moore maintains, from a wrong-headed confusion of these two distinct principles, mistaking the very dubious (2) for the quite harmless (1).

But, of course, the remark that this modal fallacy *could* have given rise to the doctrine by no means shows that it actually did so, and thus—curiously enough!—Moore's contention that the thesis (or "dogma") arose from a modal fallacy itself commits the modal fallacy of arguing from "could have" to "did." In any case, the key point remains that the core issue of the internality of relations doctrine is that of the essentiality of relational properties.

[4] "External and Internal Relations" in *Philosophical Studies* (London, 1922), pp. 276–309.

[5] *Ibid.*, pp. 283–4.

One obstacle must be set aside right at the very outset. In considering the possible essentiality of relations—of their indispensable entry into the very defining description of a thing —it is important to avoid reasoning along the following lines:

Relations must not be allowed to enter into the identificatory description of things. For the nature of the terms is a necessary precondition for a relational property even to obtain. Hence unless the terms are *first* identified we cannot possibly relate them. Thus relations are always accidental addenda to terms whose nature must *already and antecedently* be given.

This reasoning leads to the principle: "Things first and relations later." Such a temporalizing of the issue makes the mistake of thinking in causal terms about a strictly logico-conceptual issue. There is no reason why the terms and their relations cannot be specified *coordinately*, the terms being identified on the basis of (at least partly) relational information (as "the taller of the two look-alike girls we met yesterday" identifies the girl at issue in predominantly relational terms—"taller," "look-alikes"). After all, we are perfectly content to individuate things descriptively (at least in part), and have no inclination towards a principle "Things first and properties later," recognizing that the primrose path to bare particulars goes along this route.

2. THREE ALTERNATIVE DOCTRINES REGARDING THE ESSENTIALITY OF RELATIONS

It is clear that there are three basic alternative positions one could assume with respect to the internality of relations:

(1) Relations *must* be internal: *all* of the relational properties of a real, actually existing thing are (inevitably) essential to it:

$$(AR)(\forall x)(\forall y)[xRy \supset \Box xRy].$$

This is the *Doctrine of Internal Relations* in its traditional standard, strong version.

(2) Relations *cannot* be internal: *none* of the relational properties of a real thing are ever essential to it:

$$(AR)(\forall x)(\forall y)[xRy \supset \neg \Box xRy].$$

This is the *Doctrine of the Externality* (*or Accidentality*) *of Relations*, maintaining the inevitable inessentiality of relations.

(3) Relations *may or may not* be internal: *some* of the relational properties of a real thing will (or may) be internal to it, but others not:

$$(ER)(\exists x)(\exists y)(xRy \;\&\; \neg\,\Box xRy) \;\&\; (ER)(\exists x)(\exists y)(xRy \;\&\; \Box xRy).$$

This is the *Doctrine of the Contingency of Relations*, maintaining that relations may or may not be essential to their terms.

Before addressing ourselves to the question of the respective merits of these alternative doctrines, let us first consider the consequences that ensue from them. Presumably this exploration will prove of significant help in resolving the former issue.

3. THE DOCTRINE OF INTERNALITY

A relation might be characterized as internal with respect to some (arbitrary) possible world if, whenever it obtains among individuals of this world, it does so of necessity:

$$R \in \text{Int}(w) \text{ iff } (\Pi x)(\Pi y)[(x \in w \;\&\; y \in w) \supset Rw(xRy \supset \Box xRy)]$$

The doctrine of the internality of relations holds that every relation is internal with respect to the actual world.

The import of the doctrine of internal relations is seen in clearer relief against the backdrop of the preceding considerations. It maintains that all of the relationships of each real thing to every other are "internal" to its nature. The flavor of this position may be conveyed by the following passage from Blanshard:

This stone *is* unique. What makes it so is a set of relations that fix its connection with everything else in the universe. Omit these relations, all of them or indeed any of them, and you omit *some part of that which makes this stone what it is*. And with this you have admitted that it is related internally to everything else.[6]

Now if this is so—if *all* of a thing's relationships are essential

[6] Brand Blanshard, *The Nature of Thought*, Vol. II (London, 1939), p. 487.

to it—then we arrive at the upshot that *nothing can possibly differ from what it is in any respect.* The path leading to this result must be traced in detail.

To begin with, it is critically important to distinguish between abstractly *generic* and concretely *substantive* relations. A relation among individuals is *generic* if it involves no reference to any *particular* thing: "being like *something* in point of *F*" and "having *F* if *anything* else does" are examples. A relation is *substantive* if it does involve reference to a particular: "being like *a* in point of *F*" and "having *G* if *b* does" are examples.

Now if we take the view that *all* of a thing's relationships are essential to it—the substantive ones specifically included—then clearly, nothing whatsoever can be altered by any (viable) modificatory hypothesis. A single example suffices to make this clear. Consider a microworld containing individuals x_1, x_2, x_3, etc., the first two of which answer to the following descriptions:

	F	G	H
x_1	+	+	−
x_2	−	+	+

Now since x_1 will have (*ex hypothesi*) the relational property $(\lambda x)(Fx \,\&\, \bar{F}x_2)$, "being unlike x_2 in point of its lack of *F*," we cannot—if *all* the relational properties of a thing are to be essential to it—suppose x_2 to have *F*, since this would undo an essential property of x_1. And the same holds for x_1's x_2-agreeing possession of *G* and x_2-differing lack of *H*. Moreover, exactly the same situation will obtain with regard to all other individuals of our microworld. Under the hypothesis in view, one consequently cannot suppose a world in which x_1 is retained in the full panoply of its concrete relationships to other things while its environing world altered in *any* respect. Nor could we alter x_1 itself in any particular, since this would also abrogate existing relationships.

Insofar as its *concretely* substantive relationships are essential to an individual, a necessitarian essentiality thus spreads across the whole area covered by these relationships. And if *all* of these are to be essential, this serves to fix the entire world to which the thing belongs in an altogether necessitarian manner, unalterable by any hypotheses that remain within the limits of the possible. We are led to the logical determinism of necessitarian idealists like Bradley, McTaggart, and Blanshard, that all things are as they are of necessity—that everything must be just as it is, and that if *anything* were hypothetically changed from what it is, then *nothing* could remain the same. (It is, of course, hypothetical modification rather than temporal alteration that is here at issue with "change." We are not now concerned with the views of these authors on temporal processes.)

Accordingly, the doctrine of the internality of relations leads straightaway—when taken in its strong and unrestricted form—to the Leibnizian thesis that if anything in the world were different, no matter in how seemingly insignificant a respect, then *everything* would have to be different. One thus arrives at an utter rigidity of concatenation: that the full description of a single individual (with "full" construed to cover *all* of its relationships—specifically including the substantive ones) determines altogether the full description of every other individual in its environing world.

But there is, of course, a kind of cheat about this version of the doctrine, deriving from its admission of *substantive* relations, through which the features of other specific individuals are covertly introduced. Let us consider the seemingly different situation that ensues when we construe the doctrine of the internality of relations to operate in terms of *generic* relationships alone, holding merely that all the generic relationships of an individual are (inevitably) essential to it.

Suppose that x has ϕ, and that there is at least one other individual in its world, say y. Let it be that y lacks ϕ. Then x has the generic relational property of "being unlike *something* in point of this thing's lack of ϕ." And if this generic relational property is essential to x, then so is its possession of ϕ. If, on the other hand, y has ϕ, a similar argument is readily constructed. Accordingly, x's possession of ϕ (and so of any one of its properties) must be essential to it. The exclusion of substantive relations does not mend matters.

However, certain significant differences remain between these two versions of the internality doctrine: In the restricted version we can at least generally *annihilate* individuals and add novel supernumeraries (at any rate as long as (1) we do not allow a thing's existence to qualify as one of its properties, and (2) we stick to the everything/something mode of generality, and do not introduce *numerically determinate* relations of the type: "is like exactly 3 other things in also having ϕ").

4. THE DOCTRINE OF EXTERNALITY

Let us turn now to the Doctrine of the Externality of Relations, according to which all relations are always and invariably accidental. Now this is clearly infeasible in principle once we are prepared to recognize *any* properties of individuals as essential. For if (say) ϕ is essential to x and $\bar{\phi}$ essential to y then x and y will clearly stand in the relation of "being dissimilar in point of ϕ." And this relational property must (under the assumption at issue) be recognized as essential. Thus the position at issue can scarcely be maintained. In the absence of sharp qualifications and drastic restrictions, the doctrine of the inevitable accidentality of relations cannot be taken seriously.

5. THE CONTINGENCY VIEW

There now remains the contingency view, the weak thesis that relational properties are essential to a thing in *some* cases, but not inevitably so. The effect of this position is to *restrict and circumscribe* the ways in which hypothetical changes in the other things that populate the environing world of a given thing can be made—yet without blocking all such changes totally as a matter of principle.

For the sake of a concrete example, consider a microworld of three individuals answering to the following descriptions:

	F	G	H
x_1	$+$	$[+]$	$+$
x_2	$+$	$+$	$[-]$
x_3	$[-]$	$[-]$	$+$

Note that x_1 also has, quite apart from the properties indicated in its description as an isolated individual, the (derivative) relational property of "being like another individual in point of F-ness (i.e., with regard to having or lacking F)," that is, $(\lambda x)(\exists y)$ $(y \neq x \ \& \ [(Fx \ \& \ Fy) \vee (\bar{F}x \ \& \ \bar{F}y)])$. Let it now be further supposed that *this* property not only characterizes x_1, but is *essential* to it. Observe the consequences. We know from the given characterization of our (hypothetically real) microworld that the descriptions of possible individuals conform to the following inventory of actual-variant descriptive specifications:

	F	G	H	x_1	x_2	x_3	
1.	+	+	+	x_1^0			NOTE $x_1^0 = x_1$
2.	+	+	−	x_1^1	x_2^0		NOTE $x_2^0 = x_2$
3.	+	−	+				
4.	+	−	−		x_2^1		
5.	−	+	+	x_1^2			
6.	−	+	−	x_1^3	x_2^2		
7.	−	−	+			x_3^0	NOTE $x_3^0 = x_3$
8.	−	−	−		x_2^3	x_3^1	

As regards the formation of possible worlds from the possible individuals at issue here, we know, of course—by the fundamental rules of metaphysical compossibility—that we cannot *conjoin* x_1^1 and x_2^0 in one selfsame world, nor x_1^3 and x_2^2, nor x_2^3 and x_3^1. But now the particular essential relationship in view (viz., that any x_1-surrogate must be like *something* else in point of F-ness) also dictates that we cannot form a "possible world" from just the three individuals x_1^1, x_2^2, x_3^1. Various *prima facie* possible microworlds are thus ruled out by x_1's *essential* possession of the relational property in view. Nor could we have any possible world in which x_2 is annihilated, and some surrogate for x_1 combined only with some x_3-surrogate. (Though we could, of course, for all that has been said, unproblematically annihilate x_1 itself.)

6. THE QUESTION OF ACCEPTABILITY

To this point, however, we have simply considered the consequences of alternatives. The basic question of the essentiality of relations remains open, and we are still left with the problem of whether to take the position that relations are always, never, or only sometimes to qualify as essential. First off, it warrants remark that, quite on general principles, neither of the two extreme positions—that relations are *always* essential or that relations are *never* essential—exercise a great appeal. In fact, each has serious systematic shortcomings and engenders unfortunate repercussions in other areas of the metaphysical terrain.

The total-internality view of relations leads to the consequence that *all* of the properties of an individual are essential to it, so that one must forego altogether any prospect of maintaining that individuals can endure in the face of hypothetical alterations. On the other hand, the total-accidentality view of relations also leads to clearly unacceptable consequences (as implicitly indicated above).

But in the final analysis, the issue of the internality of relations is not so much one of correctness or incorrectness, but rather one relating to the wider theoretical ramifications of metaphysical systematization. What is needed is a sort of cost-benefit analysis of the consequences of alternatives. It becomes a matter of balancing the relative advantages and liabilities of the various possibilities off against one another.

The most crucial single fact is that there just is no *a priori* reason for treating relational properties differently from the ordinary, nonrelational ones in point of essentiality. It is, accordingly, well advised to return to the basic rationale for accepting certain properties as essential, and to use these considerations to govern our stance towards relational properties as well. After all, we have already committed ourselves—through the deliberations of Chapter II—to regarding the *modus operandi* of essentiality, and are at this stage no longer free to choose unconstrainedly how the ideas of essentiality and accidentality are to apply. For there is no good reason to refrain from applying these general considerations regarding the essentiality of properties in the present relational context. On this uniformitarian approach—uniform, that is, as between relational and nonrelational properties—one would adopt a policy of treating the essentiality of relational properties exactly as it was proposed to treat that of properties-in-general in the initial discussion of the problem. One would thus count a relational property of an (actual) individual as essential to it if some circumstance such as the following obtained:

(i) the relational property obtains in all the "canonical" descriptions of the (actual) individual at issue[7]

(ii) the relational property is needed to maintain the descriptive differentiation of the (actual) individual at issue from its fellows in the actual world.

(iii) the relational property is part of the typology of the taxonomic framework of descriptive identification that is in operation with respect to the range of individuals at issue and serves a natural part of the machinery by which we identify these items.[8]

All of these criteria simply apply to the special case of relational properties the various descriptive/identificatory approaches to property-essentialism treated in Chapter II. This even-handed approach certainly seems the natural way to view relational properties, and there are no theoretical grounds of general principle for departing from it.

It is worth stressing in relation to items (i) and (ii) that a thing might well be *identified* on the basis of relational properties alone, as "the one and only thing that bears the relation R to anything in the world." To be sure, it would in general be a *contingent* fact that this formally definite description succeeds in identifying. In theory, the case of several things bearing R to others could presumably always be contemplated. But this is unimportant when we are concerned to identify things within the *actual* world, for there is no need to seek a logically necessitarian guarantee of uniqueness in those cases where *de facto* uniqueness is present and is sufficient to the communicative purposes in hand. Thus when Brand Blanshard argues that "no finite set of relations confirms uniqueness" because uniqueness ensues "only when we shall have exceeded the bounds of all

---

[7] It follows that if one accepts P. F. Strawson's thesis that certain locational (spatiotemporal) relationships of (actual) particulars are requisite for their individuation, then these spatiotemporal features would, on the present approach, be essential to the individuals, and so represent internal relations. This points back to a dispute of earlier days: the internality of specifically spatial relations as affirmed by F. H. Bradley, *Appearance and Reality*, 2nd ed. (Oxford, 1897), pp. 575–6, and polemicized against by W. James, *Essays in Radical Empiricism* (New York, 1922), pp. 111–16.

[8] See Section 2 of Chapter II for other comparable approaches to essentiality.

possible repetition, and exhausted the relations of the thing to everything else in the universe,"[9] he fails to do justice to the crucial fact that within the context of a *given* world the demand for *logical* guarantees is wholly superfluous for identificatory purposes since *the facts of the case* will here presumably suffice to provide all the uniqueness that is needed.[10] As long as logical guarantees are neither issued nor demanded, there are no grounds for denying relations the power to play an identificatory role—strictly on a plane with that of properties.

It is clear that, on this strategy of assimilating the issue of the essentiality of relational properties to that of properties in general, relations can turn out to be either essential or accidental. In consequence, we reject the doctrine of internal relations in its strong classical version as well as the antithetical doctrine of the (invariable) accidentality of relations. One is accordingly led to the contingency view, taking the stance that while some of its relations will be essential to a thing, others may well fail to be so.

7. THE UPSHOT

The tenor of our position regarding relations is thus uniformitarian. It maintains a strict parity of condition: relational properties stand on the same footing as regards their essentiality (of "internality") as do properties in general, and what is sauce for the qualitative goose remains so for the relational gander. This position may not give adherents to the theory of internal relations everything they want, but it does not send them away altogether empty-handed. Their principal point, surely, was that a thing's relational properties are *just as internal* to its nature as its absolute or qualitative properties are. This is exactly our own position. And it does not lead automatically to a universal necessitarianism of relations, unless one *also* happens to hold the relation-ignoring thesis that all the qualities of a thing are

---

[9] *The Nature of Thought*, Vol. I (London, 1939), pp. 627–39.

[10] This penchant for *logical* guarantees of uniqueness in discussions of individuation even invades various recent discussions that avowedly endeavour to treat descriptively of our actually operative conceptual mechanisms for dealing with this actual world. (One case in point is P. F. Strawson, *Individuals* [London, 1959].)

essential to it, as we ourselves do not—though most of the traditional internal relationists did so (e.g., Leibniz, Bradley, Bosanquet, McTaggart, Blanshard).

We arrive at the following upshot. Two theses are at issue as components of the traditional idealist view:

I. *Internality of Relations (Proper)*
Relational properties are in general just as "internal" (essentialistic) as qualitative (non-relational) ones.

II. *Qualitative Necessitarianism*
All of a thing's qualitative (non-relational) properties are essential to it.

Only by *combining* these two theses did the idealistic internality-of-relations theorists arrive at the view that each of its relational properties is essential to a thing. But their characteristic parity thesis (No. I) can certainly be maintained in separation from their determinism thesis (No. II), and this is precisely the course we ourselves advocate.

Thus our approach does certainly and admittedly depart from the position of the traditional internality-of-relations theorists. In rejecting their thesis that all properties (categorical and relational alike) are essential to an individual, it opens up the prospect of alternative versions of an individual capable of existing within different world-environments. This step of permitting one selfsame individual to exist within different world-contexts—to continue self-identical in the face of hypothetical alterations in the world—represents a marked and decisive departure from the traditional form of the theory of internal relations. And indeed, this departure is crucial for the workings of our constructivistic approach. If we are going to proceed by determining individuals in the first instance in isolation, and only then, subsequently, to proceed to form worlds out of antecedently determined individuals, then we cannot readily take the view that the individuation of individuals invariably involves questions about the whole world-context within which they are to be positioned.

8. METAPHYSICAL INCOMPOSSIBILITY RECONSIDERED

Once *any* of its relationships are recognized as internal (essential) to a given thing, one has the upshot that a hypothetical change in *another* thing may reflect back upon it. Thus if "being alone in point of $\bar{G}$-ness" were taken as essential to some individual, we could not introduce any other G-lacking possible individual dual into a possible world without deleting the initial individual from it altogether.

Accordingly, the net effect of stipulating the essentiality of certain relations of an individual is to delimit the set of those possible worlds (i.e., *prima facie* possible worlds) into which this individual can be fitted. In effect, an essential relation circumscribes the environmental changes that are feasible, restricting the range of variant forms of *other* individuals with which the individual endowed with this relational property is mutually compatible. An internal relation accordingly restricts the compossibility of a given individual with the intrinsically feasible variant forms of others. In this sense, internal relations call for the mutual accommodation of the alternative descriptive forms of individuals. The effect is—and it is obvious enough—that the essentiality of relational properties augments the conditions under which individuals can cohabit one selfsame world—i.e., qualify as mutually compossible.

Our initial extralogical (metaphysical) rules of compossibility can now be reconsidered from this angle of approach. So regarded, they can be reinterpreted as simply specifying certain essential relationships:

Modes of Incompossibility Blockage	*Relational Essentiality-Condition*
1. Descriptive uniqueness (in the C.D.S. sense)	It is essential to every non-actual individual that it differ descriptively (i.e., with respect to its C.D.S.) from every other individual of its world.
2. Uniqueness of surrogacy	It is essential to every actual-variant individual that it not share a prototype with any other individual of its world.

3. Uniqueness of prototype   It is essential to every actual-variant individual that it have no more than one prototype in the real world.

In taking this route of reinterpreting compossibility-conditions in relational terms—as representing certain *universally and automatically essential* relational properties—it becomes feasible to absorb the metaphysical stipulations at issue within the essential relational properties of individuals, with the result of effecting a descriptive internalization of the compossibility-stipulations. In this way it becomes possible to effect a substantial reduction in the formal complexity of our apparatus. For now, the complex proceeding of maintaining a separate mechanism for M-possibility/incompossibility is done away with at one stroke, and the basic mechanisms of E-possibility/incompossibility are made to do the whole job. This reduction to one uniform mode of individual-characterizing impossibility (viz., E-impossibility) —one that is inevitable *in any case*—is clearly an attractive step.

However, it warrants note that in availing ourselves of this step as conducive to procedural uniformity and simplicity, we also commit ourselves to the position that some, at least, among the relational properties of a thing must *inevitably* be counted as essential to it. *The rules of metaphysical compossibility amount in effect to the stipulation that certain of its relations are always essential to an individual.* And by this route we are brought to espouse, at least in an attenuated form, the historic doctrine of the internality of relations.[11]

---

[11] While it is in fact helpful to look on the relationships that make for M-necessity as being actually necessary *per se* (E-necessary)—and so to assimilate metaphysical and logical compossibility—this step would *not* be coequally unproblematic with those that underwrite D- or N-necessity, since this would render as essential (and hence E-necessary) features that ought properly to be kept at the contingent level.

Chapter XI

A CONCEPTUALISTIC METAPHYSIC OF POSSIBILIA

I. THE CONSTRUCTIVE THEORY OF POSSIBILITY

The constructive theory of possibility presented here envisages the manifold of "merely possible" things as an intellectual *construct*. The starting-point of this construction is given by a theoretically informed view of "the real world," as produced in the empirical and scientific study of nature. This picture of the actual has three prime components: (A) an inventory of the (actual) *individuals*, (B) an essentialistically laden description of the actual in terms of (i) their *absolute* and (ii) their *dispositional properties*, and (C) a specification of the *laws of nature* (correlative with the preceding item), laws being viewed as universally (or quasi-universally) essential dispositions. Beginning with such a basically descriptive (albeit "theory-laden") account of the real, we then give "free rein" to the unfettered imagination in the exfoliation of combinatorial variations in its description. The manifold of alternative possibilities is viewed as answering to a descriptive elaboration of this sort. Alternative possible worlds are viewed as emerging from such an initial picture of reality through a process of intellectual construction proceeding by way of hypothetical alteration in the characterization of the real within the limits of admissibility.

The "realm of the possible" accordingly corresponds to a rational construction from descriptive mechanisms derived from and attuned to the characterization of the actual. The whole construction is, moreover, subject to the implicit constraint that the fundamental taxonomic scheme for the descriptive machinery of individual-characterizing properties is something fixed and given. The manifold of possibilia is thus viewed as the product of an intellectual construction carried out subject to certain empirically determined constraints. Above all, when our concern is with *genuine* (i.e., nomic) possibility, we impose explicitly the constraint that the actual laws of nature must continue invariant in any world that is to qualify as "genuinely," that is, *nomically* possible.[1]

2. THE GRADES OF POSSIBILITY

This theory of possibility is predicated upon a contextualistic or relativistic understanding of this concept, one according to which the possible is what is logically consistent with a certain body of stipulated fact. This basic "body of stipulated fact" can, of course, be fixed with reference to rather different sorts of stipulations (e.g., those delimiting the population of things in the world, the descriptive features of things, the laws of nature, etc.). The following tabulation categorizes the cases relevant for present purposes:

	GRADES OF POSSIBILITY		
	Change of the real population of individuals	Alterations in the descriptive make-up of the real	Modifications of the really operative laws of nature
1. actuality $(w*)$	−	−	−
2. (case impossible)	−	−	+
3. reality-transforming possibility	−	+	−
4. nomic anomaly	−	+	+
5.⎱ (negligible cases)	+	−	−
6.⎰	+	−	+
7. reality-transcending possibility	+	+	−
8. "merely logical" possibility	+	+	+

KEY: +for occurs
−for does not occur

NOTES: Cases 2 and 6 are impossible because we cannot change the laws (= quasi-universal dispositions)

---

[1] To say this is not, of course, to deny that different laws might obtain in other, more remotely "possible" worlds.

without to *some* extent altering the descriptive make up of the real. When the laws change, we must either *alter* the description of the actual individuals (Case 4) or else *replace* them altogether (Case 8). Cases 5 and 6 are negligible because we cannot retain the descriptive make-up of reality in the face of a replacement of its population, except by the trivial route of description-interchanges.

Throughout, we assume the posture that our theory is entitled to take Category 1 for granted. Categories 4 and 8 are of mitigated interest because they are "far-fetched"—in giving up the fabric of the actual laws of nature we go outside the realm of *genuine* possibilities. The cases that interest us primarily are Categories 3 and 7, in both of which we are concerned with "nomic" (i.e., law-of-nature retaining) possibility. The former deals with this "nomically realistic" sector of **v**, the latter with the case where such **s**-elements are involved. (The "unrealistic" rest of **v** and **s** are relegated to Categories 4 and 8 respectively.)

With Category 3 of "reality transforming" possibilities one assumes that the actual laws of nature continue operative and merely change the "boundary values" in the descriptions of real things. Here one has to do with *hypothetical alterations of the real* subject to constraints (viz., the retention of natural laws). However, this pivotal case splits into two major subcategories, according as we do or do not restrict the changes at issue to those relating to the inherent potentialities of the real. Accordingly, we obtain the split of Category 3 into two compartments:

3A: Potentialistic Reality-Transformations
3B: "Purely Hypothetical" Reality-Transformations

With Category 7 of "reality transcending" possibilities we again assume that the laws of nature continue operative, but now envisage changes in the *population* of individuals. We do not confine ourselves to dealing with existing things (in operating upon them with hypotheses modifying their descriptive make-up), but introduce a genuinely "new world" with altogether different things.

The net effect of these distinctions is that three major sorts of possibilities must be distinguished:

(1) Category 3A: the *unrealized potentialities* of the real inherent in the actual dispositions of things (e.g., this crushed acorn could really have grown into an oak).

(2) Category 3B: *speculatively counterfactual* possibilities which involve some wholly hypothetical changes in the properties of actual things unrelated to their operative dispositions (*you* might also be here in this room in addition to myself, though you aren't).

(3) Category 7: the *merely hypothetical* or *wholly fictional* possibilities that call for more than mere rearrangements of the characteristics of the actual, but deal with altogether nonexistent things (there might be an elephant in the room—and, at this, not just one of the actually existing ones—though there isn't).

Various strata of unrealized possibility must accordingly be discriminated. With fictions of the lowest level, the *dramatis personae* continue to be the real things of this world, doing things which, while they did not actually do them, were *genuinely* possible for them (Category 3A). At the next stratum we also deal with real things, but now cast them in roles which are too far-fetched to count as *really* possible for them (Category 3B). Finally, we arrive subjected to some hypothetical transformation, the level of the *wholly* fictional, where we deal not with actual things at all, but with "mere figments of the imagination," operating at a level where "any resemblance to actual things— past, present, or future—is purely coincidental." The distinctions operative here should by now be clear because this separation of possibilities into the "near" and the "remote" has already been dealt with at some length.

3. THE ONTOLOGY OF UNREALIZED POSSIBILITY

The issue of prime present concern can be posed in very old-fashioned terminology: What is the ontological status of non-existent possibles? How, for example, can it be said without contradiction that "there are" certain possibilia when it is said in the selfsame breath that they are *just* possibilities, and so unreal and nonexistent? In what manner do such possibilities have the "being" that is claimed for them when it is said that "they are real possibilities," since they *ex hypothesi* lack real being, i.e., existence?

Ontology—the theoretical study of the concepts revolving around such verbs as "to be" or "to exist"—is no mere logicians' game carried on for its abstract interest alone. Indeed, the ontology of possibility is of special importance—for unless the problems that arise here are somehow clarified and resolved, one cannot get an adequate account of supposition and assumption. For in the absence of a workable theory of unactualized possibles, we could not have a satisfactory mechanism for the rational manipulation of such hypothetical inferences as: "Assume the tiger in that cage were actually a unicorn; then ...." And note that our concern is not with the existential status of the *proposition* "that the unicorn is in the cage" (*qua* proposition), but rather relates to the existential status of the state of things that this proposition claims to obtain.

But just exactly what can the existential status of such possible-but-unrealized states of affairs possibly be? Clearly—*ex hypothesi*—the states of affairs or things at issue do not *exist* as such: only *actual* things or states of affairs can unqualifiedly be said to exist, and not those that are possible but unrealized. By definition, as it were, only the *actual* will ever *exist* in the world, and never the unactualized possible. For the world does not have two existential compartments, one including the actual and another that includes the unactual. Of course, unactualized possibilities can be conceived, entertained, mooted, hypothesized, assumed, etc. In this mode they do, in a way, exist—or "subsist" if one prefers—not, of course, unqualifiedly in themselves, but in a *relativized* manner, as the objects of certain intellectual processes. But it goes without saying that if their ontological footing is to rest on *this* basis—or anything like it—then they are clearly mind-correlative.

This critical point that the realm of the hypothetical things is mind-dependent must be argued in detail. Note to begin with that in the actual-existence cases we have the prospect of a dualism. There is:

(1) The actually and objectively existing thing or state of

affairs (e.g., with "that dogs have tails" we have the tailed dogs), and

(2) The thought or the entertainment or the assertion of this thing or state of affairs.

But with nonexistent possibilities (e.g., horned horses) the ontological situation becomes monistic, because item (1) is clearly lacking, since the things in question just do not exist. And this difference is crucial. For in the dualistic actual-existence cases, (1) would remain even if (2) were done away with. But with nonexistent possibles there is (*ex hypothesi*) nothing within (1) to remain, and so item (2) is determinative. Exactly this is the basis of the ontological mind-dependence of nonexistent possibles.

Our approach to the existential status of "the merely possible" is thus fundamentally conceptualistic, in that we take these possibilities to correspond to intellectual constructions, and thus to be of the status of *entia rationis* produced by certain characteristically mental processes. The move from possibilities to *possibilia* is seen to be correlative with supposition, assumption, and the like. The transition from adverbial that-possibilities of the *de dicto* variety, as with,

It is possible that there be an x that ϕ's: $\Diamond(\exists x)\phi x$

to substantive thing-possibilities of the *de re* variety, as with

There is a possible x that ϕ's: $(\Sigma x)\phi x$

is certainly feasible within the framework of our theory. For the reasoning is accomplished in the following stages:

(1) Let it be assumed that it is possible (*de dicto*) that there be an x that ϕ's: $\Diamond(\exists x)\phi x$

(2) By the Leibnizian principle that whatever is possible is realized in some possible world or other, $\Diamond P \equiv (Ew) Rw(P)$, this amounts to:

$$(Ew)Rw[(\exists x)\phi x]$$

(3) But by the construction procedure for possible worlds—and (R6) on p. 114—this is tantamount to

$$(Ew)(\Sigma x)[x \in w \ \& \ Rw(\phi x)]$$

which is equivalent with:

$$(\Sigma x)\phi x$$

Yet this transition from the *de dicto* $\Diamond(\exists x)\phi x$ to the *de re* $(\Sigma x)\phi x$ must be seen in the final analysis not as a process of logical inference at all, but as the product of the *intellectual construction* of the range of objects whose actuality, while absent *in fact*, is nevertheless capable of being *supposed*. The question: "But why speak of possible *things* at all; why give the issue an ontological dimension?" is thus answered by observing that things are correlative with possibilities through those conceptual mechanisms (like hypothesizing) by which a state of affairs can be arrived at (merely in the assumptive mode, to be sure) in which this possibility is realized. (A possibility that cannot be supposed as realized is not a possibility at all.) Accordingly, the bridge from adverbial to substantive possibility is inherently conceptualistic, and our transition to the *ontological* sphere is effected through the mediation of mind (by its capacity for hypothesizing, supposing, etc.).

As long as we remain on the side of *de dicto* possibilities ("It is possible that there be an x that ϕ's"), we do not yet encounter a possibilistic *thing*. (Though one does come *very* close to this with such a thesis as: $\neg(\exists x)\ (x = n)\ \&\ \Diamond(\exists x)\ (x = n)$, where '$n$' is a purportedly thing-referring expression.) But when we say "Let us then assume that this possibility is realized, so that there is an x that ϕ's; then of *this x* it may be said that. . .," then only here, at the level of supposition, assumption, postulation, hypothesizing, positing, etc., do we enter into the domain of *things*. For even as ostension is a thing-introducing move on the side of actualia, so supposition affords a thing-introducing move on the side of possibilia. Only with supposition (etc.) do we effect the sort of *incarnation hypothesis* that carries us from the arena of possibilities that there be such-and-such things—i.e., *de dicto* possibilities—over the threshold of the possible things that instantiate them (i.e., *de re* possibilities). The instrumentality of supposition (assumption, hypothesis, etc.) builds an effective and indestructible bridge from the sphere of *de dicto* possibilities to that of *de re* possibilia. But the things introduced by this inherently mentalistic process are inevitably mind-correlative—they cannot in the very nature of the case have an independent ontological standing outside the realm of mind. On this approach, then, the sole doorway through which entry can be made into the domain of possible individuals and possible worlds is that of a *Gedankenexperiment*: the "to be" of a possible individual or world is "to be projectible" in this way.

In dealing with the *ontology* of the merely possible, our concern is not clearly with the (very actual) *thought-of-the-possibility* but rather with the (by hypothesis unrealized) *possibility itself*, the utterly nonexistent state of affairs that is thought of. We must distinguish clearly between these two items:

    (i) the thought of the (nonexistent) possibility
   (ii) the (nonexistent) possibility thought of

When this distinction is duly observed, the "ontological" aspect of the matter becomes quite clear:

(A) The ontological status *per se* of entry (ii), the (mere) possibility at issue, is simply zero: *ex hypothesi* the item at issue—the X in view when we speak of "the mere possibility that X"—does not exist at all.

(B) Clearly entry (i), the thought of the possibility, exists unproblematically in the manner of thoughts in general. And while its object (ii) does not "exist" in reality, it does "exist" (or "subsist" or what have you) *as the object* of the thought.

(C) And then it becomes perfectly clear that *this* mode of "being"—not as a reality but solely as an object of thought—is mind-dependent.

The argument for the mind-dependency of hypothetical possibilities thus proceeds as follows: the world of mind-independent reality comprises only the actual. This world does not contain a region where nonexistent or unactualized possibilities somehow "exist." Unactualized hypothetical possibilities *ex hypothesi* do not exist in the world of objective reality at all. Nor is it feasible to hold that unactualized possibilities exist in some mind-accessible "Platonic" realm of (mind-independent) reality, existing wholly outside the world-order of natural actuality. Unactualized hypothetical possibilities lack an independent ontological footing in the sphere of objective reality: they can be said to "exist" in only a subsidiary or dependent sense—that is, only insofar as they are to be *conceived of* or *thought of* or *hypothesized* and the like. Their existence is confined to the intensional order: as the correlative objects of actual or potential thoughts (supposings, assumptions, hypotheses) *that something-or-other is so*. By hypothesis, the merely possible is unreal and does not form a constituent part of existential reality; the unreal is indeed *linked* to the real, yet not by way of inclusion, but only obliquely through the assumptive processes that minds deploy in framing suppositions, hypotheses, and the like. The key to the problem of their "ontological status" lies in the fact that the "existence" of unreal possibilities is limited by their role as objects of mental acts, so that their existential standing is mind-relative.[2]

This sketch presents the general strategy for holding that possibilities do not exist in some self-subsisting realm that is wholly "independent of the mind." The existential objectivity and autonomy of the real world does not underwrite that of the sphere of hypothetical possibility. Nature encompasses only the actual: the domain of the possible is the creation of intelligent organisms, and is a realm accessible to them alone. It is necessary always to start "from where we are" and the only route that leads from this, our actual world into the realm of possibilia is that of supposition, assumption, or the like. A "robust realism of physical objects" is all very well, but it just will not plausibly extend into the area of the hypothetical. It can plausibly be contended that it would be foolish (or philosophically perverse) to deny the thesis: "This (real) stone I am looking at would exist even if nobody ever saw it"; but one cannot reason by analogy to support the thesis: "This nonexistent but possible stone I am thinking of would be there even if nobody ever imagined it."

The fact that possible worlds are mentalistically *constructed* rather than somehow *given* for exploration means that, in a certain sense, they cannot contain genuine surprises—at any rate not for the authors of their projection. Of course, one could *assume* there to be a possible world with certain surprising features, exactly as with a work of fiction. But, however, much the fictional work may surprise its reader, it cannot surprise its author, any more than one could be surprised by the strategic

---

[2] To say this is not to drop the usual distinction between a thought and its object. If I imagine this orange to be an apple, I imagine it *as an apple* and not as an *imaginary* apple. But this does not gainsay the fact that the apple at issue *is* an imaginary apple which "exists only in my imagination."

plan deployed against one in playing a game of chess with one-self.[3] As R. C. Stalnaker very sensibly puts it:

> Writers of fiction and fantasy sometimes suggest that ima-ginary worlds have a life of their own beyond the control of their creators. Pirandello's six characters, for example, re-belled against their author and took the story out of his hands. The skeptic may be inclined to suspect that this suggestion is itself fantasy. He believes that nothing goes into a fictional world, or a possible world, unless it is put there by decision or convention; it is a creature of invention and not discovery. Even the fabulist Tolkien admits that Faërie is a land "full of wonder, but not of information." (J. R. Tolkien, "On Fairy Stories" in *The Tolkien Reader* [New York, 1966], p. 3).[4]

One point of caution is immediately necessary. We are not saying that to be a possible (but unactualized) thing requires that this must *actually* be conceived (or entertained, hypothesi-ized, etc.)—so as in fact to stand in relation to some *specific* mind. Rather, what is being said is that possible albeit un-realized *states of affairs or things* obtain an ontological footing—i.e., can be said to "exist" in some appropriately qualified way—only insofar as it lies within the generic province of minds to conceive (or to entertain, hypothesize, etc.) them. Unlike "actual" things that actually exist in their own right, unrealized possibilities exist only as objects of thought. Thus the ontological basis of "merely" possible states of affairs is mind-involving in this generic sense, that the very concept at issue is only viable in terms of conceptions whose proper analysis ultimately re-quires reference to the workings of minds. The "mere" or remote sorts of possibilities are inherently mentalistic because they root in the genuine and "near" possibilities of mental operation. The potentialities of mind for description, imagination, supposition, etc., is the only available locus of entry into the sphere of the merely possible.

---

[3] Of course, one can be surprised with unforeseen implicit consequences—in fictionalizing as in solitaire—but that's beside the point.

[4] "A Theory of Conditionals" in N. Rescher (ed.), *Studies in Logical Theory*, *American Philosophical Quarterly*, Monograph Series, No. 2 (Oxford, 1968), pp. 98–112 (see p. 111).

We have no desire to be pushed to the extreme of saying that the "being" of nonexistent "possible beings" lies in their being actually *conceived*; rather, we take it to reside in their being conceivable.[5] The "being" of an unactualized possibility does not inhere in its relation to this or that specific mind, but to its conceivability by mind-in-general, in terms of the linguistic resources that are a common capability of intelligence as we know it. This independence of any specific mind establishes the *objectivity* of nonexistent possibilities despite their mind-dependence. Just as an actual thing or state of affairs remains as such when not known, so an unactualized item is not affected if not conceived by any actual person. But this independence of specific minds does not render unactualized possibles independent of mind as such. Their mind-dependence is not a *particularistic* dependence upon a specific mind (as is that of a headache), but is *generic*: a dependence upon quintessentially mental processes and capabilities. (And, of course, generic mind-relatedness is mind-relatedness all the same.) On this perspective, then, the domain of unrealized possibility is an *intellectual projection* by mind-endowed beings, launched from a foothold in the realm of the real.

4. THE CONCEPTUALISTIC BASIS

There is plainly an absolute gulf fixed between reality and irreality, between the actual and the "merely possible." Our theory has it that this gulf can be crossed only by mentalesque acts of assumption and supposition. The sole entry-point into the realm of the unreal is via a *mind* that is capable of essentially imaginative processes like assuming, supposing, and the like. And this fact renders possibility as intrinsically mind-correlative —even the "natural possibility" inherent in the dispositional functioning of the real.

The earlier discussion (of Section 2) uncovered three strata of possibility:

[5] Or "conceivable subject to certain conditions" if genuine (e.g., physical) possibility is at issue. Note also that when the *possible* is coordinated with the *conceivable*, it is, of course, the *entire* range of possibility that is at issue, including both actualized and unactualized possibility: actual things are, of course, also conceivable. But *their* "being" cannot (*ex hypothesi*) be said to reside in this alone.

(1) *dispositional possibilities* inherent in the operational potentialities of the real,

(2) *"merely counterfactual" possibilities* involving the hypothetical variation of perfectly real things, and

(3) *purely hypothetical possibilities* involving altogether fictional things and states of affairs.

Our position is that category (1) is fundamental, and that all the variant forms of possibility are, in the final analysis, inherent in the functional potentialities of the real through the mediation of the dispositional capabilities of minds. Thus *reduction* is the key.

There is not and cannot be any "objective," mind-independent mode of *iffiness* in nature: objective states of concrete affairs must be categorical, they cannot be hypothetical (or—for that matter—disjunctive) in the final analysis. The introduction of the hypothetical mode requires—i.e., *conceptually* requires—reference to the mentalistic capabilities of assuming, supposing, or the like. Any careful analysis of possibility inevitably carries one back to the common theme that only the actual can objectively be real and that the modally variant areas of the possible and necessary depend essentially upon an invocation of mentalistic capacities.

The line of argument we have been taking may be summarized as follows:

(1) Possibility-talk is pointful only where the prospect of unrealized states of affairs is held in view.

(2) Unrealized states of affairs cannot be introduced upon the stage of consideration in any ostensive way; they must be introduced by way of assumption or hypothesis.

(3) This fact that the introduction of possibilities upon the stage of consideration inevitably calls for reference to some mind-involving capability renders the idea of possibility itself as conceptually mind-invoking (in the sense that a full-dress analysis of the meaning of this concept and its conditions of applicability ultimately drives one into making some reference to minds and their capabilities).

To a question like "Why should not the malleability of this lump of lead be every bit as real or objective as its shape or mass seemingly are?" we reply: "The issue is not one of *reality* at all, but of *objectivity*—if this 'objectivity' be construed as independence of any and all mentalistic aspect. Malleability is not just a matter of what the lead does but of *what it would do if*, and this introduces a suppositional or hypothetical element which can only be explicated in mind-invoking terms." No doubt the lead has the mind-invoking dispositional feature of malleability as a causal consequence of something it objectively and mind-independently *is*: its potentiality roots in its actuality—its "can-dos" are ultimately grounded in its "ises." But the very conceptual nature of potentiality rules out the prospect of viewing "objectively real possibility" as independent of any and all mind-invoking references, overt or covert, to the sphere of "what might be if."

Nobody wants to deny (nor is there any need for it) that there is a perfectly good sense of "possibility"—namely one articulated with reference to "the potentiality of the natural development of actual things"—in which acorns may possibly develop into oak trees but peanuts not. But the very nature of this possibility, like any other, is revealed by its conceptual unraveling to depend critically upon theses of the "what-would-happen-if" type. This claim is that: "Actual, *objective* reality (and this does and must come in explicitly) is such that if certain conditions were to be met then certain results would ensue." And just this essential reference to the consequences of the (*ex hypothesi* unrealized) meeting of "certain unactualized conditions" introduces a suppositional factor into the "objective" characterization of the properties of the acorn, so as to reveal this characterization as itself built up in mind-invoking terms. It merits reemphasis that the mind-dependency in view pertains strictly to the *conceptual* order. It is a matter of finding an implicit reference to minds in the analytical unpacking of the concepts at issue in what is being said. The key fact is that in the final analysis the iffiness of any possibilistic talk invokes "what would happen if" and so leads back into the mind-referring area of what can be supposed, hypothesized, assumed or the like.[6]

---

[6] Of course, even purely factual theses generate hypothetical consequences: e.g., if *a* has ϕ, then clearly "If something has ϕ, then it shares at least one property with *a*." But its having some mind-involving consequence is not

An objector may ask: "But why should we not say that there *really are* possibilities which determine the truth of possibility-claims just as there really are actualities determining the truth of actuality-claims?" To this one can but reply as follows: First off, we grant that the *existence* of the actualities at issue is unproblematic, since the "really is" of an actuality resides simply and straightforwardly in its existence. But this concession leads to the question: How could one conceivably construe the "really is" of the unrealized possibility in a parallel way, where the equation "really is" = "actually exists" is *ex hypothesi* broken? The "really is" of an unrealized possibility is intelligible only in hypothetical terms—with reference to suppositions and their consequences—and accordingly introduces an ineradicably mind-correlative factor. The crucial issue regards not *that* possibilities really are but *what* they really are, and relates to their nature and conceptual status.

Another possible objection must be dealt with:

> Your analysis of (unrealized) possibility in terms of suppositions and hypotheses is surely deficient. Anything that is *logically* possible may be supposed, but some things are *actually* possible and others not. Your approach avoids the issue of the truth or the reality of the possibility at issue. An acorn can properly be supposed to develop into an oak tree (even should it fail) but a peanut not.

This objection overlooks the crucial issue of the *background or context* of a supposition. Any discussion of what is possible proceeds against the background of a substantial body of continued and unaltered rational commitments—some view as to the fundamental facts regarding how things work in nature. Given that I want to retain the sizes of things, I cannot assume that there are 10,000 people in this room. Given that I want to retain *the basic facts as to how things work in the world,* I cannot assume peanuts develop into oak trees. The difference between "real" and "merely speculative" possibilities does *not* turn on

---

sufficient to establish the mind-involvingness of the thesis at issue, any more than its having some hypothetical consequences prevents a categorical thesis from being categorical. The operative issue is that of the analytical make-up of the thesis itself.

the fact that the latter are suppositional and the former not; *both* are in fact suppositional, although different contexts of background or frames of reference are operative with respect to the suppositions in the two cases.

Our approach does not obliterate the distinction between different types of possibility (e.g., near and remote), but prepares the ground for it. For it is held that possibilistic discourse is to be regarded as context-relative against a "background"—one that is empty when merely *logico-conceptual possibilities* are at issue, and variously filled in for the other cases. In the context of fixed invariants in the "background," some assumptions will obviously be blocked. And insofar as our standard conceptual scheme for viewing natural reality has a whole cluster of rather fundamental commitments, there will, of course, be many possibilities that one will have to dismiss as "merely speculative" and unable to qualify as "genuine possibilities."

The presently operative conception might thus be characterized as the *compatibility theory of possibility*: the logically possible is that which is compatible with itself; and all other modes of possibility (physical possibility, technical possibility, etc.) are matters of compatibility with some coordinated context of "background" stipulations (laws of nature, the technology of the time, etc.). We do not deny the existence of such significantly diverse modes of possibility as the "purely speculative" and the "natural," but insist that, because of their essentially hypothesis-invoking character, all of these types rest on assumptions, suppositions, etc., in such a way as to introduce the characteristic capabilities of minds upon the stage of consideration.

It cannot be overemphasized that the mode of mind-invocation at issue in our thesis regarding the mind-dependency of possibility is strictly conceptualistic. Thus, consider the objection that—"Surely it was possible before there were any minds in the universe that there should be minds; hence possibilities antedate minds and are accordingly not mind-dependent." This objection misses its target if aimed at our position. Its entire approach is altogether misleading. Our present preoccupation is not with a point of conjectural natural history, but is strictly *conceptual* in character. The conceptual unraveling of the idea of "hypothetical possibilities" demands deployment of mind-related conceptions. Thus the dependence at issue is conceptual and not causal. We are certainly not saying that the "real world" (the extra-mental world—whatever it is) somehow becomes different with the introduction of minds. The whole issue of historico-causal dependencies is entirely beside the point, and even to talk of a mental *creation* of possibility is to set up something of a straw man. Let it be granted—by way of analogy—that there were colors (in the sense of phenomenal colors) in the universe long before there were any sight-endowed beings; this in no way prevents phenomenal color from being *conceptually* sight-referring, e.g., that orange is the color a visually normal person sees when looking at an orange under normal conditions of lighting, etc. In fine, it is a *conceptual* dependency upon mind-referring notions, rather than any *causal* dependency upon the functionings of minds, that is at issue in our discussion. The mind-dependency of a possibility is *not* like that of a headache.

5. THE LINGUISTIC FOUNDATION OF UNREALIZED POSSIBILITY

The essential role of descriptive mechanisms in the identificatory specification of "mere possibilities" indicates the indispensable part played in this connection by the descriptive instrumentalities of our language—its stock of adjectives, verbs, and adverbs. Now while *these* are doubtless tied to reality, the link to reality is attenuated when we move from universals to particulars and from their features to the things themselves. Once we have enough descriptive machinery to describe something real (e.g., to describe this pen, which is pointed, blue, 6 inches long, etc., etc.), we are *ipso facto* in a position to describe nonexistents (e.g., a pen in other respects like this one but 10 inches long). It is in principle impossible to design a language whose descriptive mechanisms suffice for discourse about real things alone, without affording the means for introducing nonexistents into discussion (if only because any genuine language comprises the instrumentalities of negation). The mechanisms of reference to nonexistents are an inherent linguistic feature. Any linguistic vehicle for communication adequate to a discussion of the real cannot but burst the bounds of reality.

Nonexistent possibilities thus have an amphibious ontological basis: they root in the capability of minds to perform certain operations—to conceive or describe and to hypothesize (assume, conjecture, suppose)—operations to which the use of *language* is essential, so that both thought processes and language enter the picture.[7] Their foothold in language is the factor that gives to unrealized possibilities the *objective* ontological basis which they undoubtedly possess. *It is the actuality of minds capable of deploying by way of hypotheses and assumptions the descriptive mechanisms of language that provides the ontological basis of nonexistent possibilities.* For such possibilities can be said to "exist" only insofar as they are statable or describable in the context of their being supposed, assumed, posited, or the like. A "merely possible" individual is (*ex hypothesi*) not real; it is a *hypothetical* individual, a *supposed* individual, a *purported* individual—and all these italicized qualifications make manifestly clear the mind-referential character of the issue.

Possible *things* do not exist in their own right, but their existence is linked to the resources and processes of the actual world. Specifically, possibilia are "projected" by minds in a process that involves two elements: (1) the descriptive conceptualization of certain thing-specifications, and (2) the assumption (supposition hypothesis, etc.) of their actualization. This mind-relative sort of "being" is the only mode of existence to which possibilia can lay claim since (by hypothesis) they do not exist as such. On such a view, then, the only *existence* that characterizes nonexistent individuals and worlds is the "existence" they can have *for* the mind-endowed beings of this actual world who are capable of projecting (positing, supposing, hypothesizing imagining, conceiving, etc.) them.[8] To emphasize by repetition: the realm of possibilia (of possible objects and worlds) is the product of intellectual projection by thought-capable creatures from within the vantage point of the real.

[7] In this discussion we have taken a distinctly verbal (i.e., description-centered) view of unrealized possibilities. We have neglected, for example, the prospect of unreal things or states of affairs as presented quasi-visually (for example in hallucination). This is no serious deficiency because in such cases of illusion (rather than hypothesis) the mind-dependency aspect of the matter is all the more clear and noncontroversial.

[8] This mind-dependency ontology of possibilia contrasts with an existential neutrality theory according to which the "mere possibilities" of one world

Possible worlds, then are—in point of their "ontological status" or "mode of being"—the potential products of intellectual projections that can be made with respect to descriptive specifications by real-world beings possessed of such intellectual capacities as assumptions, hypotheses, or the like.[9] This conceptualistic approach to possible worlds is at odds with a realistic approach, such as that recently defended by David Lewis by the following argument:

> It is said that realism about possible worlds is false because only our own world, and its contents, actually exist. But of course unactualized possible worlds and their unactualized inhabitants do not *actually* exist. To actually exist is to exist and to be located here at our actual world—at this world that we inhabit. Other worlds than ours are not our world, or inhabitants thereof. It does not follow that realism about possible worlds is false. Realism about unactualized possibles is exactly the thesis that there are more things than actually exist.[10]

A realism that maintains, as Lewis insists, that "there are more things than actually exist" is simply wrong, for what it says just

---

exist as the realities of another. (Think, for example, of Jorge Luis Borges' idea that we ourselves might be fictions imaginatively projected by the real beings of another world.) The crucial fact remains that— whatever may be supposed as "existing for" the members of another world—since we ourselves are *in* this world we must also be *of* it, and cannot help taking a conceptualist stance towards other, from our vantage point, *unrealized* possibilities.

[9] This conceptualistic stance towards the *ontological status* of possible worlds does not block agreement with possible world realists as to their *nature*. Thus David Lewis writes: "When I profess realism about possible worlds, I mean to be taken literally. Possible worlds are what they are, and not some other thing. If asked what sort of thing they are, I cannot give the kind of reply my questioner probably expects. . . . I can only ask him to admit that he knows what sort of thing our actual world is, and then explain that other worlds are more things of *that* sort, differing not in kind but only in what goes on at them." (*Counterfactuals*, [Oxford, 1973], p. 85). There is nothing in this "realism-expounding" passage that cannot be accepted from the standpoint of the present "conceptualistic" approach.

[10] *Op. cit.*, p. 86.

is false. There simply *are* not more things than actually exist. But, of course, there *might* be—i.e., one could *defensibly assume* (*suppose* or *hypothesize*—but NOT *correctly state*) that there are. And just this assumptive aspect lies at the core of the conceptualism expounded here.

The quarrel reduces to this: We maintain that the only "existence" that unactualized possible worlds has a relativized *existence-for*, that is, for the assumption-capable beings of this real world; independent existence in their own right is not within their grasp. And it is difficult to see how the possible-world realist can dissent from this and concede to unrealized possibilities an "existence in their own right." To grant them such existence—not to be sure in this world, but somehow "in their own sphere"—is to be misled by the mistaken spatial analogy that something not in fact located in one realm must be located in another. But there exists only one real world—the actual one: there is no extant superworld in which various possible worlds can be existentially juxtaposed, the real one along with others.

Our view of the "ontology" of the matter can now be put into brief compass. *Ex hypothesi*, whatever is an *unrealized possibility* does not "exist" pure and simple. What exist are—*inter alia*—minds and their capabilities, and, so, accordingly, also languages and their rules. Unrealized possibilities are *projected* by minds, and so can be said to "exist" only in a secondary and dependent sense, as actual or potential objects of language-deploying thought. From this standpoint, the realm of (mere) possibility is seen as the correlative product of mentalistic capabilities. All the possibilities there are are possibilities that can in principle be "projected" from within the actual world.

To be a possibility is to answer, by way of supposition or hypothesis, to a certain description—one that is framed by means of the language-grounded taxonomic and nomic machinery designed to cope with "the real world." The entire manifold of possible things is the product of an *intellectual construction*. The ontological status of possibilities is thus fundamentally mind-dependent, the domain of the possible being a mental construct.

But consider the following line of objection which might be developed against this view.

You say that minds project possibilities (i.e., unrealized possibilities) through the use of language. Presumably, this means (*inter alia*) that possibilities are individuated as (potential) states of affairs corresponding to (certain) expressions of a language. Now, for one thing, this makes possibility relative to specific languages. And further, how can the contrast between the possible and the impossible then be preserved at all? Given the open and developmental character of languages, there is—quite possibly—nothing sayable that a "language" can't say. Metaphor and the other ways of extending a language by the diversified mechanisms of the symbolic process seemingly make the concept of "the unsayable" a dubious one. (And if the only contrast one can get is between that which can only be said *easily* in a language and that which can only be said complexly, then the matter of the "possibilities relative to the language" rests on a very shaky and unsatisfactory foundation.) Thus a conception of possibility in terms of the equation *possible = sayable* cannot have much discriminative bite to it.

Here the second part of the objection effectively answers the first: since, presumably, nothing sayable cannot in principle somehow be said in a language, the factor of language-relativity-to-*specific*-languages is removed. And as regards the second argument, the contrast-objection, there is just no warrant for making the pair possible/impossible run parallel the pair sayable/unsayable. Even the impossible may well be described or stated, and need not be altogether ineffable. The key consideration is not that the impossible cannot be said, but that it cannot be said without in the final analysis espousing some sort of absurdity or contradiction: that it cannot correspond to a "meaningful thought." And just this essential correlation with "meaningful thought" is the basis of the mind-dependence of the merely possible. To repeat: Unrealized possibilities are mind-dependent not because they can only be stated in language—that's trivial, *anything* can only be stated in language—but because they can only be said to "exist" in a secondary and dependent sense, as available objects of thought.

It must, of course, be recognized that language is a contingent phenomenon. Not only might existing languages be radically different from what they are—there might be no existing languages whatsoever. In that case, nonexistent possibles would appear to lose their ontological footing—no languages: no discussion, no discourse, no *entia rationis*. "But," so an objector might argue, "are nonexistent possibilia in fact as vulnerable as all that? Is the non-existence of nonexistent possibles a prospect we can meaningfully contemplate?" The objection rests on drawing an unwarranted consequence. It fails to heed one distinction between *speech* and *speakability*, between *discussion* and *discussibility*. Like yet unactualized possibilities, nonexistent possibles inhere in the very *possibility* of language: we need not conceive of their depending on the historical vagaries of actual language-use.

In this connection, too, it is worthwhile to return to the point of p. 62 above and recall that since there is nothing inherently finitistic about our linguistic resources, our thesis that possibilia inhere in the imaginatively projective proliferation of linguistic combinations does not impose upon them any conditions of finitude (or denumerability).

The position we have ourselves taken here with respect to the status of nonexistent possibles is thus a complex one. Basically its tendency is nominalistic, in that it finds nonexistent possibles to be rooted in the language-using capacity of minds. But it is also conceptualistic in embracing possible as well as actual languages, stressing the need to consider not only actual language-utterances, but also what is potentially utterable by language users. Indeed this emphasis on what is possible—on the *discussible* rather than more narrowly upon the *discussed*—even endows our seemingly nominalistic position with a faintly realistic coloration.

It is important to distinguish between mere possibilities at the wholesale level of generic reference (as in the claim "There may well be possibilities no one will ever think of") and at the retail level of specific and individuated possibilities (such as the possible red-haired man in the doorway). Our thesis is that any *instance* of possibilia—i.e., specific and individuated possibilities —must actually be projected by a hypothesizing mind because to identify or specify a possibility is to hypothesize it. But at the wholesale level of merely potential possibilities, it is generic conceivability rather than particularized conception that enters in. Here we are concerned not with the activities of this or that possibility-projecting mind, but with the possibility-projective capabilities of minds in general. The crucial point is that on our view individuated possibilities correspond to actual conceptual constructions and generic possibilities correspond to potential conceptual constructions.

A *rigoristic* conceptualism with reference to nonexistent possibilities, holding that for such possibilities *To be is to be conceived*—that their *esse* is *concipi*—is not an appealing position. The generically-oriented notion of *unthought-of-possibilities* is certainly too viable to be so easily dismissed. (Note that while "it is possible though not conceived" is a perfectly viable locution, "it is possible though not conceivable" is not viable, at any rate not in the *quasi-logical* rather than *psychological* sense of "conceivability" that is relevant to our present discussion.[11] For at the generic level of possibility—in contrast with the specific level of individuated possibilities—we are concerned not with what people will in fact conceive, but with what is conceivable-in-principle.) And nonexistent possibilities would seem to have a solidity and objectivity of status that we hesitate to subject to the vagaries of what is and is not in fact thought of. We have ourselves preferred to move in the direction of going from "to be *conceived*" to "to be *conceivable*"—construing this in a broad sense that includes imaging and imagining. And, once this approach has been purged of its psychological connotations, we have moved near to the nominalistic realm of what can be described and discussed, assumed and stated. For mind-involvement of possibility is not idiosyncratic or somehow bound up with the personal, private side of the "mental life" of people, but is entirely public and interpersonal through its objectification in language. Just here, in the sphere of linguo-centric considerations, we reach the ground which is in any rate most congenial to contemporary philosophers. The fashionably "modern" view that the ultimate foundation for nonexistent individuals is linguistic (in a broadly functional and potentialistic rather than strictly actualistic manner) comes close to returning in a full circle to the language-orientated

---

[11] Regarding the issue of psychologism that arises here see Chapter VIII of N. Rescher, *Essays in Philosophical Analysis* (Pittsburgh, 1969).

conceptualism expounded in classical antiquity by the Stoics in their theory of *lekta* ("meanings"). The problem of nonexistent possibles once more illustrates the fundamental continuities of *philosophia perennis*.

The conceptualistic construction of possibilities thus roots in the contingent features of the actual—viz., the actual capacities of actual minds. The whole of the construction rests on a basis (in terms of properties and laws) which is factual and contingent. (For neither the properties taken to characterize things, nor the laws taken to govern their behavior, are necessary in any absolutistic sense.) On such an approach, the manifold of possibilia is a rational construct carried out by means of reality-descriptive resources. And the materials of this conceptualistic construction are inherently contingent, precisely because they are ultimately reality-derived.

This line of thought appears to lie open to the serious-seeming objection that might be made along the following lines:

> You have made the horizons of the possible far too narrow in treating possible things (and hence possible worlds) as conceptual constructions exfoliated projectively from the machinery of actuality-description requisite for coping with the actual world. Science, after all, advances constantly into new regions of what previously was just *terra incognita*. The physics of Aristotle, of Newton, and of Einstein provide a substantial diversity of conceptual schemes, and possibilities can be envisioned in the later stages of knowledge that were beyond the grasp of the earlier. Why should we treat the present state of knowledge as final, and its correlative conceptual scheme as exhaustively determinative of the limits of the possible?

To begin with, it must be said that the only possibilities *for us* are those which can be projected in terms of *our* conceptual scheme. This point is trite and true, but also indecisive for present purposes. For as a matter of fact it is not being maintained that the *presently* conceptualizable possibilities are the only ones there are.

Caesar presumably could not imagine radiotelescopes. Our assumptive prospects are limited by the horizons of our conceptual framework. Care must be taken not to confine the boundaries of the possible to that which *we can imagine here and now*, but to that which can be imaginatively projected *überhaupt*. There are indeed more things in the realm of possibility than are dreamt of in our imaginings, but this fact does not detach the realm of possibility from that of assumptive conceptualization construed open-endedly across-the-board.

In thus rooting possibilities in the groundwork of a reality-oriented taxonomic and conceptual scheme, we arrive at a position where it makes perfectly good sense to say (in agreement with ordinary usage) that certain possibilities do not exist for a given individual because the conceptual means for their projection are beyond that person's reach, in exactly the same way that the technical means for the projection of certain possibilities (e.g., telephonic communication) lay outside the conceptual reach of Julius Caesar.

There is no question that it makes perfectly good sense to speak (of course, from an *epistemic* angle of approach) of "opening up new—and hitherto undreamt of—possibilities," and there are no grounds for denying present applicability to this historic prospect. We certainly need not limit the projection of possibilities to those *immediately* projectable from our actuality-oriented conceptual scheme, since other variant conceptual schemes might be supposed (though, of course, and this is important—the ultimate basis of these projections must always be our—actuality oriented—conceptual scheme). Nor even need we limit the basis of projectability to that millennially ultimate conceptual scheme to which our science may (or may not) attain in a Peircean long run. All these limitations construe our insistence on an actualistic basis in too actualistic terms. For the import of our present actualism should itself be construed in the possibilistic terms of the conceptualizing capacities and capabilities of actual beings. The crucial point is that in rooting the ontology of possible things in terms of what is "conceivable," we mean conceivable *per se*, and not "conceivable in terms of the conceptual mechanisms currently in hand." The charge of over-restrictedness articulated in the objection thus fails to tell against the position in view.

6. A PROBLEM OF CIRCULARITY

Does one not reason in some sort of a circle in saying that possibility (be it actualized or not) is tantamount to conceivability, something which in turn requires reference to the possible —to what *can be conceived*? Isn't the specification of possibility-in-general in terms of mentalistic possibilities a nonproductive circumambulation? Not really. For our position is not *circular* but *reductive*: its stance is that *all* possibilities are in the final analysis inherent in and derivative from mental possibility. We maintain that the "reality" of unrealized, *merely possible things and states of affairs* is dependent upon the reality of the possibility-involving processes of actual things viz., mind-endowed beings) through the *construction* of descriptions, and the hypothesizing (assuming, postulating) of their existence. It is maintained that when the-possibility-of-the-thing is its only "reality," then this "reality" inheres in a possibilistic intellectual process. Here, actuality is indeed prior to possibility—the actuality of one category of things (viz., minds with their characteristic modes of functioning) underwrites the *construction* of the totality of nonexistent possibles that can be contemplated.

Several key conclusions emerge from this standpoint. *Substantive* possibility, the possibility of altogether hypothetical unrealized states of affairs and things, is conceptually consequent upon *functional* possibility, the possibility inherent in the "can do" of processes and capabilities—specifically mentalistic ones. And at this stage we arrive at mind-involvement of an overt and blatant sort.

Mind-correlative possibilities are thus seen as being fundamental: the basic category of possibilities are possible *descriptions*—language-enshrined concepts—and are consequently items that are in substantial measure linguistic in nature (construing language in the broad sense of the symbolic process in general). Accordingly, whatever "being" or "quasi-reality" nonexistent possibilities have is consequent upon the actuality of minds and their modes of functioning, for it is based upon and derivative from a real functional potentiality of mental processes: the mental capacities for assuming, supposing, and the like. In affording the mechanisms of conceivability minds come to be functionally operative in such a way as to render the whole range of (mere) possibility as such mind-involving.

On this view, the fundamentality of mentalistic *capability* is the locus of the mind-dependency of possibility in general. Entity-possibility inheres in performance-possibility: the possibility of things derives from possibilistic processes. Our motto is: *Unrealized possibility ultimately roots in the mind-correlative capabilities of the real.* Thus while we hold that possible individuals and possible worlds are intellectual artifacts whose ontological status is that of mere *entia rationis*, we are certainly not committed to attributing such fictiveness to the operative possibilities inherent in the mode of functioning of real things. *Au contraire*, on our view this *functional* possibility provides the existential basis for the *substantive* possibility of unactualized *possibilia*.

7. RELATIONS OF THE REAL TO THE "MERELY" POSSIBLE

We must face the implications of a recognition of the contingency of the real. Reality is, of course, to be viewed as simply one among alternative possibilities: that one which *actually* happens to be realized (though not "*just* happens," since the reasons for this realization can presumably be inquired into). But does not this recognition of reality as simply one sector of the possible block a theory that sees the possible as derivative from the real? Not at all. The primacy of the actual lies in the *conceptual* order, not the order of explanation. There is no reason why, once we have the concept of alternative possibilities in hand, we cannot take the view that there is nothing *existentially* inevitable or necessary about the real world that precludes us from taking the view that *in the causal/explanatory order* it emerged contingently from a spectrum of possibilities. On this view, the Aristotelian dictum that "actuality is prior to possibility" applies in the *conceptual* and not necessarily in the *explanatory* order.

Once one has used the real as a conceptual basis for the possible one can certainly take retrospect, viewing the real as one among many possibilities, and seeking for an explanatory accounting of this actuality regarded as merely one among alternative possibilities.

Nothing in our theory blocks the prospect that one can view the real as one among perfectly genuine alternatives. No vicious circle is generated, because the primacy of the real over the possible is seen to lie in the conceptual order, but that of the possible over the real in the order of explanation.

The following objection against the mind-involvement theory of possibility could also be attempted:

> If possibility is (as your analysis has it) essentially mind-correlative, then the extra-mental world is devoid of potentiality. It then seems that there are no longer contingent events in (extra-mental) nature—events possibly other than what they actually are. But *then* one can no longer distinguish between what is actual and what is necessary, and we are driven to the fatalistic result that whatever happens must happen.[12]

But this objection will not stand. Our analysis does not show that actuality and necessity somehow *coincide* in the sphere of mind-independent reality (so that whatever is actual here is also necessary). It shows that the entire distinction possible/actual/necessary is (categorially) inoperative in this sphere as a *distinction*, because *in principle* only the actual can (virtually *ex hypothesi*) exist simply and as such. No fatalistic result ensues from this, however. Because the sphere of altogether mind-independent reality includes only the actual—and no "unrealized possibilities" can exist within it—it does not follow that what belongs to this sphere belongs to it of necessity. To claim this would be to confuse the necessity of consequence with absolute necessity, because being a consequence of the *ex hypothesi* actual with a necessity relativized to this actuality is certainly not tantamount to necessity pure and simple. To say that the conception of alternative possibilities is mind-dependent is not to say that these possibilities are unreal in the sense of improper (let alone impossible).

Although we have taken a conceptualistic line in holding that possibilities are mind-involving, we do not want to say that this role of mind is a matter of individual volition and idio-

---

[12] Compare Lee C. Rice, review of *Essays in Honor of Carl G. Hempel*, ed. by N. Rescher *et al.*, *The Modern Schoolman*, vol. 48 (1971), pp. 179–81 (see p. 181).

syncratic whim. Though the reality of possibilities resides only in the mind's conception thereof, the critical fact remains that the mind proceeds in this constructive enterprise in a restricted and canalized way, by use of the structured and structuring framework of a conceptual scheme and the linguistic machinery that gives it concrete embodiment. The realm of the possible is a construct, but the construction is made with the perfectly real materials of the conceptual and theoretical mechanisms of the conceptual schemes we use in our description and rationalization of the real world about us. And the availability of these "materials" is not confined to the limited resources of what actually lies to hand. They themselves have a possibilistic dimension—in the area of the possibility of process of what can be forged by the real conceptualizing mechanisms. We return again to the crucial recognition that the ontological basis of inexistent possibilistic *things* and states of affairs lies in the existential reality of possibilistic *processes* (of an inherently mentalistic nature).[13]

[13] The conceptualist/idealist approach to possibility in this chapter is developed further, and placed within its wider idealistic context in N. Rescher, *Conceptual Idealism* (Oxford, 1973). Parts of the present chapter are drawn from discussions given there.

Appendix

SUMMARY OF FUNDAMENTAL RELATIONSHIPS

I. INDIVIDUATION

$$x \sim \langle [\mathscr{P}_x, \mathscr{E}_x], \xi_x \rangle$$

with

$$\xi = \begin{cases} i_x \text{ for the actual individuals in } w^* \\ \rho_x \text{ for the actual-variant individuals in } \mathbf{v} \\ \star \text{ (the null individual) for the supernumeraries in } \mathbf{s} \end{cases}$$

II. IDENTITY AND SURROGACY

1. If x and y are both actual individuals (i.e., both $x \in w^*$ and $y \in w^*$), then:

$$x \doteq y \text{ iff } i(x) \text{ and } i(y) \text{ both indicate one} \\ \text{and the same item in the actual world}$$

2. If one of x and y is actual and the other is actual-variant (i.e., if either $[x \in w^* \ \& \ y \in \mathbf{v}]$ or $[x \in \mathbf{v} \ \& \ y \in w^*]$), then:

$$x \cong y \text{ iff either } \rho(x) = y \text{ or } \rho(y) = x$$

3. If both x and y are actual-variants (i.e., if both $x \in \mathbf{v}$ and $y \in \mathbf{v}$), then:

$$x \cong y \text{ iff } \rho(x) = \rho(y)$$

4. If both x and y are supernumeraries (i.e., if both $x \in \mathbf{s}$ and $y \in \mathbf{s}$), then:

$$x \cong y \text{ iff both } \mathscr{P}(x) = \mathscr{P}(y) \text{ and } \mathscr{E}(x) = \mathscr{E}(y)$$

5. Individuals are identical iff one of the four preceding conditions obtain, that is iff $x \doteq y$ or $x \cong y$ holds in one of the preceding senses.

6. The individual y is the surrogate of the (actual) individual x in the possible world w iff y is an element of w and is identical with x

$$S_{yx}^{w} \text{ iff both } y \in w \text{ and } y \cong x, \text{ where } x \in w^{*}$$

III. PRINCIPLES OF METAPHYSICAL INCOMPOSSIBILITY

Let $x \sim \langle d_x, \xi_x \rangle$ and $y \sim \langle d_y, \xi_y \rangle$ both be non-actual. Then:

(1) $(d_x = d_y \, \& \, \rho_x \neq \rho_y) \supset$ M-Incomposs $\{x, y\}$
(2) $(d_x \neq d_y \, \& \, \rho_x = \rho_y) \supset$ M-Incomposs $\{x, y\}$

IV. REALIZATION IN WORLDS

(R1) $Rw(\neg P) \equiv \neg Rw(P)$
(R2) $Rw(P \, \& \, Q) \equiv [Rw(P) \, \& \, Rw(Q)]$
(R3) $(Aw) \, Rw'[(Rw(P))] \equiv Rw'[(Aw)Rw(P)]$
(R4) $P \equiv Rw^{*}(P)$
(R5) $Rw'[Rw(P)] \equiv R\langle w' \star w \rangle (P)$
(R) If $\vdash P$, then $\vdash Rw(P)$
(R†) $Rw \, (\phi x) \equiv (\Sigma y)[y \in w \, \& \, y \cong x \, \& \, \phi \in \mathscr{P}(y)]$
(R6) $Rw[(\forall x)\phi x] \equiv (\Pi x)[x \in w \supset Rw(\phi x)]$
(R7) $Rw[\Box \phi x] \equiv (Aw')(\Pi y)[(y \in w' \, \& \, y \cong x) \supset Rw'(\phi y)]$, where $x \in w^{*}$

V. ESSENTIALITY AND MODALITY

1. Whenever $x \in w^{*}$: $\phi! x$ iff $(\Pi y)[y \cong x \supset \phi \in \mathscr{P}(y)]$
   Corollary: If $x \in w^{*}$, then: $\phi! x$ iff $(Aw)(\Pi y)[S_{yx}^{w} \supset Rw(\phi y)]$ iff $\Box \, \phi x$.
2. Whenever $x \in w^{*}$: $\phi? x$ iff $(\Sigma y) \, [y \cong x \, \& \, \phi \in \mathscr{P}(y)]$
   Corollary: If $x \in w^{*}$, then: $\phi? x$ iff $(Ew)(\Sigma y)[S_{yx}^{w} \, \& \, Rw(\phi y)]$ iff $\Diamond \, \phi x$.

VI. DISPOSITIONS

Whenever $x \in w^{*}$:

$(\psi/\phi)x$ iff $(Aw)(\Pi y)[(w \in \Delta_x \, \& \, S_{yx}^{w}) \supset Rw(\phi y \supset \psi y)]$
$(\psi/\phi)! x$ iff $(\Pi y)[y \cong x \supset [\phi \in \mathscr{P}(y) \supset \psi \in \mathscr{P}(y)]]$
$(\psi/\phi)! x$ iff $(Aw)(\Pi y)[S_{yx}^{w} \supset Rw(\phi y \supset \psi y)]$
$\phi\P x$ iff $(\Pi y)[y \in D_x \supset \phi \in \mathscr{P}(y)]$
$(\psi/\phi)x$ iff $\phi? x \, \& \, (\phi \supset \psi)\P x$

VII. LAWS

$\phi \Rightarrow \psi$ iff $(\forall x)[\phi ? x \supset (\psi/\phi) x]$

$\phi \Rightarrow \psi$ iff $(\Pi x)[x \in \mathcal{N} \supset \psi/\phi \in \mathscr{P}(x)]$

$\phi \Rightarrow \psi$ iff $(\mathrm{A}w)[w \in \varXi \supset (\Pi x)[x \in w \supset \mathrm{R}w(\phi x \supset \psi x)]]$

$\phi \dagger x$ iff $(\mathrm{A}w)[w \in \varXi \supset (\Pi y)[(y \in w \,\&\, y \cong x) \supset \mathrm{R}w(\phi y)]]$

$\phi \Rightarrow \psi$ iff $(\forall x)(\phi \supset \psi) \dagger x$

VIII. INTERNAL RELATIONS

$R \in \mathrm{Int}(w)$ iff $(\Pi x)(\Pi y)[(x \in w \,\&\, y \in w) \supset \mathrm{R}w(Rxy \supset \Box Rxy)]$

BIBLIOGRAPHY

A. Essentialism

Bennett, Daniel
   "Essential Properties," *The Journal of Philosophy*, vol. 66
      (1969), pp. 487–99.
Blanshard, Brand
   The Nature of Thought (London, 1939), Vol. II, p. 487
Cartwright, Richard
   "Some Remarks on Essentialism," *The Journal of Philosophy*,
      vol. 65 (1968), pp. 615–26.
Chisholm, Roderick M.
   "Identity Through Possible Worlds: Some Questions," *Nous*,
      vol. 1 (1967), pp. 1–8.
Gale, Richard M.
   "On What There Isn't," *The Review of Metaphysics*, vol. 25
      (1971–1972), pp. 459–88.
Harman, G. H.
   "A Nonessential Property," *The Journal of Philosophy*, vol. 67
      (1970), pp. 183–5.

Kripke, Saul
"Naming and Necessity" in D. Davidson and G. Harman (eds.), *Semantics of Natural Language* (Dordrecht, 1972), pp. 252–355 and 763–9.

Leonard, Henry
"Essences, Attributes and Predicates," *Proceedings and Addresses of the American Philosophical Association: 1963–1964* (Yellow Springs, 1964), pp. 25–51.

Lewis, David
"Counterpart Theory and Quantified Modal Logic," *The Journal of Philosophy*, vol. 65 (1968), pp. 113–26.

Linsky, Leonard
"Reference, Essentialism, and Modality," *The Journal of Philosophy*, vol. 66 (1969), pp. 687–700. Reprinted in L. Linsky (ed.) *Reference and Modality* (Oxford, 1971).

Marcus, Ruth Barcan
"Modalities and Intensional Languages," *Synthese*, vol. 13 (1961), pp. 303–22.
"Essentialism in Modal Logic," *Nous*, vol. 1 (1967), pp. 91–6.
"Essential Attribution," *The Journal of Philosophy*, vol. 68 (1971), pp. 187–202.

Nagel, Ernest
Sovereign Reason (Glencoe, Ill., 1954), pp. 271–7.

Parsons, Terence
"Grades of Essentialism in Quantified Modal Logic," *Nous*, vol. 1 (1967), pp. 181–91.
"Essentialism and Quantified Modal Logic," *The Philosophical Review*, vol. 78 (1969), pp. 35–52.

Plantinga, Alvin
"World and Essence," *The Philosophical Review*, vol. 79 (1970), pp. 461–92.

Putnam, Hilary
"The Analytic and Synthetic" in *Minnesota Studies in the Philosophy of Science*, Vol. III, ed. by H. Feigl and W. Sellars (Minneapolis, 1962).

Quine, W. V. O.
"Notes on Existence and Necessity," *The Journal of Philosophy*, vol. 40 (1943), pp. 113–27.
Word and Object (Cambridge, Mass., 1960).

"Two Dogmas of Empiricism," reprinted in *From a Logical Point of View* (New York, 1963), pp. 20–46.

"Three Grades of Modal Involvement" in *Ways of Paradox* (New York, 1966).

Rorty, Amelie Oksenberg
"Essential Possibilities in the Actual World," *The Review of Metaphysics*, vol. 25 (1972), pp. 607–24.

Smiley, Timothy
"Relative Necessity," *Journal of Symbolic Logic*, vol. 28 (1963), pp. 113–34.

Sprigge, Timothy
"Internal and External Properties," *Mind*, vol. 71 (1962), pp. 199–207.

Stine, Gail C.
"Essentialism, Possible Worlds, and Propositional Attitudes," *The Philosophical Review*, vol. 82 (1973), pp. 471–82.

Woods, John
"Essentialism, Self-Identity and Quantifying" in *Identity and Individuation*, ed. by M. Munitz (New York, 1971).

B. REFERENCE AND IDENTIFICATION

Chisholm, Roderick M.
"Intentionality and the Theory of Signs," *Philosophical Studies*, vol. 3 (1952), pp. 56–63.

Davidson, Donald
"The Individuation of Events" in N. Rescher (ed.), *Essays in Honor of Carl G. Hempel* (Dordrecht, 1969).

Donnellan, K. S.
"Reference and Definite Description," *The Philosophical Review*, vol. 75 (1966), pp. 281–304.

"Proper Names and Identifying Descriptions," *Synthese*, vol. 21 (1970), pp. 335–58.

Fitch, F. B.
"Some Logical Aspects of Reference and Existence," *The Journal of Philosophy*, vol. 57 (1960), pp. 640–7.

Hintikka, Jaakko
"Existential Presuppositions and Existential Commitments," *The Journal of Philosophy*, vol. 56 (1959), pp. 125–37.

"Towards a Theory of Definite Descriptions," *Analysis*, vol. 19 (1959), pp. 79–85.

"Modality and Quantification," *Theoria*, vol. 27 (1961), pp. 119–28.

Knowledge and Belief (Ithaca, 1962).

"The Modes of Modality," *Acta Philosophica Fennica*, fasc. 16 (1963), pp. 66–7.

"Studies in the Logic of Existence and Necessity: I. Existence," *The Monist*, vol. 50 (1966), pp. 55–67.

"Individuals, Possible Worlds and Epistemic Logic," *Nous*, vol. 1 (1967), pp. 33–62.

Kaplan, David

"Demonstratives and Proper Names," unpublished lectures delivered at Princeton (May, 1971).

"Bob and Ted and Carol and Alice," in J. Hintikka, *et al.* (eds.), *Approaches to Natural Language* (Dordrecht, 1973), pp. 490–518.

Kripke, Saul

"Identity and Necessity" in M. Munitz (ed.), *Identity and Individuation* (New York, 1972).

"Naming and Necessity" in D. Davidson and G. Harman (eds.), *Semantics of Natural Language* (Dordrecht, 1972), pp. 253–355 and 763–9.

Lambert, Karl

"Quantification and Existence," *Inquiry*, vol. 6 (1963), pp. 357–72.

Lambert, Karl and Bas van Fraassen

"On Free Description Theory," *Zeitschrift für Mathematische Logik und Grundlagen der Mathematik*, vol. 13 (1967), pp. 225–44.

Leonard, Henry

"The Logic of Existence," *Philosophical Studies*, vol. 7 (1956), pp. 49–64.

Linsky, Leonard

"Reference, Essentialism, and Modality," *The Journal of Philosophy*, vol. 66 (1969), pp. 687–700. Reprinted in L. Linsky, *Reference and Modality* (Oxford, 1971).

Martin, R. M.

"On Denotation and Ontic Commitment," *Philosophical Studies*, vol. 13 (1962), pp. 35–8.

Mates, Benson
"Leibniz on Possible Worlds" in B. van Rortselaar and J. F. Staal (eds.), *Logic, Methodology and Philosophy of Science*, Vol. III (Amsterdam, 1968), pp. 507–29.

Menne, Alfred
"The Logical Analysis of Existence," *Logico-Philosophical Studies*, A. Menne (ed.), (Dordrecht, 1962), pp. 88–96.

Mondadori, Fabrizio
"Reference, Essentialism, and Modality in Leibniz's Metaphysics," *Studia Leibnitiana*, vol. 5 (1973), pp. 74–101.

Pap, Arthur
"Logic, Existence, and the Theory of Descriptions," *Analysis*, vol. 13 (1952–1953), pp. 97–111.

Parfit, Derek
"Personal Identity," *The Philosophical Review*, vol. 80 (1971), pp. 3–27.

Popper, Karl
"Names, Negation, and Nothing," *Philosophical Studies*, vol. 15 (1964), pp. 49–56.

Purtill, Robert
"About Identity Through Possible Worlds," *Nous*, vol. 2 (1968), pp. 87–9.

Quine, W. V. O.
"Designation and Existence," *The Journal of Philosophy*, vol. 36 (1939), pp. 701–49. Reprinted in H. Feigl and W. Sellars (eds.), *Readings in Philosophical Analysis* (New York, 1949), pp. 44–51.
"Notes on Existence and Necessity," *The Journal of Philosophy*, vol. 40 (1943), pp. 113–27. Reprinted in L. Linsky (ed.), *Semantics and the Philosophy of Language* (Urbana, 1952), pp. 77–91.
"The Problem of Interpreting Modal Logic," *Journal of Symbolic Logic*, vol. 12 (1947), pp. 43–48.
"Quantifiers and Propositional Attitudes" in *The Ways of Paradox* (New York, 1966).
From a Logical Point of View (Cambridge, Mass., 1953, and 1961; New York, 1963); see especially "Reference and Modality," pp. 139–159.
"Meaning and Existential Inference," *From a Logical Point of View* (Cambridge, Mass., 1953), pp. 160–7.

"Quantification and the Empty Domain," *The Journal of Symbolic Logic*, vol. 19 (1954), pp. 177–9.

Word and Object (Cambridge, Mass., 1960).

Rorty, A. O.

"The Transformations for Persons," *Philosophy*, vol. 48 (1973), pp. 261–75.

Russell, Bertrand

"On Denoting," *Mind*, vol. 14 (1905), pp. 479–93.

Scott, Dana

"Existence and Description in Formal Logic," *Philosopher of the Century*: *Essays in Honor of Bertrand Russell*, R. Schoenman (ed.), (London, 1967).

Searle, John R.

"Proper Names," *Mind*, vol. 67 (1958), pp. 166–73.

Smullyan, Arthur

"Modality and Description," *Journal of Symbolic Logic*, vol. 13 (1948), pp. 31–7.

Stahl, Gerold

"Le probleme de l'existence dans la logique symbolique," *Revue philosophique de la France et de l'étranger*, vol. 150 (1960), pp. 97–104.

Strawson, P. F.

"On Referring," *Mind*, vol. 59 (1950), pp. 320–44.

Introduction to Logical Theory (London, 1952).

Individuals: An Essay in Descriptive Metaphysics (London, 1959).

"On Referring" in *Philosophy and Ordinary Language*, ed. by C. E. Caton (Urbana, 1963).

"Identifying Reference and Truth Values," *Theoria*, vol. 30 (1964), pp. 96–118.

Thomason, Richmond

"Modal Logic and Metaphysics," *The Logical Way of Doing Things*, ed. by K. Lambert (New Haven, 1968).

Thomason, R. H. and R. C. Stalnaker

"Modality and Reference," *Nous*, vol. 2 (1968), pp. 359–372.

van Fraassen, Bas

"Singular Terms, Truth-Value Gaps, and Free Logic," *The Journal of Philosophy*, vol. 63 (1966), pp. 481–95.

van Fraassen, Bas and Karel Lambert

"On Free Description Theory," *Zeitschrift für Mathematische Logik und Grundlagen der Mathematik*, vol. 13 (1967), pp. 225–40.

Wiggins, David
"Identity Statements" in R. Butler (ed.), *Analytic Philosophy* (New York, 1962).
"Individuation of Things and Places," *Proceedings of the Aristotelian Society* Supplementary Volume XXXVII (London, 1963), pp. 177–202.
Identity and Spatio-Temporal Continuity (Oxford, 1971).

Williams, B. A. O.
"The Self and the Future," *The Philosophical Review*, vol. 79 (1970), pp. 161–80.

Wilson, Neil
"Designation and Description," *The Journal of Philosophy*, vol. 50 (1953), pp. 369–83.
"Existence Assumptions and Contingent Meaningfulness," *Mind*, vol. 65 (1956), pp. 336–45.

Woods, John
"Essentialism, Self-Identity and Quantifying-in" in *Identity and Individuation*, ed. by M. Munitz (New York, 1971).

Ziff, Paul
Semantic Analysis (Ithaca, 1960).

C. Nonexistents and "Merely Possible" Objects

Ayer, A. J.
"On What There Is," *Proceedings of the Aristotelian Society*, Supplementary Volume XXV (1951), pp. 137–48.

Braithwaite, R. B.
"Imaginary Objects," *Proceedings of the Aristotelian Society*, Supplementary Volume XII (1933), pp. 44–58.

Cartwright, Richard
"Negative Existentials," *The Journal of Philosophy*, vol. 57 (1961), pp. 629–39.

Chisholm, Roderick M.
"Intentionality and the Theory of Signs," *Philosophical Studies*, vol. 3 (1952), pp. 56–63.
"Identity Through Possible Worlds: Some Questions," *Nous*, vol. 1 (1967), pp. 1–8.

Copp, David
"Leibniz's Thesis that Not All Possibles are Compossible," *Studia Leibnitiana*, vol. 5 (1973), pp. 26–42.

Crittenden, Charles
"Fictional Existence," *American Philosophical Quarterly*, vol. 3 (1966), pp. 317–21.
"Ontology and the Theory of Descriptions," *Philosophy and Phenomenological Research*, vol. 31 (1970), pp. 85–96.
"Thinking About Non-Being," *Inquiry*, vol. 16 (1973), pp. 290–311.

Ebersole, F. B.
"Whether Existence is a Predicate," *The Journal of Philosophy*, vol. 60 (1963), pp. 509–23.

Feldman, Fred
"Counterparts," *The Journal of Philosophy*, vol. 68 (1971), pp. 406–9.

Findlay, J. N.
Meinong's Theory of Objects (London, 1933). Second edition as *Meinong's Theory of Objects and Value* (London, 1963).

Fitch, F. B.
"Actuality, Possibility and Being," *The Review of Metaphysics*, vol. 3 (1950), pp. 367–84.

Gale, Richard
"On What There Isn't," *The Review of Metaphysics*, vol. 25 (1971–1972), pp. 459–88.

Geach, P. T.
"On What There Is," *Proceedings of the Aristotelian Society*, Supplementary Volume XXV (1951), pp. 125–36.

Goodman, Nelson
"About," *Mind*, vol. 70 (1961), pp. 1–24.

Grossman, Reinhardt
"Acts and Relations in Brentano," *Analysis*, vol. 21 (1960–1961), pp. 1–5.

Hacking, Ian
"Possibility," *The Philosophical Review*, vol. 76 (1967), pp. 143–68.

Hailperin, Theodore
"Quantification and Empty Individual Domains," *The Journal of Symbolic Logic*, vol. 18 (1953), pp. 197–200.

Hailperin, Theodore and Hughes Leblanc
"Nondesignating Singular Terms," *The Philosophical Review*, vol. 68 (1959), pp. 239–43.

Hintikka, Jaakko
"Existential Presuppositions and Existential Commitments,"
The Journal of Philosophy, vol. 56 (1959), pp. 125-37.
"Individuals, Possible Worlds and Epistemic Logic," *Nous*,
vol. 1 (1967), pp. 33-62.
"The Semantics of Modal Notions and the Indeterminacy of
Ontology" in D. Davidson and G. Harman (eds.),
Semantics of Natural Languages (Dordrecht, 1972), pp. 398-
414.

Khatchadourian, Haig
"On Existence," *Methodos*, vol. 9 (1957), pp. 65-76.
"About Imaginary Objects," *Ratio*, vol. 8 (1966), pp. 77-89.

Kröner, F.
"Zu Meinongs 'unmöglichen Gegenständen'," *Meinong
Gedenkschrift*, Schriften der Universität Gräz, Vol. I
(Graz, 1952), pp. 67-79.

Lambert, Karl and Bas van Fraassen
"Meaning Relations, Possible Objects, and Possible Worlds,"
in K. Lambert (ed.), *Philosophical Problems, Some Recent
Developments* (Dordrecht, 1970).

Leblanc, Hughes and Theodore Hailperin
"Nondesignating Singular Terms," *The Philosophical Review*,
vol. 68 (1959), pp. 239-43.

Leibniz, G. W.
Philosophische Schriften, ed. by C. I. Gerhardt, 7 vols. (Berlin,
1875-1890).

Lejewski, Casimir
"Logic and Existence," *British Journal for the Philosophy of
Science*, vol. 5 (1954), pp. 1-16.

Lewis, David
"Counterpart Theory and Quantified Modal Logic," *The
Journal of Philosophy*, vol. 65 (1968), pp. 113-26.
"Anselm and Actuality," *Nous*, vol. 4 (1970), pp. 175-188.
"Counterparts of Persons and Their Bodies," *The Journal of
Philosophy*, vol. 68 (1971), pp. 203-11.

Mates, Benson
"Leibniz on Possible Worlds" in B. van Rootselaar and J. F.
Staal (eds.), *Logic, Methodology and Philosophy of Science*, Vol.
III (Amsterdam, 1968), pp. 507-29.

Meinong, Alexius von
Ueber Möglichkeit und Wahrscheinlichkeit (Leipzig, 1915).
Meyer, Robert and Karl Lambert
"Universally Free Logic and Standard Quantification Theory," *The Journal of Symbolic Logic*, vol. 33 (1968), pp. 8–26.
Montague, Richard
"Pragmatics" in R. Klibansky (ed.), *Contemporary Philosophy*: *La Philosophie contemporaire*, Vol. I (Florence, 1968), pp. 102–122.
"On the Nature of Some Philosophical Entities," *The Monist*, vol. 53 (1969), pp. 159–94.
Moore, G. E.
"Imaginary Objects," *Proceedings of the Aristotelian Society*, supp. Vol. XII (1933), pp. 59–70.
Morton, Adam
"The Possible in the Actual," *Nous*, vol. 7 (1973), pp. 394–407.
Owens, Joseph
"The Range of Existence," *Proceedings of the Seventh Inter-American Congress of Philosophy* (Quebec, 1967), pp. 44–59.
Plantinga, Alvin
The Nature of Necessity (Oxford, 1974).
Popper, Karl
"Names, Negation, and Nothing," *Philosophical Studies*, vol. 15 (1964), pp. 49–56.
Prior, A. N.
"Nonentities," *The Philosophical Review*, vol. 70 (1961), pp. 120–32. Reprinted in R. J. Butler (ed.), *Analytical Philosophy* (New York, 1962).
"Possible Worlds," *The Philosophical Quarterly*, vol. 12 (1962), pp. 36–43.
Purtill, Robert
"About Identity Through Possible Worlds," *Nous*, vol. 2 (1968), pp. 87–9.
Quine, W. V. O.
"Designation and Existence," *The Journal of Philosophy*, vol. 36 (1939), pp. 701–49. Reprinted in H. Feigl and W. Sellars (eds.), *Readings in Philosophical Analysis* (New York, 1949), pp. 44–51.

"Notes on Existence and Necessity," *The Journal of Philosophy*, vol. 40 (1943), pp. 113–27. Reprinted in L. Linsky (ed.), *Semantics and the Philosophy of Language* (Urbana, 1952), pp. 77–91.

"On What There Is," *The Review of Metaphysics*, vol. 2 (1948), pp. 21–38. Reprinted in L. Linsky (ed.), *Semantics and the Philosophy of Language* (Urbana, 1952), pp. 189–206.

"On What There Is," *Proceedings of the Aristotelian Society*, supp. Vol. XXV (1951), pp. 149–60.

Word and Object (Cambridge, Mass., 1960.)

"Propositional Objects" in *Ontological Relativity and Other Essays* (New York, 1969).

Rescher, Nicholas
"On the Logic of Existence and Denotation," *The Philosophical Review*, vol. 68 (1959), pp. 157–80.

Rescher, Nicholas and Zane Parks
"Possible Individuals, Trans-World Identity, and Quantified Modal Logic," *Nous*, vol. 7 (1973), pp. 330–50.

Routley, Richard
"Some Things Do Not Exist," *Notre Dame Journal of Formal Logic*, vol. 7 (1966), pp. 251–76.

Russell, Bertrand
The Philosophy of Logical Atomism (Minneapolis, 1949). A collection of papers reprinted from *The Monist* (1918–1919), the last of which is entitled "Excursus into Metaphysics: What There Is."

Ryle, Gilbert
"Systematically Misleading Expressions," *Proceedings of the Aristotelian Society*, vol. 32 (1932), pp. 139–70.

"Imaginary Objects," *Proceedings of the Aristotelian Society*, Supplementary Volume XII (1933), pp. 19–43.

Scholz, Heinrich
Metaphysik als strenge Wissenschaft (Köln, 1941).

Scott, Dana
"Existence and Description in Formal Logic," *Bertrand Russell: Philosopher of the Century*, ed. by R. Schoenman (Boston, 1967), pp. 181–200.

Stine, Gail C.
"Essentialism, Possible Worlds, and Propositional Attitudes," *The Philosophical Review*, vol. 82 (1973), pp. 471–82.

Strawson, P. F.
  "On Referring," *Mind*, vol. 59 (1950), pp. 320–44.
  "Identifying Reference and Truth Values," *Theoria*, vol. 30 (1964), pp. 96–118.
Taylor, Richard
  "Negative Things," *The Journal of Philosophy*, vol. 49 (1952), pp. 433–49. [The article is concerned primarily with negative facts: nonexistent or "negative" *things* come in for only incidental mention.]
Toms, Eric
  Being, Negation and Logic (Oxford, 1962). See especially chap. III on "Non-existence and Universals."

D. Is Existence a Predicate?

Ebersole, Frank B.
  "Whether Existence is a Predicate," *The Journal of Philosophy*, vol. 60 (1963), pp. 509–23.
Harré, Rom
  "A Note on Existence Propositions," *The Philosophical Review*, vol. 65 (1956), pp. 548–9.
Kiteley, Murray
  "Is Existence a Predicate?", *Mind*, vol. 73 (1964), pp. 364–73.
Kneale, William
  "Is Existence a Predicate?", *Aristotelian Society*, Supplementary Volume XV (1936), reprinted in *Readings in Philosophical Analysis*, ed. by H. Feigl and W. Sellars (New York, 1949), pp. 29–43.
Leonard, Henry
  "The Logic of Existence," *Philosophical Studies*, vol. 7 (1956), pp. 49–64.
  "Essences, Attributes and Predicates," *Proceedings and Addresses of the American Philosophical Association: 1963–1964* (Yellow Springs, 1964), pp. 25–51.
Menne, Alfred
  "The Logical Analysis of Existence," *Logico-Philosophical Studies*, A. Menne (ed.), (Dordrecht, 1962), pp. 88–96.
Nakhnikian, George and Wesley C. Salmon
  "'Exists' as a Predicate," *The Philosophical Review*, vol. 66 (1957), pp. 535–42.

Pap, Arthur
"A Note on Logic and Existence," *Mind*, vol. 56 (1947), pp. 72–6.
"Logic, Existence, and the Theory of Descriptions," *Analysis*, vol. 13 (1952–1953), pp. 97–111.
Quine, Willard V.
"Designation and Existence," *The Journal of Philosophy*, vol. 36 (1939), pp. 701–49. Reprinted in H. Feigl and W. Sellars (eds.), *Readings in Philosophical Analysis* (New York, 1949), pp. 44–51.
Rescher, Nicholas
"Definitions of 'Existence'," *Philosophical Studies*, vol. 8 (1957), pp. 65–9.
"Al-Farabi on the Question: Is Existence a Predicate?" in *Studies in the History of Arabic Logic* (Pittsburgh, 1963), pp. 39–42.
"The Logic of Existence" in *Topics in Philosophical Logic* (Dordrecht, 1968), pp. 138–61.
"On the Logic of Existence and Denotation," *The Philosophical Review*, vol. 68 (1959), pp. 157–80. Reprinted in H. Feigl and W. Sellars and K. Lehrer (eds.), *New Readings in Philosophical Analysis* (New York, 1972).
Russell, Bertrand
"The Existential Import of Propositions," *Mind*, vol. 14 (1905), pp. 398–401.
"On Denoting," *Mind*, vol. 14 (1905), pp. 479–93.
Shearman, A. T.
"Note on Logical Existence," *Mind*, vol. 14 (1905), pp. 440.
Strawson, P. F.
"On Referring," *Mind*, vol. 59 (1950), pp. 320–44.
Introduction to Logical Theory (London, 1952).

E. Modal Logic and Modality "de re" and "de dicto"

Bressan, Aldo
A General Interpreted Modal Calculus (New Haven, 1972).
Camp, Joseph
"Plantinga on De Dicto and De Re," *Nous*, vol. 5 (1971), pp. 215–25.

Carnap, Rudolf
"Modalities and Quantification," *The Journal of Symbolic Logic*, vol. 11 (1942), pp. 33–64.
Meaning and Necessity (Chicago, 1947).

Føllesdal, Dagfinn
"Quantification into Causal Contexts" reprinted in L. Linsky (ed.), *Reference and Modality* (Oxford, 1971), pp. 57–62.

Hintikka, Jaakko
"Modality as Referential Multiplicity," *Ajatus*, vol. 20 (1957), pp. 49–64.
Knowledge and Belief (Ithaca, 1962).
"The Modes of Modality," *Acta Philosophica Fennica*, fasc. 16 (1963), pp. 66–7.
"Quantifiers in Deontic Logic," *Societas Scientiarum Fennica, Commentationes Humanarum Litterarum*, vol. 23 (1957), no. 4, 23 pp.

Kneale, William
"Modality *de dicto* and *de re*" in E. Nagel, P. Suppes, and J. Tarski (eds.), *Logic, Methodology and Philosophy of Science: Proceedings of the 1960 International Congress* (Stanford, 1962), pp. 622–33.

Kripke, Saul
"A Completeness Theorem in Modal Logic," *Journal of Symbolic Logic*, vol. 24 (1959), pp. 1–14.
"Semantic Considerations on Modal Logic," *Acta Philosophica Fennica*, fasc. 16 (1963), pp. 83–94.
"Identity and Necessity" in M. Munitz (ed.), *Identity and Individuation* (New York, 1971).
"Naming and Necessity" in D. Davidson and G. Harman (eds.), *Semantics of Natural Language* (Dordrecht, 1972).

Lewis, David
"Counterpart Theory and Quantified Modal Logic," *The Journal of Philosophy*, vol. 65 (1968), pp. 113–26.
"Counterparts of Persons and Their Bodies," *The Journal of Philosophy*, vol. 68 (1971), pp. 203–11.

Linsky, Leonard
"Reference, Essentialism, and Modality," *The Journal of Philosophy*, vol. 66 (1969), pp. 687–700. Reprinted in L. Linsky (ed.), *Reference and Modality* (Oxford, 1971).

Marcus, Ruth Barcan
"Modalities and Intensional Languages," *Synthese*, vol. 13 (1961), pp. 303–22. Reprinted in Marx Wartofsky (ed.), *Boston Studies in the Philosophy of Science* (Dordrecht, 1963).
et al., "Discussion on the Paper of R. B. Marcus," *Synthese*, vol. 14 (1962), pp. 132–43. Reprinted in Marx Wartofsky (ed.), *Boston Studies in the Philosophy of Science* (Dordrecht, 1963).
"Essentialism in Modal Logic," *Nous*, vol. 1 (1967), pp. 91–6.

Montague, Richard
"Logical Necessity, Physical Necessity, Ethics, and Quantifiers," *Inquiry*, vol. 3 (1960), pp. 259–69.

Parsons, Terence
"Essentialism and Quantified Modal Logic," *The Philosophical Review*, vol. 78 (1969), pp. 35–52.

Plantinga, Alvin
God and Other Minds (Ithaca, 1967).
"*De Re* and *De Dicto*," *Nous*, vol. 3 (1969), pp. 235–58.
"What George Could Not Have Been," *Nous*, vol. 5 (1971), pp. 227–32.

Quine, W. V. O.
"Notes on Existence and Necessity," *The Journal of Philosophy*, vol. 40 (1943), pp. 113–27.
"The Problem of Interpreting Modal Logic," *Journal of Symbolic Logic*, vol. 12 (1947), pp. 43–8.
From A Logical Point of View (Cambridge, Mass., 1953, and 1961; New York, 1963); see especially "Reference and Modality," pp. 139–59.
Word and Object (Cambridge, Mass., 1960).
"Three Grades of Modal Involvement" in *The Ways of Paradox* (New York, 1966), pp. 156–74.

Rescher, Nicholas and Zane Parks
"Possible Individuals, Trans-World Identity, and Quantified Modal Logic," *Nous*, vol. 7 (1973), pp. 330–50.

Scott, Dana
"Advice on Modal Logic" in K. Lambert (ed.), *Philosophical Problems in Logic: Some Recent Developments* (Dordrecht, 1970).

F. Laws and Dispositions

Alexander, H. Gavin
"General Statements as Rules of Inference" in H. Feigl, G. Maxwell and M. Scriven (eds.), *Minnesota Studies in the Philosophy of Science*, vol. 2 (Minneapolis, 1958).

Alston, William P.
"Dispositions and Occurrences," *Canadian Journal of Philosophy*, vol. 1 (1971), pp. 125–54.

Ayer, A. J.
"What is a Law of Nature?" in *The Concept of a Person*, A. J. Ayer (London, 1963).

Burks, A. W.
"Dispositional Statements," *Philosophy of Science*, vol. 22 (1955), pp. 175–93.
"The Logic of Causal Propositions," *Mind*, vol. 60 (1951), pp. 363–83.

Campbell, Norwood R.
"The Structure of Theories" in N. R. Campbell, *Physics: The Elements* (Cambridge, Mass., 1920), reprinted in H. Feigl and M. Brodbeck (eds.), *Readings in the Philosophy of Science* (New York, 1953).

Carnap, Rudolf
"Testability and Meaning," *Philosophy of Science*, vol. 3 (1936), pp. 419–71 and vol. 4 (1937), pp. 1–40.

Chisholm, R. M.
"Law Statements and Counterfactual Inference," *Analysis*, vol. 15 (1955), pp. 97–105.

Fisk, Milton
"Are There Necessary Connections in Nature?", *Philosophy of Science*, vol. 37 (1970), p. 385.

Goodman, Nelson
Fact, Fiction, and Forecast (Cambridge, Mass., 1955).

Grünbaum, Adolf
"Law and Convention in Physical Theory" in H. Feigl and G. Maxwell (eds.), *Current Issues in the Philosophy of Science* (New York, 1961).

Harré, Rom
Theories and Things (London, 1961).

Hempel, Carl G.
"The Function of General Laws in History," *The Journal of Philosophy*, vol. 39 (1942), pp. 35–48.
"Explanation and Prediction by Covering Laws" in B. Baumrin (ed.), *Philosophy of Science: The Delaware Seminar*, vol. 1 (New York, 1963).
"Studies in the Logic of Confirmation" in *Aspects of Scientific Explanation and Other Essays in the Philosophy of Science* (New York, 1965).

Hilpinen, Risto
Rules of Acceptance and Inductive Logic (Amsterdam, 1968; *Acta Philosophica Fennica*, fasc. 22).

Kneale, William
"Natural Laws and Contrary-to-Fact Conditionals," *Analysis*, vol. 10 (1950), pp. 123–5. Reprinted in M. MacDonald (ed.), *Philosophy ond Analysis* (Oxford, 1955).

Körner, Stephan
"On Laws of Nature," *Mind*, vol. 62 (1963), pp. 218–29.

Lundberg, G. A.
"The Concept of Law in the Social Sciences," *Philosophy of Science*, vol. 5 (1938), pp. 189–203.

Mandelbaum, Maurice.
"Societal Laws," *British Journal for the Philosophy of Science*, vol. 8 (1957), pp. 211–24.

Nagel, Ernest
The Structure of Science (New York, 1961).
"The Logical Character of Scientific Laws" in above, pp. 47–78.
"Experimental Laws and Theories" in above pp. 79–105.
"The Cognitive Status of Theories" in above, pp. 106–52.

Pap, Arthur
"Disposition Concepts and Extensional Logic" in H. Feigl, M. Scriven, and G. Maxwell (eds.), *Minnesota Studies in the Philosophy of Science*, vol. 2 (Minneapolis, 1958).
An Introduction to the Philosophy of Science (New York, 1962).

Peirce, C. S.
The Collected Works of C. S. Peirce, ed. by C. Hartshorne, P. Weiss, and A. Burks (8 vols.; Cambridge, Mass, 1933–58).

Peierls, R. E.
The Laws of Nature (New York, 1956).

Pietarinen, Juhani
Lawlikeness, Analogy, and Inductive Logic (Amsterdam, 1972).
Popper, Karl R.
"A Note on Natural Laws and So-called 'Contrary-to-Fact' Conditionals," *Mind*, vol. 58 (1949), p. 62.
The Logic of Scientific Discovery (London, 1959).
"A Revised Definition of Natural Necessity," *The British Journal for the Philosophy of Science*, vol. 18 (1967), p. 316.
Reichenbach, Hans
Experience and Prediction (Chicago, 1938).
Nomological Statements and Admissible Operations (Amsterdam, 1954). See the review by C. G. Hempel in *The Journal of Symbolic Logic*, vol. 26 (1956), pp. 50–4.
Rescher, Nicholas
Hypothetical Reasoning (Amsterdam, 1964).
Scientific Explanation (New York, 1970).
"Counterfactual Hypotheses, Laws, and Dispositions," *Nous*, vol. 5 (1971), pp. 157–78.
Conceptual Idealism (Oxford, 1973).
Rorty, Amelie Oksenberg
"Essential Possibilities in the Actual World," *The Review of Metaphysics*, vol. 25 (1972), pp. 607–24.
Schlick, Moritz
"Are Natural Laws Conventions?" in H. Feigl and M. Brodbeck (eds.), *Readings in the Philosophy of Science* (New York, 1953).
Sellars, Wilfrid
"Counterfactuals, Dispositions, and the Causal Modalities" in H. Feigl, M. Scriven, and G. Maxwell (eds.), *Minnesota Studies in the Philosophy of Science*, vol. II (Minneapolis, 1958), pp. 225–308.
Stegmüller, Wolfgang
"Der Bergriff des Naturgesetzes," *Studium Generale*, vol. 19 (1966), pp. 649–57.
Wissenschaftliche Erklärung und Begründung (Berlin, Heidelberg and New York, 1969).
Storer, Thomas
"On Defining 'Soluble'," *Analysis*, vol. 11 (1950–51), pp. 134–7.

Walters, R. S.
"The Problem of Counterfactuals," *Australasian Journal of Philosophy*, vol. 39 (1961), pp. 30–46.
"Laws of Science and Law-Like Statements," *The Encyclopedia of Philosophy*, vol. IV (New York, 1967), pp. 410–14.

Wigner, Eugene
"Events, Laws of Nature, and Invariance Principles," *Science*, vol. 145 (1964), pp. 995–8.

G. ASSUMPTIONS AND HYPOTHESES

Bradley, F. H.
Principles of Logic (London, 1883).

Dorolle, Maurice
"La valeur des conclusions par l'absurde," *Revue philosophique*, vol. 86 (1918), pp. 309–13.

Erdmann, Benno
Logik, 2 vols. (2nd edition, Halle, 1907, 1908).

Findlay, J. N.
Meinong's Theory of Objects and Values (Oxford, 1933; 2nd edn., 1963).

Görland, Albert
Die Hypothese (Göttingen, 1911).

Hall, Roland
"Assuming: One Set of Positing Words," *The Philosophical Review*, vol. 67 (1958), pp. 52–75.

Heath, Sir Thomas L.
The Thirteen Books of Euclid's Elements, 3 Vols. (Cambridge, 1908; 2nd edn., 1925).

Heyting, Arent
Les fondements des mathématiques: Intuitionisme—Théorie de la démonstration (Paris and Louvain, 1955).
Intuitionism (Amsterdam, 1956).

Jaskowski, Stanislaw
"On the Rules of Suppositions in Formal Logic," *Studia Logica*, No. 1 (Warszawa, 1934).

Kerler, Dietrich Heinrich
Ueber Annahmen: Eine Streitschrift gegen A. von Meinongs gleichnämiger Arbeit (Ulm, 1910).

Kneale, William and Martha Kneale
The Development of Logic (Oxford, 1962).
Meinong, Alexius von
Ueber Annahmen (Leipzig, 1902).
Prantl, Carl
Geschichte der Logik, vol. 1 (Graz, 1855).
Rescher, Nicholas
"Belief-contravening Suppositions," *The Philosophical Review,*
vol. 70 (1961), pp. 176–95.
Hypothetical Reasoning (Amsterdam, 1964).
The Coherence Theory of Truth (Oxford, 1973).
Russell, Bertrand
"Meinong's Theory of Complexes and Assumptions," *Mind,*
vol. 13 (1904), pp. 204–19 (Part I), 336–54 (Part II), 509–
24 (Part III).
Sigwart, Christoph
Beiträge zur Lehre vom hypothetischen Urtheil (Tübingen, 1870).
Vaihinger, Hans
Die Philosophie des Als Ob (Berlin, 1911).
Vailati, G.
"Sur une classe remarquable de raisonnements par réduction
à l'absurde," *Revue de métaphysique,* vol. 12 (1904), pp. 799–
809.
Ziehen, Theodor
Lehrbuch der Logik (Bonn, 1920).

H. COUNTERFACTUALS

Anderson, A. R.
"A Note on Subjunctive and Counterfactual Conditionals,"
Analysis, vol. 12 (1951), p. 35.
Ayers, M. R.
"Counterfactuals and Subjunctive Conditionals," *Mind,* vol.
74 (1965), p. 347.
Braithwaite, R. B.
Scientific Explanation (Cambridge, 1953).
Burks, A. W.
"Dispositional Statements," *Philosophy of Science,* vol. 22
(1955), pp. 175–93.

Chisholm, Roderick M.
"The Contrary-to-Fact Conditional," *Mind*, vol. 55 (1946), pp. 289–307.
"Law Statements and Counterfactual Inference," *Analysis*, vol. 15 (1955), pp. 97–105.
Cooley, John C.
"Professor Goodman's 'Fact, Fiction, and Forecast'," *The Journal of Philosophy*, vol. 54 (1957), pp. 293–311.
D'Alessio, J. C.
"On Subjunctive Conditionals," *The Journal of Philosophy*, vol. 64 (1967), p. 306.
Diggs, B. J.
"Counterfactual Conditionals," *Mind*, vol. 61 (1952), pp. 513–27.
Goodman, Nelson
"The Problem of Counterfactual Conditionals," *The Journal of Philosophy*, vol. 44 (1947), pp. 113–28. Reprinted in L. Linsky (ed.), *Semantics and the Philosophy of Language* (Urbana, 1952), with minor changes in N. Goodman, *Fact, Fiction and Forecast* (Cambridge, Mass., 1955).
"On Infirmities of Confirmation Theory," *Philosophy and Phenomenological Research*, vol. 8 (1947), pp. 149–51.
Greef, Jan de
"Professor Halberstadt on Counterfactual Conditionals and Modality," *International Logic Review*, vol. 4 (1973), pp. 126–34.
Halberstadt, W. H.
"A New Look at Counterfactual Conditional Statements," *International Logic Review*, vol. 1 (1970), pp. 99–105.
Hampshire, Stuart
"Subjunctive Conditionals," *Analysis*, vol. 9 (1948), pp. 9–14. Reprinted in M. MacDonald (ed.), *Philosophy and Analysis* (Oxford, 1955).
Hempel, Carl G.
"Studies in the Logic of Confirmation," *Mind*, vol. 54 (1945), pp. 1–26, 97–121.
Hiz, Henry
"On the Inferential Sense of Contrary-to-Fact Conditionals," *The Journal of Philosophy*, vol. 48 (1949), pp. 586–7.

Johnson, W. E.
  Logic, Part III (Cambridge, 1924).
Kneale, William
  Probability and Induction (Oxford, 1949).
  "Natural Laws and Contrary-to-Fact Conditionals," *Analysis*,
    vol. 10 (1950), pp. 123–5. Reprinted in M. MacDonald
    (ed.), *Philosophy and Analysis* (Oxford, 1955).
Lewis, C. I.
  An Analysis of Knowledge and Valuation (La Salle, 1946).
Lewis, David K.
  Counterfactuals (Oxford, 1973).
  "Counterfactuals and Comparative Possibility," *Journal of
    Philosophical Logic*, vol. 2 (1973), pp. 418–46.
Mackie, J. L.
  "Counterfactuals and Causal Laws" in R. J. Butler (ed.),
    Analytical Philosophy (New York, 1962), pp. 66–80.
Milmed, B. K.
  "Counterfactual Statements and Logical Modality," *Mind*,
    vol. 64 (1957), pp. 453–70.
Nagel, Ernest
  The Structure of Science (New York, 1961).
Pap, Arthur
  An Introduction to the Philosophy of Science (New York, 1962).
Pietarinen, Juhani
  Lawlikeness, Analogy, and Inductive Logic (Amsterdam, 1972).
Popper, Karl R.
  "A Note on Natural Laws and So-Called Contrary-to-Fact
    Conditionals," *Mind*, vol. 58 (1949), pp. 62–6.
Reichenbach, Hans
  Nomological Statements and Admissible Operations (Amsterdam,
    1954).
Rescher, Nicholas
  "A Factual Analysis of Counterfactual Conditionals,"
    Philosophical Studies, vol. 11 (1960), pp. 49–54.
  "Belief-Contravening Suppositions," *Philosophical Review*,
    vol. 70 (1961), pp. 176–95.
  Hypothetical Reasoning (Amsterdam, 1964).
  "Counterfactual Hypotheses, Laws, and Dispositions," *Nous*,
    vol. 5 (1971), pp. 157–78.
  The Coherence Theory of Truth (Oxford, 1973).

Schneider, Erna F.
"Recent Discussions of Subjunctive Conditionals," *The Review of Metaphysics*, vol. 6 (1952), pp. 623–47.

Sellars, Wilfrid
"Counterfactuals, Dispositions, and the Causal Modalities" in H. Feigl, M. Scriven and G. Maxwell (eds.), *Minnesota Studies in the Philosophy of Science*, Vol. II (Minneapolis, 1958), pp. 225–308.

Stalnaker, Robert
"A Theory of Conditionals," *Studies in Logical Theory* (Oxford, 1968).
"Pragmatics" in D. Davidson and G. Harman (eds.), *Semantics of Natural Language* (Dordrecht, 1972).

Stegmüller, Wolfgang
"Conditio Irrealis, Dispositionen, Naturgesetze und Induktion," *Kantstudien*, vol. 50 (1958–59), pp. 363–90.
Wissenschaftliche Erklärung und Begründung (Berlin, Heidelberg, and New York, 1969).

Storer, Thomas
"On Defining 'Soluble'," *Analysis*, vol. 11 (1950–51), pp. 134–7.

Thomason, R. H.
"A Semantic Analysis of Conditional Logic," *Theoria*, vol. 36 (1970), pp. 23–42.

von Wright, G. H.
Logical Studies (London, 1957).
"On Conditionals" in G. H. von Wright, *Logical Studies* (London, 1957), pp. 127–65.

Walters, R. S.
"The Problem of Counterfactuals," *Australasian Journal of Philosophy*, vol. 39 (1961), pp. 30–46.
"Laws of Science and Law-Like Statements," *The Encyclopedia of Philosophy*, Vol. IV (New York, 1967), pp. 410–14.

Weinberg, Julius R.
"Contrary-to-Fact Conditionals," *The Journal of Philosophy*, vol. 48 (1951), pp. 17–22.

Will, F. L.
"The Contrary-to-Fact Conditional," *Mind*, vol. 56 (1947), pp. 236–49.

I. INTERNAL RELATIONS

Blanshard, Brand
The Nature of Thought, Vol. II (London, 1939), p. 484.
Reason and Analysis (London, 1961), pp. 483–4.
Bosanquet, Bernard
Knowledge and Reality (London, 1892).
Bradley, F. H.
Appearance and Reality (2nd edn., Oxford, 1930).
Essays on Truth and Reality (Oxford, 1914).
Broad, C. D.
Examination of McTaggart's Philosophy, 3 Vols. (Cambridge, 1933–1938).
Ewing, A. C.
Idealism: A Critical Survey (London, 1934), chap. IV, sec. I.
James, William
"The Thing and its Relations," chap. III of *Essays in Radical Empiricism* (New York, 1912).
Joachim, H. H.
The Nature of Truth (London, 1906).
Logical Studies (Oxford, 1948).
Leibniz, G. W.
Philosophische Schriften, ed. by C. I. Gerhardt, 7 vols. (Berlin, 1875–1890).
McTaggart, J. M. E.
The Nature of Existence (Cambridge, 1921–1927), sect. 85; see also chap. V and sections 80–1 and 86.
Moore, G. E.
"Internal and External Relations" in *Philosophical Studies* (London & New York, 1922), pp. 276–309.
Rorty, R. M.
"Internal and External Relations," *Encyclopedia of Philosophy*, vol. 7 (New York, 1970), pp. 129 ff.
Russell, Bertrand
"Logical Atomism" in *Contemporary British Philosophy*, First Series (New York, 1924), pp. 358–383.
Ryle, R. M.
"Internal Relations," *Proceedings of the Aristotelian Society*, supp. Vol. XIV (1935), pp. 164–5.

Sprigge, Timothy
  "Internal and External Properties," *Mind*, vol. 71 (1962),
    pp. 199–207.
Taylor, A. E.
  Elements of Metaphysics (London, 1907).

Name Index

Subject Index